THE GREAT AMERICAN EDUCATION-INDUSTRIAL COMPLEX

"This book offers readers the alarming facts about the influence that private, for-profit organizations and companies have on education policy and practices in the United States. Providing a cogent and thorough analysis and critique the authors have written an important and useful book in the name of reclaiming education for the good of our nation."

Ron Scapp, College of Mount Saint Vincent, USA

The Great American Education-Industrial Complex examines the structure and nature of national networks and enterprises that seek to influence public education policy in accord with their own goals and objectives.

In the past twenty years, significant changes have taken place in the way various interest groups seek to influence policies and practices in public education in the United States. No longer left to the experience and knowledge of educators, American education has become as much the domain of private organizations, corporate entities, and political agents who see it as a market for their ideas, technologies, and ultimately profits. Picciano and Spring posit that educational technology is the vehicle whereby these separate movements, organizations, and individuals have become integrated in a powerful common entity, and detail how the educational–industrial complex has grown and strengthened its position of influence. Offering a new formulation of an important dimension of the educational dynamic in the United States, this timely, carefully documented, well argued book brings together Picciano's perspective and expertise in the field of technology and policy issues and Spring's in the history and politics of education in a unique critical analysis of the education-industrial complex and its implications for the future.

Anthony G. Picciano is Professor and Executive Officer, Ph.D. Program in Urban Education, Graduate Center, and Professor, Hunter College, City University of New York.

Joel Spring is Professor, Queens College and Graduate Center, City University of New York.

Sociocultural, Political, and Historical Studies in Education
Joel Spring, Editor

Peshkin • *Places of Memory: Whiteman's Schools and Native American Communities*

Hemmings • *Coming of Age in U.S. High Schools: Economic, Kinship, Religious, and Political Crosscurrents*

Spring • Educating the Consumer-Citizen: A History of the Marriage of Schools, Advertising, and *Media*

Ogbu • Black American Students in an Affluent Suburb: A Study of Academic Disengagement

Benham/Stein, Eds. • *The Renaissance of American Indian Higher Education: Capturing the Dream*

Hones, Ed. • *American Dreams, Global Visions: Dialogic Teacher Research with Refugee and Immigrant Families*

McCarty • *A Place to Be Navajo: Rough Rock and The Struggle for Self-Determination in Indigenous Schooling*

Spring • *Globalization and Educational Rights: An Intercivilizational Analysis*

Grant/Lei, Eds. • *Global Constructions of Multicultural Education: Theories and Realities*

Luke • *Globalization and Women in Academics: North/West–South/East*

Meyer/Boyd, Eds. • *Education Between State, Markets, and Civil Society: Comparative Perspectives*

Roberts • *Remaining and Becoming: Cultural Crosscurrents in an Hispano School*

Borman/Stringfield/Slavin, Eds. • *Title I: Compensatory Education at the Crossroads*

DeCarvalho • *Rethinking Family-School Relations: A Critique of Parental Involvement in Schooling*

Peshkin • *Permissible Advantage?: The Moral Consequences of Elite Schooling*

Spring • *The Universal Right to Education: Justification, Definition, and Guidelines*

Nieto, Ed. • *Puerto Rican Students in U.S. Schools*

Glander • *Origins of Mass Communications Research During the American Cold War: Educational Effects and Contemporary Implications*

Pugach • *On the Border of Opportunity: Education, Community, and Language at the U.S.-Mexico Line*

Spring • *Education and the Rise of the Global Economy*

Benham/Heck • *Culture and Educational Policy in Hawai'i: The Silencing of Native Voices*

Lipka/Mohatt/The Ciulistet Group • *Transforming the Culture of Schools: Yu'pik Eskimo Examples*

Weinberg • *Asian-American Education: Historical Background and Current Realities*

Nespor • *Tangled Up in School: Politics, Space, Bodies, and Signs in the Educational Process*

Peshkin • *Places of Memory: Whiteman's Schools and Native American Communities*

Spring • *The Cultural Transformation of a Native American Family and Its Tribe 1763–1995*

For additional information on titles in the Sociocultural, Political, and Historical Studies in Education series visit **www.routledge.com/education**

THE GREAT AMERICAN EDUCATION-INDUSTRIAL COMPLEX

Ideology, Technology, and Profit

Anthony G. Picciano
Joel Spring

Routledge
Taylor & Francis Group

NEW YORK AND LONDON

First published 2013
by Routledge
711 Third Avenue, New York, NY 10017

Simultaneously published in the UK
by Routledge
2 Park Square, Milton Park, Abingdon, Oxon OX14 4RN

Routledge is an imprint of the Taylor & Francis Group, an informa business

Library of Congress Cataloging in Publication Data
Picciano, Anthony G., author.
    The great American education-industrial complex : ideology, technology, and profit / Anthony G. Picciano, Joel Spring.
    pages cm — (Sociocultural, political, and historical studies in education)
    Includes bibliographical references and index.
    1. Academic-industrial collaboration—United States. I. Spring, Joel H., author. II. Title.
    LC1085.2.P53 2013
    378.1'035—dc23
    2012015129

ISBN13: 978-0-415-52413-1 (hbk)
ISBN13: 978-0-415-52414-8 (pbk)
ISBN13: 978-0-203-12061-3 (ebk)

Typeset in Bembo and Stone Sans by
EvS Communication Networx, Inc.

Printed and bound in the United States of America on sustainably sourced paper by IBT Global

CONTENTS

PREFACE

This book on the education–industrial complex emerged following a series of collaborations between the two authors. In addition to their many discussions, the authors have together offered seminars at their home institution, the City University of New York Graduate Center, on the topics and issues presented in this book. It is important to mention that the authors approach issues related to education policy, privatization, and technology from different perspectives. Anthony Picciano has spent his career as a proponent of policies and practices that integrate technology and innovation into education at all levels. He has published and lectured extensively on these themes, emphasizing instructional quality, respect for educators, and the primacy of student learning. In coauthoring this book, his goal was to examine the forces that are pushing technology on American education with a certain unbridled enthusiasm and often without enough evaluation. Joel Spring is interested in the social and economic forces shaping global education policy. He is concerned about the rapid growth of global education businesses and their increasing profits gained from public monies spent on schooling.

The book opens in chapter 1 with a general discussion of the components of the education–industrial complex including the powerful role of networks that link education businesses to government policies and the public purse.

Chapter 2 comprises a discussion of the people who move through these networks connecting foundations, think tanks, education businesses, for-profit education trade organizations, international organizations such as the World Economic Forum, and government bureaucracies.

This theme is continued in chapter 3 with an examination of the role of technology in the education–industrial complex and how it might increase the profits of education technology firms regardless of technology's actual benefits.

Chapter 4 examines how government education policies, particularly No Child Left Behind, have promoted the role of for-profit businesses in education including for-profit educational management companies and supplementary education services resulting in the commercialization of school life. Chapter 4 also explores the free market ideology used to justify these policies.

Chapter 5 continues this theme with an examination of the privatization movement in K–12 education, the growth of online businesses selling tutoring services, virtual schools, course management software, and the services providing testing and assessment software. In addition, chapter 5 discusses the increasing privatization of higher education.

In chapter 6, the authors analyze the role of ideology in supporting the expansion of the education-industrial complex. They discuss the organizations that promote certain ideologies, including foundations practicing venture philanthropy such as the Bill and Melinda Gates Foundation, and think tanks such as the American Enterprise Institute. Chapter 7 examines the role of the media in selling education products to schools and homes as well as its lack of critical perspective on education. In this context, chapter 7 discusses the growth of edutainment that is the attempt to make education entertaining through the sale of learning software and games, particularly to homes. In the final chapter, chapter 8, the authors offer some possible solutions to the exploitation of government monies by for-profit companies.

1

INTRODUCTION TO THE EDUCATION-INDUSTRIAL COMPLEX AND THE POWER OF NETWORKS

On January 17, 1961, at 8:30 in the evening, Dwight D. Eisenhower delivered his farewell address to a nation that had respected him as its general, president, and leader. While the address evoked many memories of his lifetime of service to his country, the words which are best remembered from that night may be these:

> we must guard against the acquisition of unwarranted influence, whether sought or unsought, by the military–industrial complex. The potential for the disastrous rise of misplaced power exists and will persist.
>
> (Eisenhower, 1961, p. 1035)

These words were spoken by a soldier prophet who personified the ideals of the U.S. military. He saw weapons and armaments being developed not to secure our country's defense but for the sake of their own development. He saw the associated costs and profits of such weaponry escalating, and feared the temptations that they provided. Fifty years later we know without a doubt that the military–industrial complex is thriving and has a significant influence on the country's military policy and expenditures. In a talk commemorating Dwight D. Eisenhower, Secretary of Defense Robert Gates commented on America's insatiable appetite for more and more weapons:

> Does the number of warships we have, and are building, really put America at risk, when the U.S. battle fleet is larger than the next 13 navies combined—11 of which are our partners and allies?
>
> Is it a dire threat that by 2020, the United States will have only 20 times more advanced stealth fighters than China?

These are the kinds of questions Eisenhower asked as commander-in-chief. They are the kinds of questions I believe he would ask today.

(Gates, 2010)

The Merriam–Webster Dictionary defines the military–industrial complex as "an informal alliance of the military and related government departments with defense industries that is held to influence government policy." This book is not about the military–industrial complex but a similar alliance that exists today in American education. One of the authors of this book first used the term *education-industrial complex* in 1994 to refer to the networks and alliances that were forming to promote the use of technology and related services in American K-12 education (Picciano, 1994). In that article, he described the education–industrial complex as being in its infancy but contended that within the next ten or more years, a major new thrust would occur that would become "very visible." The banking industry changed from the 1970s to the 1990s with automated-teller machines (ATMs) replacing human tellers for much of the routine processing of customer transactions, such as making deposits to and withdrawals from savings or checking accounts. It was difficult, but not impossible, to imagine an automated teaching machine that would replace the teacher in front of the classroom leading a lesson or delivering a lecture. The teaching machine did not materialize but Internet-based online learning has ushered in a new era of technology in American education.

While technology remains an important part of the education–industrial complex, the sphere of the complex has expanded to include ideological components and an array of for-profit corporations and service providers. The education–industrial complex can now be defined as networks of ideological, technophile, and for-profit entities that seek to promote their beliefs, ideas, products, and services in furtherance of their own goals and objectives. This complex is fueled by significant resources and advocacy provided by companies, foundations, and the media that want to shape American education policy to conform to their own ideals and that also stand to profit significantly from its development. Furthermore, the education–industrial complex is not simply a single entity conspiring to influence education policy. In fact, it is made up of multiple networks that sometimes share agendas but frequently operate independently and compete with one another for contracts and sales of goods and services.

The Components of the Education-Industrial Complex

The education–industrial complex revolves around three major components: ideology, technology, and profit-making (see Figure 1.1). These components interact with one another and are made up of multiple networks and alliances of agencies, organizations, and corporations (see Figure 1.2). In most cases, they overlap in their interests and goals.

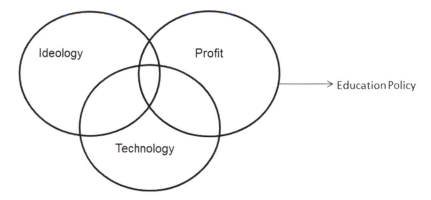

FIGURE 1.1 The Components of the American Education-Industrial Complex

School Governance and Organization

Today, American schools operate on a business model in a network of relationships which decrease voters' control. The schools didn't start out with limited voter input and modeled on a corporate structure. In their early days American schools were locally controlled by elected school boards with state and federal involvement limited to laws creating school districts, general regulations, and the collection of statistics (Tyack, 1974, pp. 37–40). By the end of the 19th

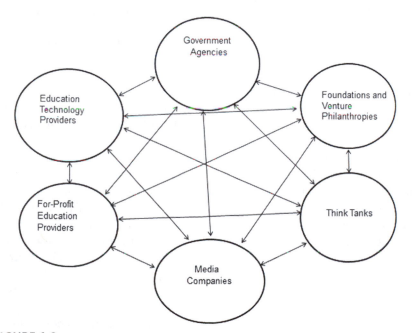

FIGURE 1.2 Networks and Alliances of the American Education–Industrial Complex

century schools adopted a corporate model with school administrators recast as corporate managers and school boards, particularly urban school boards, as boards of directors (Tyack, 1974, pp. 128–144). The new school board organization included fewer members, at-large elections of members, and, in many cases, elections held separately from general state and federal elections. This reorganization favored the election of the wealthy and the socially elite to school boards (Cronin, 1973). Only the "best" citizens, it was argued, should be trusted with the care of school children (Counts, 1927).

After World War II direct voter control of schools began to decline as federal and state governments expanded their influence over local schools through legislation such as the National Defense Education Act (1958) and the Elementary and Secondary Education Act (1965). The increasing centralization of school authority in state legislatures and Congress was challenged by free market ideologies and the reaction of some Christians and Whites displeased with U.S. Supreme Court rulings requiring the end to racial segregation, school prayer, and classroom Bible reading. This disaffected population joined with free marketers to propose school choice. Proponents of free markets wanted competition between schools to improve education and advocated a number of measures, including privatization of public schools, vouchers, and education tax credits. On the surface school choice promised democratically controlled education by letting parents "vote with their feet." Nineteenth century school elections promised democratic representation, while school choice promised direct parental control of their children's education (Spring, 2011, pp. 358–454). Choice certainly sounded democratic but in reality it was compromised by the continual expansion of state and federal involvement in schools.

By the 21st century actual democratic control slipped away as the federal legislation No Child Left Behind opened an era of national curriculum standards and mandated standardized testing. In most cases school choice was limited to choosing the school that best achieved the goals of the state curriculum. In this framework, parental choice did not include actual choice of instructional content for their children (Spring, 2010, pp. 121–127).

Today American schools are entangled in conflicting political and economic ideologies. Free market economists would like to privatize schooling with regulation turned over to the "invisible hand of the marketplace." Those advocating a limited free market approach to schools favor choice of public schools and charter schools that would teach a standardized state curriculum and tests. Clinging to more traditional ideas others seek to limit choice and privatization by asserting that schools should serve public goals and reflect public control. Corporate models of school organization persist even to the extent of opening school administrative ranks to those who have proven successful in the business world.

Those favoring the corporate model of schooling argue that schools should function like a business and that their balance sheets should be driven largely by accountability as measured by assessments and testing. Decisions should be made based on clearly defined outcomes and driven by efficient data-delivery systems. Students and parents are viewed as customers rather than partners in the common good. In addition, competition is seen as desirable and if a school is not performing, it should be closed down, transformed, or its students be allowed to attend other schools. Furthermore, privatization of public education in the form of government funding, directly or indirectly, of for-profit schools and private education management companies, should be considered as policy options for reforming schools. Associated with this thinking are desires to limit the privileges and influence of teachers' unions. Tenure, seniority rights, union shops, and teacher evaluation procedures are some of the issues that are sources of contention fostered by the educational-industrial complex. Teachers' unions affiliated with the American Federation of Teachers (AFT) and the National Education Association (NEA) became powerful in the 1960s and have tried to maintain their influence by endorsing and funding political candidates at all levels of government. The rational and corporate entities of the educational-industrial complex seek to counter the unions' influence on elections by supporting candidates who agree with their own views. It would be easy to say that the teachers unions typically support the candidates of the Democratic Party and the rational and corporate entities support candidates of the Republican Party, but this is not always the case and a good deal of overlapping exists. Teachers' unions themselves have to be considered players in the educational-industrial complex that vie with rational and corporate ideological entities. They seek to preserve prerogatives that have been negotiated and established in their collective bargaining agreements. For example, a major player in the education–industrial complex is the Democrats for Education Reform (n.d.), a political action committee whose "mission is to encourage a more productive dialogue within the Democratic Party on the need to fundamentally reform American public education centered on matters of greater accountability of schools, principals, and teachers." It has frequently clashed with the NEA and AFT over matters of teacher evaluations and seniority rules.

It should be mentioned that social conservative organizations have also been involved in the education-industrial complex. Rather than being focused on rational or managerial models of decision making, they have focused on issues such as school prayer, sex education, and the teaching of creationism. They have also been active and successful in organizing at the grassroots level to influence education policy. David Brock (2003) observed that fundamentalist Christians had working majorities on perhaps hundreds of school boards around the country where they influence "decisions on everything from curricula to condoms." While acknowledging their presence, this book will focus for the most part on those entities within the education-industrial complex that promote rational decision processes, accountability, school choice, and privatization.

Technology

Another important component of the education-industrial complex is technology. The use of technology in education has been evolving for decades. In higher education, technology has been widely used for research and administration applications since the 1960s. In K-12 education, the implementation of technology for administrative uses has been increasing steadily since the 1970s, but really did not make much of an impact on instructional uses until the 1990s when educational technology software such as simulations, games, and integrated learning systems became popular. The ubiquitous Internet has provided a plethora of educational uses and has lifted the dependence on technology to new heights. This applies to all applications whether administrative or instructional as well as for research and scholarship at the college level. The Internet has spurred new educational applications in online learning, credit-recovery, and data-driven decision making that did not exist 20 years ago. In K-12 education, several million students take online courses every year (Picciano & Seaman, 2010). The Florida Virtual High School alone enrolled more than 122,000 students in its programs in the 2010–2011 academic year. In higher education, fully online programs have become commonplace with over 6 million students or 30% of the total higher education student population taking a fully online course in any given year (Allen & Seaman, 2011). Technology is fundamentally transforming much of education from what it was in the 1990s and is an important aspect of a maturing education-industrial complex.

Steven Brill, a writer who has written extensively on education issues, in his latest book, *Class Warfare: Inside the Fight to Fix America's Schools* (2011), examined school reform from the point of view of those who deeply believe in charter schools and the need to limit the influence of teachers unions. The importance of technology is for the most part not mentioned at all until the very last chapter. In an interview with David Levin, founder of the KIPP schools which are among the most successful charter schools in the country, he discussed how can some of the successful experiments in KIPP schools be scaled up to improve teaching in American education. Levin's answer is enlightening that basically you cannot expect the KIPP model to be scaled up for all schools and teachers. Instead you have to devise support systems that rely extensively on good management and "great technology" (Brill, 2011, pp. 6862–6871).

Believers in the benefits of technology have developed extensive networks at all levels of government and across all political parties to push for greater reliance on and investment in educational technology in education, particularly in K-12. They see technology as something good and feel that the more it is used the better. Given the Internet's ease of use, availability, and general adoption in most public and private endeavors, the technology component of the education-industrial complex is very strong and will continue to grow.

Profit-Making

The third component of the education–industrial complex is made up of entities that profit by providing goods and services to schools and colleges. Textbook publishers, testing and tutoring services, education management companies, and for-profit colleges are significant players in the education–industrial complex. They should not all be looked upon as unscrupulous profiteers, although some could justifiably be characterized as such. To the contrary, many provide valuable services upon which schools and colleges absolutely rely. Corporate America embodies the capitalistic aspect of American culture and has been influencing American institutions since the Revolution. In 1835, Alexis de Tocqueville in his treatise, *Democracy in America*, stated:

> I know of no country, indeed, where the love of money has taken stronger hold on the affections of men and where a profounder contempt is expressed for the theory of the permanent equality of property.
>
> (De Tocqueville, Ch. 3)

All aspects of federal, state, and local political systems including education have been influenced historically, one way or other, by the business sector. However, in the past 20 years, corporate America has become more involved in and has tried to wield more influence on education policy than was ever the case in the past. Major companies and their officers have become outspoken on their views of American education and have geared many of their positions to influence overall education policy but also to benefit their products and services. Corporate executives such as Louis Gerstner Jr. (IBM and the Carlyle Group) have called for and organized education summits. Corporate-affiliated foundations such as the Gates Foundation are investing billions of dollars in school "reform" initiatives. Think tanks such as the American Enterprise Institute and the Heritage Foundation that receive substantial contributions from corporate sponsors regularly present extensive policy papers and briefs. These position papers promulgate the need for changes in education if America is to compete internationally for economic development, new industries, and professional talent. Media conglomerates, such as the Washington Post Company and News International that control television, radio, and Internet services as well as invest in educational services, promote products and services beneficial to their investments. The New York Times Company holds conferences on "Schools for Tomorrow" that focus on "bringing technology into the classroom." In a recent such conference 37 speakers were listed on the program 29 of whom represented corporations, advocacy organizations, and technology suppliers. Eight speakers were from colleges and universities, most of whom were directors of technology centers or initiatives. Not one individual on the program was a current public school teacher or administrator (*New York Times*, 2011).

In sum, the education–industrial complex is a series of networks and alliances that strive to influence the creation or modification of policies at all levels of government consistent with views and ideas that support extensive uses of technology and are profitable for its members.

Points of Influence—American Education Policy

The points of influence in the education–industrial complex are different from those in the military-industrial complex. The policy leadership of the military and defense organizations has always been centralized in the federal government, the Pentagon being the symbol of this central leadership. Industries and contractors serving the military interact with the federal government and officials appointed or elected to national office. Most senior-level appointed officials in the military are based in Washington DC. Members of the House and Senate, while they have offices in their home districts and states, conduct much of their business in offices in Washington, DC. In sum, the main points of policy formulation for the American military are generally accepted to exist in the nation's capital.

The education–industrial complex operates in a much more dispersed manner. While the U.S. Department of Education (USDOE) is a most important point of influence in education policy formulation, it is not the only one. The USDOE is relatively new, beginning operation in 1980, while the 50-state education departments and the 15,000 school districts have been in existence much longer and maintain significant influence in the development of policy and the allocation of resources in the nation's schools. Public and private colleges and universities operate as independent entities with oversight by state education departments and independent, mostly regional, accrediting bodies. In terms of K–12 financial policy, the federal government provides approximately 8 to 9% of funding with the remainder provided by the states and local school districts (Aud et al., 2011). The governing organizations of local school districts are not very consistent. The school district of Hawaii for instance encompasses the entire state. In Maryland, every school district is managed and operates at the county or municipal level. In New York, the vast majority of its 800 school districts operate independently of any other county or municipal governing body. With so many school districts, many important policy decisions including the selection of textbooks, the purchase of educational software, and the selection of testing services are made by school board members, most of whom are members of the community and are influenced primarily by parents, neighbors, and other constituents. At this level, an active Parent-Teacher Association (PTA) and even a local collective-bargaining agency can wield significant influence. With so many stakeholders dispersed over wide geographic areas, the mass media can become important in swaying decisions about education policy. In New York, there were substantial mass media campaigns in 2011 for and against the expansion of the number of charter schools that can operate in the state. In addition to promoting the movie, *Waiting for Superman*, pro charter school organizations held a Charter School Advocacy Day on February 7, 2011, to influence state legislators. Opponents to the expansion of charter schools such as the United Federation of Teachers (UFT) and the National Association for the Advancement of Colored People (NAACP) mounted their own anticharter school media campaigns in response.

An important aspect of the formulation of education policy, given the many points of influence, is the struggle for power among the policy makers. The USDOE since its inception has been trying to wield more influence on education policies throughout the country. Using financial aid as incentives, it has sought common core curricula and standards, new teacher evaluation systems, and the establishment of school "report cards." Some states have supported the USDOE in this respect, but others have resisted this intrusion and invoked the U.S. Constitution which reserves to the states the right and power to govern education.

The Power of Networks

The education–industrial complex is made up of a series of networks that evolve and grow in many ways. Personal contacts, regular meetings, social gatherings, and associations in formal organizations are examples of network behavior. However, over the past 20 years, technology in the form of digital communications as exemplified by the Internet and its social media capabilities, has added a whole new dimension to the concept of networking. Far beyond their ability to move data more rapidly throughout an organization, networks have profound effects on how people work with one another, on how the cohesion of a group can be maintained, and ultimately on accomplishing the group's goals and objectives. Watts (2003) and Barabasi (2002) have studied the effects of networks on various people-intensive processes. What they found is that networks enable individual behavior to aggregate into collective behavior. Something special happens when individual entities such as nodes, components, and people, are able to interact to form larger wholes such as networks, systems, and communities. Furthermore, the "interaction effect" or collective behavior may result in a far more productive environment than individuals acting by themselves; one individual working with another individual does not simply comprise two individuals but a third more powerful collaborating entity which can extend the benefits beyond two. Modern data communications networks now make it possible for many individuals to share ideas, work with one another, and organize collective behavior to achieve common goals and objectives. Perhaps one of the best examples of this is the revolution that occurred in Egypt in January 2011. Internet-based networking and social media such as Facebook, Twitter, and text-messaging were important tools of the revolution's organizers. These tools sped up the process by helping to organize the revolutionaries, to transmit their message and to galvanize support. In a piece that appeared in *Wired Magazine*, Sascha Meinrath, director of the New America Foundation's Open Technology Initiative commented:

> In the same way that pamphlets didn't cause the American Revolution, social media didn't cause the Egyptian revolution…. Social media have become the pamphlets of the 21st century, a way that people who are frustrated with the status quo can organize themselves and coordinate protest, and in the case of Egypt, revolution.
>
> (cited in Gustin, 2011)

While most observers saw the Egyptian revolution as a sudden, spur of the moment event, insiders such as Lawrence Pintak (2011), author of *The New Arab Journalist*, pointed out in a CNN interview that despite the speed with which the Mubarak regime fell, bloggers and digital activists have been working toward reform in the Middle East for years. "This is a digital revolution that has been happening for quite a while…" (Gustin, 2011). In response, Egyptian President Hosni Mubarak attempted to cut off Internet access to Facebook, Twitter, laptops, and smartphones. Iran and other countries in the Middle East and elsewhere have also been using Internet tools to monitor antigovernment activity (Shane, 2011). Likewise the networks of the education-industrial complex are attuned to the new social media technologies and have been using them extensively in conjunction with traditional people-networking to influence what happens in American education.

A Brief Look at the State of American Education

All of the important growth indicators (enrollment, revenues and expenditures, teachers and employees, number of graduates), show that American education is at an all-time high and is continuing to grow. The U.S. Department of Education, *Digest of Education Statistics* (2010) shows that enrollment in American education at all levels (pre-K through graduate school) in 2010 is almost 76 million students and it is projected to increase to more than 82 million students by 2019, with 58.5 million in K-12 schools and 23.5 million in postsecondary education. The increase is due primarily to the expected increase in the size of the national school-age population and there is nothing on the horizon that will change this projection.

In terms of teachers and other support staff, approximately 10 million people were employed in education in 2010 with 7 million employed in K-12 and 3 million in postsecondary education. If we combine student enrollment with the number of individuals employed, the combined number of people directly involved in education is 86 million, or about 27% of the total population (312 million people) in the United States.

With respect to the educational attainment of the population between 2000 and 2010, the percentage of the adult population 25 years of age and over who had completed high school rose from 84% to 87%, and the percentage of adults with a bachelor's degree increased from 26% to 30%. High school completers include those people who graduated from high school with a diploma, as well as those who completed high school through equivalency programs (i.e., GED programs). The percentage of young adults (25- to 29-year-olds) who had completed high school in 2010 was about the same as it was in 2000 (89 and 88%, respectively). The percentage of young adults who had completed a bachelor's degree increased from 29% in 2000 to 32% in 2010.

Funding the American education enterprise in 2010 reached in excess of $1.1 trillion with $650 billion provided for K-12 schools and $461 billion for postsecondary education. To provide a comparison, the military budget for the United States was $685 billion in 2010. Assuming that the level of expenditures match the growth in enrollment, the total cost for education at all levels will be in excess of $1.2 trillion by 2019. Over the next 10 years, more than $11 trillion will be spent on education.

The size and scope of the American education enterprise is enormous and far-reaching. It is growing and supports many individuals, businesses, and other enterprises. While the numbers and projections paint the picture of a vibrant growing system, there are many concerns about the quality of American education. Student performance on international assessments, high school graduation rates, time to degree at the postsecondary level, funding equity, and the cost of education have been well-documented issues that tend to dominate any discussion of American education and are an important part of the story that underlies the American education–industrial complex.

Organization of this Book

It is fair to say that many others including Henry Giroux, Stanley Aronowitz, Kenneth Saltman, and Kevin Kinser have written about particular parts of the education–industrial complex without naming it as such. It is our intention to offer a more complete critique of this complex by thoughtfully spelling out the full connections to be made and the consequences of such connections.

This book contains eight chapters designed to explore the American education–industrial complex. This chapter provides an introduction, definition, and background for the further exploration of the education–industrial complex. It draws upon the military-industrial complex, which is older and more established, as a way to introduce the concept of networks of ideological, technological, and for-profit entities that seek to promote their beliefs, ideas, products and services in accord with their own goals and objectives.

Chapter 2, "The Flat World as Shaped by the Shadow Elite," draws on Janine Wedel's framework of the "shadow elite" as used in her (2009) book.

This chapter will provide a template that tracks those who move between government, private companies, and other organizations promoting and influencing policies and practices related to American education. Specific examples will be drawn from companies such as textbook publishers, software providers, and other education services designed to operate at significant profit for their stockholders and parent companies.

Chapter 3 looks at the state of "Technology in American Education." Technology is a major aspect of the education–industrial complex and has facilitated its growth and operations. Billions of dollars are expended each year on educational technology, yet conclusive benefits of its uses are questioned. The advent of the Internet and online instruction has seen significant expansion of the use and investment in technology at all levels of education. This chapter will review the state of technology as applied in K-12 schools and colleges, focusing specifically on the growing development and demand for online learning environments.

Chapter 4, "Corporate Influences: No Child Left Behind, Privatization, and Commercialization," examines the role of corporate America in the education–industrial complex. Corporate America is a major player in the education–industrial complex, whether publishing textbooks, selling consulting services, or running for-profit educational entities. As such, it stands to benefit significantly from policies that promote the use of their products and services. Education in America has become big business with enormous expenditures to acquire the people, products, and services that make it function. While most businesses provide necessary and important products and services needed in schools and colleges, others are questionable revenue generators for private investors. This chapter will examine the role and objectives of corporations as major operators in the education–industrial complex.

Chapter 5 takes a close look at "Profits, Products, and Privatization." An important cornerstone of the education–industrial complex is the movement to privatization of public schools and colleges and their replacement by for-profit entities. The use of vouchers in K-12 education under the ideological guise of increasing competition and school choice are prime examples. For-profit colleges and universities have evolved as major players as well as competitors for public financial aid programs. This chapter will examine for-profit entities and compare their contribution to the public good with their private gain.

Chapter 6 considers the role of "Foundations and Think Tanks: Policies and Ideas Supporting the Educational-Industrial Complex," in the education–industrial complex. Funding many of the initiatives within the education–industrial complex are private foundations that have used their resources to "reform" education to conform to their own views. These foundations are further supported by think tanks, some of which are completely partisan in their views, the positions they take, and the studies that they publish. This chapter will specifically look at the role of several of the major foundations and think tanks that fund and promote the ideas of the players in the education-industrial complex.

Chapter 7 examines, "Media: News Media, Edutainment, and the Education-Industrial Complex," in supporting the education-industrial complex. The Internet, talk radio, and cable news networks provide platforms for sending messages that support the ideology and positions of the education-industrial complex to the public. The media become especially important given the dispersed nature of the governance of American education that exists in state and local bodies as well as in Washington DC. In this chapter, a "fair and balanced" look at how the media function as indoctrinating voices for the education-industrial complex will be examined.

Chapter 8, "Conclusion: 'A Nation at Risk' Redux," will integrate the ideas and positions established in the preceding chapters. It will ask a fundamental question about the mission of the education system we want in this country: Is it one based on capitalist principles of competition and profit-making or is it one based on the need to nurture students and their minds? It concludes that the nation is indeed once again at risk, not because of the quality of our schooling but because we may be selling our children's education out to private interests.

References

Allen, I. E., & Seaman, J. (2011). *Going the distance: Online education in the United States, 2011.* Babson College Survey Research Group and The Sloan Consortium. Retrieved from http://www.babson.edu/Academics/centers/blank-center/global-research/Pages/babson-survey-research-group.aspx

Aud, S., Hussar, W., Kena, G., Bianco, K., Frohlich, L., Kemp, J., & Tahan, K. (2011). *The condition of education 2011* (NCES 2011-033). U.S. Department of Education, National Center for Education Statistics. Washington, DC: U.S. Government Printing Office.

Barabasi, A. L. (2002). *Linked: The new science of networks.* Cambridge, MA: Perseus.

Brill, S. (2011). *Class warfare: Inside the fight to fix America's schools* [Kindle version]. New York: Simon & Schuster.

Brock, D. (2003). *Blinded by the right.* New York: Crown.

Counts, G. (1927). *The social composition of boards of education: A study of the social control of public education.* Chicago: University of Chicago Press.

Cronin, J. (1973). *The control of urban schools: Perspectives on the power of educational reformers.* New York: Free Press.

Democrats for Education Reform. (n.d.). Retrieved from http://www.dfer.org/about/

De Tocqueville, A. (1835). *Democracy in America.* Retrieved from http://xroads.virginia.edu/~HYPER/DETOC/1_ch03.htm

Eisenhower, D. E. (1961). Farewell address. *Public papers of the presidents* (pp. 1035–1040). Retrieved from http://www.h-net.org/~hst306/documents/indust.htm

Gates, R. M. (2010, May 8). *Remarks on defense spending.* Retrieved from http://www.defense.gov/speeches/speech.aspx?speechid=1467

Gustin, S. (2011, February 11). Social media sparked, accelerated Egypt's revolutionary fire. *Wired Magazine.* Retrieved from http://www.wired.com/epicenter/2011/02/egypts-revolutionary-fire/

Merriam-Webster Online Dictionary. Military-industrial complex. Retrieved from http://www.merriam-webster.com/dictionary/military-industrial

New York Times. (2011). Schools for tomorrow—Bringing technology into the classroom. Retrieved from http://www.nytschoolsfortomorrow.com/speakers.html

Picciano, A. G. (1994). Technology and the evolving education-industrial complex. *Computers in the Schools, 11*(2), 85–101.

Picciano, A. G., & Seaman, J. (2010). *Class connections: High school reform and the role of online learning.* Babson Survey Research Group, Babson College. Retrieved from http://www3.babson.edu/ESHIP/research-publications/upload/Class_connections.pdf

Pintak, L. (2011). *The new Arab journalist*: Mission and identity in a time of turmoil. London: I.B. Tauris & Co. Ltd.

Shane, S. (2011, January 29). Spotlight again falls on Web tools and change. *New York Times.* Retrieved from http://www.nytimes.com/2011/01/30/weekinreview/30shane.html?_r=1&nl=todaysheadlines&emc=tha26

Spring, J. (2010). *Political agendas for education* (4th ed.). New York: Taylor & Francis.

Spring, J. (2011). *The American school: A global context from the Puritans to the Obama Era, eighth edition.* New York: McGraw-Hill.

Tyack, D. (1974). *The one best system: A history of American urban education.* Cambridge, MA: Harvard University Press.

U.S. Department of Education, National Center for Education Statistics. (2010). *Digest of education statistics.* Retrieved from http://nces.ed.gov/programs/digest/d10/

Watts, D. (2003). *Six degrees: The science of a connected age.* New York: Norton .

Wedel, J. (2009). *Shadow elite: How the world's new power brokers undermine democracy: Government, and the free market.* New York: Basic Books.

2

THE FLAT WORLD AS SHAPED
BY THE SHADOW ELITE

"Welcome to the Human Network," invites the information and communication technology (ICT) giant Cisco, "When we're all connected, great things happen" (Cisco, 2011). The "Human Network" could represent what Janine Wedel, a professor of public policy, considers a new form of global governance based on networks of governments, educational institutions, and for-profit companies (Wedel, 2009). *Flexians* are what Wedel calls the actors moving through the networks between these global institutions. In global networks, flexians promote their own interests and sometimes those of for-profit companies. Flexians also network with educational institutions and private foundations, such as the Gates Foundation. The link between flexians and government bureaucracy involves flexians having personal relationships with bureaucrats. Some flexians may have at one time worked for a government agency. In a global context, flexians often have more allegiance to themselves and their networks than to a particular nation–state. Wedel argues that these networks represent a new form of global governance, particularly with increasing privatization of government services including education services.

For example, when U.S. Secretary of Education, Arne Duncan introduced the U.S. National Education Technology Plan, "Transforming American Education: Learning Powered by Technology," he recognized the important role in its development of Karen Cator, Director of the Office of Educational Technology, U.S. Department of Education. When announcing the plan Secretary Duncan stated, "Our team here, led by Karen Cator, who is doing a fantastic job, is absolutely committed to supporting the work necessary to bring this plan to life" (U.S. Department of Education, 2010).

Karen Cator exemplifies the life of a flexian who networks with private industry and government. Prior to joining the U.S. Department of Education, she directed Apple's "leadership and advocacy efforts in education" (U.S. Department of Education, 2011b). She joined Apple in 1997 after working on ICT for the Alaskan state government. Further illustrating the often entangled networks between government and business, she has served on the board of a major education for-profit lobbying group Software & Information Industry Association (SIIA)—Education (U.S. Department of Education, 2011b). This group lobbies government for laws and regulations that support the work of the industry, including the use of government money to purchase software for schools and laws allowing for increased K-12 online instruction. The SIIA describes its efforts to represent the industry:

> The Software & Information Industry Association is the principal trade association for the software and digital content industries. SIIA provides global services in government relations, business development, corporate education and intellectual property protection to the leading companies that are setting the pace for the digital age.

> **Principal Missions:**

> Promote the Industries: SIIA promotes the common interests of the software and digital content industries.

> Protect the Industries: SIIA protects the intellectual property of member companies, and advocates a legal and regulatory environment that benefits the industries.

> Inform the Industries: SIIA informs the industries and the broader public by serving as a resource on trends, technologies, policies and related issues that affect member firms and demonstrate the contribution of the industries to the broader economy.

> (Software & Information Industry Association, 2011a)

Another example of a flexian is Cator's colleague in the U.S. Department of Education, James H. Shelton, Assistant Deputy Secretary for Innovation and Improvement who works with learning technology. He has networked between private foundations, government positions, and business. Before taking a position in the federal government's Department of Education, Shelton worked as Program Director for the Gates Foundation. His education business connections are extensive as reported in his official biography posted on the U.S. Department of Education's website (2011a).

Coincidence of Interests

It is not our intention or Wedel's to portray careers like those of Cator and Sheldon as being sinister or conspiratorial. The networks they form between governments, business, and private foundations are a realistic portrait of current educational governance. Key to this network is what Wedel calls a "coincidence of interests" between personal, government, and nongovernment groups. First, Cator and Sheldon share a personal interest in ICT and, of course, advocate for its use. Second, this common interest is shared with the U.S. Secretary of Education Arne Duncan and it is reflected in the government's report *National Education Technology Plan 2010* that advocates for greater use of ICT in schools. A coincidence of interests is shared between Cator and Sheldon and the ICT companies they are associated with currently and in the past. This coincidence of interests also involves financial gain and the potential of financial gain for Cator and Sheldon and their associated ICT business connections.

It would be wrong to consider a coincidence of interests as resulting in corrupt actions or intentional bilking of government funds for for-profit companies, though this issue might be raised regarding Cator's association with the lobbying organization Software & Information Industry Association—Education. We can probably assume that both Cator and Sheldon are sincere advocates of ICT in schools and they believe it will improve schools. They would probably not see their actions as nefarious but as work that is doing good. In fact, their work might actually result in school improvement.

Another example of coincidence of interests between government policies (Core Standards) and the ICT industry is the *National Education Technology Plan 2010*'s recommendations for the national standardization of the curriculum and learning through the creation of Common Core Standards. It is not our intention to make a judgment about having national standardization of the curriculum but to point out how the Common Core intersects with the interests of the education business. It is easier to develop software learning programs to be sold in a national market if all states agree to a common set of curriculum standards. The Plan states, "The lack of common standards affects the quality of tools because developers limit their R&D investments into narrow markets and are not able to leverage overall market advancements in research and development. Interoperability standards are essential to resolving these issues" (U.S. Department of Education, 2010, p. xx).

A New Form of Governance?

Janine Wedel suggests that flexians and their networks are creating new forms of governance where decisions are made and discussions take place outside of normal government channels. For instance, the 2010 U.S. Department of Education's *National Education Technology Plan* is not a law but is intended to influence future federal government involvement in promoting ICT in schools. As a government policy statement it could potentially affect any future government involvement in schools. The report, as discussed below, was written by flexians with networks running through higher education, for-profit companies, private foundations, and government.

What is different today, as compared to the past, is the increasing privatization of government services. Wedel calls the bureaucracies of government involved in privatizing services "Swiss-cheese" to symbolize the holes left in government as services are turned over to private companies. There are two forms of "Swiss-cheese" governments, with the first involving turning over traditional government services to for-profit industries and the second being the initiation of new services by first hiring outside agencies.

The holes in Swiss-cheese government bureaucracies represent the reduction in government staff as services are privatized leaving fewer bureaucrats to regulate these privatized services. Wedel writes (2009),

> Because the number of government contracts and contractors has risen, while the number of civil servants available to supervise them has proportionately fallen, thus decreasing the government's capacity to oversee the process, even when government officials sign on the dotted line, they are sometimes merely rubber stamping the work of contractors.
>
> (p. 86)

Therefore, Wedel's description of the new governance system, including the governing system for education, involves linkages between privatized for-profit government services and flexians. In the United States, these linkages were made possible by the federal legislation No Child Left Behind (2001) which specifically provides for the hiring of for-profit companies. For instance, the section of the legislation dealing with failing schools provides for technical assistance which "shall include assistance in analyzing data ... [which] may be provided ... by ... a private not-for-profit organization or *for-profit organization* [emphasis added], an educational service agency, or another entity with experience in helping schools improve academic achievement" (No Child Left Behind, 2002).

The concept of a coincidence of interests becomes more powerful once the door is open for privatization of government services. For example, Karen Cator, Director of the Office of Educational Technology in the U.S. Department of Education, as previously discussed, was on the board of the Software & Information Industry Association—Education. While Cator is no longer on the board, the organization exemplifies the linkages between public policy and for-profit industries. The organization describes its intersection with government policies:

> SIIA's Public Policy program aggressively promotes and protects the interests of its member companies in legal and public policy debates by working with state, federal and international policymakers, organizing grassroots activism and participating in landmark legal decisions. SIIA

is the leading voice on key issues affecting the software and information industry, particularly with regards to electronic commerce and the digital marketplace.

(Software & Information Industry Association, 2011b).

The SIIA-Education describes its actions as: "SIIA's Education Division participates, shapes and supports the education industry by providing leadership, advocacy and critical marketing information to promote the success of education technology and content providers" (2011b). The education division's public policy is given as:

> SIIA supports a comprehensive, life-long learning strategy to prepare our citizenry with the knowledge and skills necessary for 21st Century success. Public policies should support: (1) integration of technology into education and training to provide anytime, anywhere and individualized learning; and (2) education and training in computing, mathematics, engineering and the sciences to meet our high-tech workforce needs.
>
> (Software & Information Industry Association–Education, 2011b)

In summary, in Wedel's model of a new governance system many government decisions are made not by elected representatives but within a network of private industries, flexians, and a personalized bureaucracy. Elected representatives play a smaller role as government services are privatized and decision making is made within these new networks. In the above examples, there is a common interest in increasing the use of ICT in education which would benefit for-profit companies providing these services. Promoting this coincidence of interests, Karen Cator moves in a network between government and for-profit industries, works with SIIA to ensure legislation and regulations favorable to the industry, supports government purchases of ICT from for-profit companies, and works on a government report that calls for more money for ICT usage in education.

Personalized Bureaucracy

Janine Wedel also argues that under this form of governance there develops a "personalized bureaucracy" where people working outside of government have personal relationships with those in government. These personal contacts are a result of flexian movement between business, private foundations, and government. When a person works in business or in another nongovernment organization she or he establishes a network of personal contacts. When a person in this category moves into a government bureaucracy this network of personal contacts might follow them, particularly if the bureaucracy where that person works serves his or her former industrial employment or organizational membership.

Karen Cator's career exemplifies the possibility of a personalized bureau-cracy. Her career at Apple and membership on the board of the Software & Information Industry Association–Education probably created a network of contacts in ICT industries. We use the word *probably* because there is no record of her actual personal contacts. We are assuming that her very appointment to the board of the Software & Information Industry Association–Education indicates she has some network of relations in the industry. Her work at Apple involved, as indicated before, leadership and advocacy efforts in education. Essentially, her efforts for Apple were to promote educational use of the company's products. This role would lend itself to creating networks among educators involved in the application of ICT in schools.

Consequently, when Cator was hired as a Washington bureaucrat, Director of the Office of Educational Technology in the U.S. Department of Education, she brought with her networks of relationships that could personalize her relationship with the very industry served by her government position. In turn, many in these networks might be on a first name basis with her. They might feel free to contact her about anything their private companies or organizations might want regarding federal education technology policies.

The possibility of personalized relations regarding the *National Education Technology Plan* between the bureaucracy of the U.S. Department of Education and nongovernment organizations is illustrated by the role of Barbara Means of SRI International who guided the 15-member technical group working on the plan. SRI, originally called the Stanford Research Institute, describes itself as "an independent, nonprofit research institute conducting client-sponsored research and development for government agencies, commercial businesses, foundations, and other organizations. SRI also brings its innovations to the marketplace by licensing its intellectual property and creating new ventures" (SRI, 2011). SRI's staff pursues grants from both government and commercial businesses. This means that the staff of SRI pursues network relationships with governments and business to ensure funding.

Barbara Means is codirector of SRI's Center for Technology in Learning. The 15-person technical working group on the *National Education Technology Plan* included Professor Roy Pea of Stanford University and codirector of SRI's Center for Innovations in Learning. Prior to joining the Stanford faculty in 2001 he served from 1996 to 2001 as SRI International Director of the Center for Technology in Learning. Currently, Pea is director and cofounder of Teach-Scape (Stanford Center for Innovations in Learning, 2011). TeachScape, where Professor Pea is director, is a for-profit company selling learning software, and its board of directors includes representatives from the financial industry: Phil Clough, ABS Capital Partners; Paul Mariani, ABS Capital Partners; and Robert Finzi, Sprout Group (Teachscape, 2011). Pea is also director of VIP Tone, another for-profit learning corporation, whose website (2011) states,

VIP Tone helps educators create world-class school environments with one integrated solution for their learning, communication and collaboration needs. Founded by Robert Iskander in April 2000, VIP Tone, Inc. is a privately held Delaware Corporation headquartered in Alameda, California, with an Australian subsidiary, VIP Tone Australia, PTY, Ltd., based in Adelaide, South Australia.

(VIP Tone, 2011)

The company claims that it sells products that serve 3,600,000 students and over 100,000 teachers around the globe (VIP Tone, 2011). Cator, Means, and Pea exemplify a network of personalized relationships that link the U.S. Office of Education to for-profit companies and private research organizations receiving government contracts. The network also exemplifies the coincidence of interests between technology firms that want to sell software to schools; research institutions like SRI that seek government grants and develop software for for-profit companies, and members of the U.S. Department of Education. Not surprisingly the *National Education Technology Plan* contains no criticisms of technology use in education and asserts: "The NETP presents a model of learning powered by technology, with goals and recommendations in five essential areas: learning, assessment, teaching, infrastructure, and productivity. The plan also identifies far-reaching 'grand challenge' R&D problems that *should be funded and coordinated at a national level* [emphasis added]" (U.S. Department of Education, 2010, p. x).

Shadow Government: The Gates Foundation

Another element in this new governance system is private foundations that influence public policy by supporting particular ideological positions, scholars, research, and policy reports. As the world's richest foundation, the Gates Foundation is linked to a shadow elite network that supports online instruction aligned with Common Core Standards and promotes increased use of ICT in schools. This is not surprising given the ICT orientation of Bill Gates who founded Microsoft and the foundation. As an example of the Gates Foundation's involvement in national education policy, the foundation gave money to Achieve, Inc. to coordinate the writing of tests to be aligned with the Common Core Standards. Achieve was created "by the nation's governors and corporate leaders ... [to] raise academic standards and graduation requirements, improve assessments and strengthen accountability" (Dillon, 2011). In addition, the Gates Foundation funded Teach Plus which lobbies state legislatures to eliminate protection of senior teachers during layoffs; most teacher union contracts and many state policies favor layoffs based on seniority. The Gates Foundation has also funded groups such as the New Teacher Project to support changes in the way teachers are evaluated. As we will discuss later in this chapter, the

Gates Foundation supports the Foundation for Educational Excellence, a major advocacy group for expanding online instruction by changing state education laws, and it funds the Pearson Foundation to create online courses aligned with the Common Core Standards. *New York Times* investigative reporter Sam Dillon wrote about the attempt by Teach Plus to change state laws favoring senior teachers during layoffs: "In Indiana, some lawmakers accused the group [Teach Plus] of being 'part of a conspiracy by Gates and hedge fund managers' to undermine the [teacher] unions' influence" (Dillon, 2011).

A flexian who has a personalized relationship with the Gates Foundation is Cator's colleague in the U.S. Department of Education, James H. Shelton, Assistant Deputy Secretary for Innovation and Improvement. His office deals with learning technology. Prior to joining government, he was Program Director for the Gates Foundation. His education business connections are extensive as reported in his official biography posted on the U.S. Department of Education's website and LearnNow, Edison Schools, and McKinsey.

Sheldon exemplifies Wedel's description of a flexian with his movement between government, private industry, and the Gates Foundation. It reflects a coincidence of interests between government, for-profit companies, and non-profit foundations. Through his work with the Gates Foundation and private industry, Sheldon has a network of personal relations interested in his government work. This raises two questions: How many people in the for-profit education business and the Gates Foundation feel they can approach Sheldon on a first name basis? Does his network extend to his colleague in the Department of Education, Karen Cator?

Coincidence of Interests and Financial Gain

Sometimes the coincidence of interests in flexian networks is tied to financial gain. We use the word *sometimes* because people within a network of relationships might share professional interests and beliefs with financial rewards being a low priority. For instance, Karen Cator's networks created through her work in the Alaskan government, Apple, and the U.S. Department of Education appears to have less to do with major financial gain, except for possible increases in salary, than with her dedicated interest in promoting the value of ICT in education. The coincidence of her interests with those of foundations, for-profit ICT companies, and government policies appears to be based on a shared interest in enhancing the role of ICT in education.

However, there are other examples of network relationships that do reflect a coincidence of interests involving financial gain. In the following example promotion of increased online instruction involves connections between the Foundation for Excellence, Gates Foundation, Pearson Foundation, and Pearson publishing. As we will discuss, Pearson publishing has the greatest financial interest in this network of relationships through the selling of online courses that are aligned with the national Common Core Standards along with other for-profit ICT companies.

The Foundation for Excellence is headed by Jeb Bush, former governor of Florida and brother of ex-President George W. Bush. The major goal of the Foundation for Excellence is to increase the availability of online instruction. Foundation for Excellence in Education is urging legal changes that will expand opportunities for online education offered by both public and for-profit organizations. The Foundation's action report *Digital Learning Now* (2011a) lists in its "10 Elements of High Quality Digital Learning" actions that should be taken by lawmakers and policymakers. These actions include state legislation providing online courses to K-12 students. The proposed laws require that online courses be aligned with the Common Core Standards and that all providers are treated equally, meaning that for-profit companies will be treated the same as public schools (Foundation for Excellence in Education, 2011a). The Foundation's action plan calls for states to *not* place limits on the number of credits earned online; to allow students to take all or some of their courses online; and to make online instruction available all year and at any time.

The above legal changes would open the floodgates to online K-12 instruction in the United States. An important part of this plan is the elimination of any laws that put a cap on the size of class enrollments. This opens the door to replacing teachers with online instruction since the elimination of class size requirements would allow schools to put all their students, if they make the choice, online for their education. *Digital Learning Now* states, "Actions for lawmakers and policymakers: 'State does not restrict access to high quality digital content and online courses with policies such as *class size ratios and caps on enrollment or budget* [emphasis added]'" (Foundation for Excellence in Education, 2011a, p. 7).

Proposals to expand online instruction and, as a result, reduce the cost of teachers' salaries, are presented as answers to declining state education budgets. Digital Learning Now states that budget crises open the door to educational changes like the expansion of online learning: "Growing budget deficits and shrinking tax revenue present a tremendous challenge for the nation's Governors and lawmakers, especially when education sometimes consumes up to half of a state's budget. However, what might appear to be an obstacle to reform can also present a great opportunity for innovation" (Foundation for Excellence in Education, 2011a, p. 5). Another cost cutter in Digital Learning Now is the proposal that textbooks be replaced with digital content. In 2011, Bush hit the road carrying the message of the Foundation's Digital Learning Now to state governments. The message was simple—the economic crises provided an opportunity to reduce school budgets by replacing teachers with online courses (Trip, 2011).

The sources of the Foundation for Excellence's funding reveal networks between foundations. Their major funder is the Gates Foundation along with the Walton Family Foundation and the Broad Foundation. The Walton Family Foundation was established by Sam Walton the founder of the global retail chain Wal-Mart. One area of funding of the Walton Family Foundation is education, with a primary concern of promoting school choice. The Walton Foundation website states, "The Walton Family Foundation invests in programs that empower parents to choose the best education for their children.... We are interested in helping children to receive high-quality educations in public, charter and private school" (Walton Foundation, 2011). One choice option is of course online learning.

The other major funder of the Foundation for Excellence is the Broad Foundation established by Eli and Edythe Broad who made their money in real estate and financial services through the creation of two Fortune 500 companies—KB Home and SunAmerica (Broad Foundation, 2011b). *Forbes* lists Eli Broad as the 132nd among the world's billionaires (*Forbes*, 2010). Part of the work of the Broad Foundation is devoted to education, including support for school choice options that are the same as Jeb Bush's Foundation: "We are interested in helping children to receive high-quality educations in public, charter and private schools" (Broad Foundation, 2011a).

Illustrating the intertwined network relations is the fact that the Broad Foundation receives support from the Gates Foundation for its Broad Residency Program in Urban Education. The residency program trains executives from business and civic organizations to assume leadership roles in education at every level of government. In other words, the Residency Program trains flexians who will be able to move between private for-profit companies and government positions in schools.

> The Broad Residency is a management development program that places talented executives with private and civic sector experience and advanced degrees from top business, public policy and law schools into two-year, full-time, paid positions at the top levels of urban school districts, state and federal departments of education and leading charter management organizations.
>
> (Broad Center, 2011)

The goal of training flexians and Broad's connection to the Gates Foundation is highlighted in a Broad Center news release, "Record Number of Broad Residents Take on Local, State, and Federal Roles Managing Education Reform" (Broad Center, 2011). This news release reports the extent of Gates Foundation involvement in training members of this shadow elite: "The Broad Center has received a $3.6 million grant from the Bill & Melinda Gates Foundation to recruit and train as many as 18 Broad Residents over the next 4 years to, "Provide management support to school districts and charter management organizations addressing the issue of teacher effectiveness" (Broad Center, 2011).

Another supporter of the Foundation for Education for Excellence who would financially gain from the Foundation's agenda is IQity, a provider of online learning platforms. IQity is a sustaining contributor to the Foundation for Excellence in Education (the Gates, Walton, and Broad foundations are founding contributors). IQity website describes the company's work:

> The IQity e-Learning Platform is the most complete solution available for the electronic search and delivery of curriculum, courses, and other learning objects. Delivering over one million courses each year, the IQity Platform is a proven success for students, teachers, school administrators, and district offices; as well as state, regional, and national education officials across the country.
>
> (IQuity, 2011)

Other supporters are the publishing house giants Houghton Mifflin Harcourt and McGraw-Hill. Listed as Friends of the Foundation for Educational Excellence are ICT companies involved in education, namely Apex Learning, Cisco, Learning3.Com, Pearson Foundation, and SMART (Foundation for Excellence in Education, 2011b).

The Pearson Foundation, one of the funders of the Foundation for Excellence in Education, also receives funds from the Gates Foundation to write online courses based on Common Core Standards which in turn helps its parent company Pearson to create and sell online courses based on the same standards.

Foundation for Excellence, Pearson, and the Gates Foundation: Coincidence of Interests

The relationship between the Foundation for Excellence, and the Pearson and Gates foundations highlights how organizations mutually reinforce each other's policy objectives and promote an economic interest in online instruction. In other words, it is a coincidence of interests that include both a belief and dedication to the importance of ICT in education and financial gain. On April 27, 2011 the Pearson Foundation announced that it had received a grant from the Gates Foundation to aid in the creation of 24 online courses in math and reading/English arts that would be aligned with the Common Core Standards (Pearson Foundation, 2011b). The courses are to be implemented in 2013 (Gates Foundation, 2011).

The economics of the relationship between the two foundations demonstrates how opportunities are created by nonprofits to help for-profits increase their earnings. The Pearson Foundation was established by the global publishing and ICT company Pearson. The Pearson Foundation explains this relationship as: "The Pearson Foundation is the philanthropic arm of Pearson, one of the world's leading media and education companies. Pearson Foundation extends Pearson's commitment to education by partnering with leading nonprofit, civic, and business organizations to provide financial, organizational, and publishing assistance across the globe" (Pearson Foundation, 2011).

The money given by the Gates Foundation to the Pearson Foundation will allow for the free distribution of 4 of the planned 24 online courses. Pearson, the company, will be able to sell the other 20 online courses. In their announcement of the award to the Pearson Foundation, the Gates Foundation stated (2011), "Funding from the Bill & Melinda Gates Foundation will support the development of this robust system of courses, including four—two in math and two in English language arts—to be available at no cost on an open platform for schools" (Gates Foundation, 2011).

Pearson, the company, describes itself as the world's leading for-profit education company: "Pearson is the world's leading education company. From pre-school to high school, early learning to professional certification, our curriculum materials, *multimedia learning tools and testing programs help to educate more than 100 million people worldwide—more than any other private enterprise* [emphasis added]" (Pearson, 2011). Pearson reports that 60% of their sales are in North America though it sells books and tests in 60 countries. Its publishing subsidiaries are Scott Foresman, Prentice Hall, Addison-Wesley, Allyn and Bacon, Benjamin Cummings, and Longman.

Pearson, the company, does have an economic stake in the relationship between its Pearson Foundation and the Gates Foundation in the creation of online courses to meet Common Core Standards. A huge market for online courses aligned to the Common Core Standards is being created by the U.S. Department of Education's implementation of the *National Technology Education Plan* and Jeb Bush's lobbying of state governments to implement the recommendations in *Digital Learning Now*. Pearson wants to sell products in this burgeoning market. The company has a past history of marketing online courses with claims that they are one of the world's largest providers and the company boasts on its website that: "We are also a leading provider of electronic learning programs and of test development, processing and scoring services to educational institutions, corporations and professional bodies around the world" (Pearson Education, 2011).

The Pearson Foundation is candid that Pearson, the company, will use the Foundation's work to market products to local school districts. The foundation and company are not embarrassed at what on the surface appears illegal with a tax-exempt foundation creating materials that will eventually be sold by a for-profit company. This intention is clearly stated in Pearson Foundation's announcement of the money it is receiving from the Gates Foundation.

> Pearson, the nation's leading education technology company, will offer these courses to school districts, complete with new services for in-person professional development for teacher transition to the Common Core and next-generation assessment. The Pearson Foundation will also work

with other partners to explore opportunities for additional commercial development and distribution.

(Pearson Foundation, 2011b)

Pearson will also earn money from assessments aligned with the Common Core Standards. These aligned assessments promise to be another major source of revenue. Pearson already claims:

> We are also the largest provider of educational assessment services and solutions in the US (Pearson Educational Measurement), developing, scoring and processing tens of millions of student tests every year. We mark school examinations for the US federal government, 20 American states, and score more than 100 million multiple-choice tests and 30 million essays every year. Pearson also scores the National Assessment of Educational Progress (the only federal nationwide test), and college entrance exams

(Pearson Education, 2011b).

As an example of a coincidence of interests involving financial gain, the Gates Foundation plays a crucial role. The money given to the Pearson Foundation is only part of what the Gates Foundation refers to as a "suite of investments." This suite of investments focuses on using ICT to implement the Common Core Standards. In the announcement of this suite of investments, including the money going to the Pearson Foundation, the Gates Foundation states it will support the following activities to be aligned with the Common Core Standards: "game-based learning applications; math, English language arts and science curricula built in to digital formats; learning through social networking platforms; and embedded assessments through a real-time and engaging environment of experiences and journeys" (Gates Foundation, 2011).

Pearson Foundation, Pearson, and State Commissioners of Education: Coincidence of Interests

Another example of a coincidence of interests is the Pearson Foundation's funding of state commissioners of education to take global junkets to hear sales pitches from Pearson publishing. *New York Times* investigative reporter Michael Winerip wrote in a September 19, 2011 article,

> In recent years, the Pearson Foundation has paid to send state education commissioners to meet with their international counterparts in London, Helsinki, Singapore and, just last week, Rio de Janeiro. The commissioners stay in expensive hotels, like the Mandarin Oriental in Singapore. They spend several days meeting with educators in these places. They also meet with top executives from the commercial side of Pearson,

which is one of the biggest education companies in the world, selling standardized tests, packaged curriculums and Prentice Hall textbooks.

(Winerip, 2011)

For example, Illinois state education superintendent Christopher A. Koch traveled at the Pearson Foundation's expense to Pearson conferences in Helsinki in 2009 and to Rio de Janeiro. At the time, Illinois was paying Pearson $138 million to develop and administer tests that are aligned with the Common Core Standards. Nine state education executives received an all-expense paid trip to Singapore to attend a Pearson conference. At the Singapore conference were the president of Pearson Education South Asia, the president of Pearson Brazil, three corporate vice presidents and chief marketing officers. According to Winerip, a Pearson produced videotape of the Singapore Conference includes "Steve Dowling, the executive vice president for corporate development at the time, saying, 'Pearson, through the Pearson Foundation, has brought this group together'" (Winerip, 2011). Other states having contracts with Pearson whose education executives attended Pearson conferences include Florida, Virginia, California, Georgia, Michigan, Iowa, and South Dakota (Winerip, 2011).

Both Pearson Foundation executives and state education officials claim that their behavior was not unethical but represented an attempt to improve education. The disingenuous responses of state and Pearson officials may be a result of believing that these behind the scenes activities are the normal way of conducting government business. As an example of the shadow elite, the above scenario illustrates the networking of government officials, foundations, and for-profit companies in a global arena. Reporter Winerip quotes Jack Jennings of the Center on Education Policy, who believes that a "wall" should be created between for-profit education companies and state officials, "We shouldn't let these companies—that make tests, textbooks, curriculum materials—buy the loyalty of educators the way the drug companies have bought the loyalty of doctors" (Winerip, 2011).

ICT and the Shadow Elite: A New System of Governance?

Is Janine Wedel correct that the type of networks existing in the world of ICT and education represent a new form of governance? In an ideal situation for democratic control, which seldom happens because of the amount of information and complicated issues that are usually involved, the voting public would be making direct decisions either through voting or pressure on elected representatives. Given the sheer quantity of activities that the government is involved in it is hard for the average voter to keep abreast of government decisions and minutiae that might be associated, for example, with environmental, health, defense, financial and education issues. A system of representative government primarily works by voters selecting representatives who then deal with the details of governance. Many of the actions of elected representatives take place outside the public eye except for those diligent voters who spend their days following government activities (Spring, 2011b).

Consequently, one could argue that a large number of decisions made by modern governments are done outside the direct purview of voters. Does this represent actions by shadow elites or is Wedel's concept of the shadow elite something new? As discussed previously, Wedel claims that today public decisions are made by organizations and people outside of government as a result of privatization of government services and the global networking made possible by ICT. For instance, in the early history of U.S. school governance was primarily a function of local school boards with state governments increasing their governance role in the late 19th and early 20th centuries. Consequently, the public had the opportunity to be more directly involved in educational decisions. Direct citizen power diminished in the 20th century as the federal and state governments expanded their roles in educational governance (Spring, 2011a, chapters 6, 10, 13, 15). Privatization of government services made the decision-making process further removed from public scrutiny and control. With the benefit of ICT the decision making now has a global dimension that involves international organizations and education companies.

Let's consider this new governing structure by looking at the role of the Gates Foundation. Its funding decisions affect educational systems around the world. Most importantly these decisions are not publicly controlled. However, Gates Foundation funding sometimes targets the changing of government laws. For instance, the Gates Foundation is one funder of Foundation for Excellence in Education, which, as previously mentioned, advocates changing state laws to create a more favorable environment for online instruction. The Gates Foundation also supports other efforts to change state laws providing for online instruction. It also provides support for Florida's Virtual School which was founded in 1997 as the first statewide system of K–12 online instruction. The courses are offered globally with Florida residents taking the courses for free while non-Florida residents pay tuition (Florida Virtual School, 2011). The legal parallels between Florida's Virtual School laws and those advocated by the Foundation for Excellence in Education are highlighted in a memorandum issued on January 8, 2009 by Florida's Commissioner of Education Eric Smith. The memorandum explains Florida's legal requirements, including "that school districts may not limit student access to FLVS courses" and that there are "no limits on the number of credits a student may earn at FLVS during a single school year or multiple school years" (Smith, 2009). While the Foundation for Excellence in Education promotes online courses as solutions to school budget problems, Florida law allows for the use of the Florida Virtual Schools by local school districts "to help ease overcrowding" (Smith, 2009).

Affecting global math instruction, the Gates Foundation funds a joint Russian and United States nonprofit initiative for online math instruction called

Reasoning Mind (2011a). With offices in Moscow and Houston, Reasoning Mind cites the mantra that: "First-rate math and science skills are essential for success in the 21st century workforce. Unless we can come together to take our nation's math education to the next level, the United States will quickly lose its leading role in industry and innovation" (Reasoning Mind, 2011a). Reasoning Mind is supported by a host of foundations besides the Gates Foundation. Reasoning Mind is a nonprofit organization, but it receives sponsorship from global for-profit technology firms having an interest in online instruction, including Cisco, Google, Oracle, FairIsaac, Sungard, and Atlassian (Reasoning Mind, 2011b). Reasoning Mind has linkages to global firms, including Russia's oil and gas industry. The founder and CEO of Reasoning Mind is Alexander Khachatryan who in 1992 founded and became President of Russian Petroleum Consultants Corporation and in 1999 became Vice President of Operations of the ICT company Logexoft. Khachatryan's career stretches back to the Soviet period when he earned degrees from the Moscow Oil and Gas Institute. Consequently, it is not surprising that the American branch of Reasoning Mind is located in the oil and gas center of Houston Texas.

The Gates Foundation also influences literacy instruction by funding 20 literacy based programs developed by the Digital Youth Network for online instruction (Digital Youth Network, 2011). Also funded is the Institute of Play (2011) to apply game design to instructional methods and curriculum. The Institute of Play is a nonprofit corporation founded in 2007 "by a group of game designers looking to apply game design principles to challenges outside the field of commercial game development. Within six months funding was secured to start up an innovative new public school in New York City, called Quest to Learn" (Institute of Play, 2011). The application of game design to education was also the purpose of the Gates Foundation grant to Quest Atlantis to create video games for math, science, and literacy. Quest Atlantis serves 50,000 children in 22 states and 18 countries. As described on its website it "is an international learning and teaching project that uses a 3D multi-user environment to immerse children, ages 9 to 16, in educational tasks" (Quest Atlantis, 2011). It was created by the Center for Research on Learning and Technology at the School of Education, Indiana University.

The Gates Foundation also supports the creation and use of the Common Core Standards. As noted earlier, the foundation gave money to Achieve, Inc. to coordinate the writing of tests to be aligned with the Common Core Standards. Achieve was created "by the nation's governors and corporate leaders... [to] raise academic standards and graduation requirements, improve assessments and strengthen accountability" (Dillon, 2011). Directly influencing the adoption of Common Core Standards, the Gates Foundation announced the funding of Portfolio of Innovative Grants to Develop New Teaching and Learning Tools: "All these applications will support the Common Core Standards" (Gates Foundation, 2011). In addition, the Gates Foundation is funding

Educurious Partners to develop high school courses based on Common Core Standards using a social network Internet application and Next Generation Learning Challenges to develop embedded assessments aligned with the Common Core Standards.

Exemplifying its effect on governments, the Gates Foundation funded Teach Plus which has been lobbying state legislatures to eliminate protection of senior teachers during layoffs; most teacher union contracts and many state policies favor layoffs based on seniority.

In summary, the Gates Foundation is part of a network of foundations, for-profit ICT companies, and government bureaucrats making important decisions that are designed to change or enact new laws. The support of creation and implementation of Common Core Standards and aligned assessments are examples as also are the network's funding efforts to have states enact laws similar to those in Florida and create schools similar to the Florida Virtual School. As exemplified by the Gates funding of the Pearson Foundation, this funding supports the involvement of ICT for-profit companies in preparing online instruction aligned with the Common Core Standards.

International Association for K-12 Online Learning: Lobbying Government to Support an Industry

The International Association for K-12 Online Learning exemplifies the attempt by companies to influence public opinion, government policies, and school funding. As a trade association its membership includes some of the big names in the field of online learning: Blackboard, K12, Inc., Connections Academy, EdisonLearning, and the ubiquitous company Pearson (iNACOL, 2011b). There are many other online companies that belong to this trade group. Throughout the following chapters of this book we will be exploring the work of these companies, particularly Pearson, which seems to have its hand in every aspect of education including textbooks, online learning, data management, and assessment. For the purposes of this chapter, we want to focus on the network and advocacy role of the International Association for K-12 Online Learning.

The President and CEO of the International Association for K-12 Online Learning, Susan Patrick, is networked with the previously discussed Karen Cator and the *National Education Technology Plan*. As former Director of the U. S. Department of Education's Office of Educational Technology under President George W. Bush, she contributed to publishing the U.S. *National Education Technology Plan* (iNACOL, 2011a). Also, she cochaired the U.S. government's Advanced Technologies Working Group for Education and Training. Prior to her U.S. government job, she worked on technology policy and legislation for Arizona's Governor Jane Dee (iNACOL, 2011a). As President and CEO she is now linked to all the for-profit online education companies who are members of the trade association.

Interestingly, the International Association for K-12 Online Learning supports changes in state and federal laws that parallel the recommendations of Jeb Bush's Foundation for Excellence report *Digital Learning Now.* In answer to the question "What Can Congress and the Federal Government Do to Promote Quality Online Learning Opportunity for All Students?" the trade association recommends: "Make removal of online learning enrollment caps and restrictions a condition and requirement for states to receive grants from US ED Office of Innovation and Improvement" (iNACOL, 2009b). Also, in the economic interests of its members, the trade association advocates that the federal government, "Assist states/districts in moving away from funding based on seat-time toward mastery learning" (iNACOL, 2009b). This recommendation would ensure that students could take online courses without worrying about having to spend a certain amount of time in a brick and mortar school to meet graduation requirements.

Similar to the Foundation for Excellence, this trade association claims that the financial crisis opened the door to more online learning in schools. In one of the most blatant examples of pushing the economic interests of online companies during a period when teachers were losing their jobs because of budget cuts, the International Association for K-12 Online Learning issued a statement with the revealing title, "K-12 Online Learning: A Smart Investment NOW More Than Ever" (2011a).

> In times of great economic challenge, citizens look to policymakers for solutions that lay the foundation for a brighter tomorrow. In K-12 education, one of the most promising and cost-effective solutions is quality online learning. Many states have made an important initial investment in online learning. Since every dollar spent this year must count even more than ever, now is the time to preserve and expand investments in online learning.
>
> (iNACOL, 2009a)

The Nation's reporter Lee Fang claims that there is a connection between right-wing organizations and the virtual online education industry. He writes, "Lobbyists for virtual school companies have also embedded themselves in the conservative infrastructure" (Fang, 2011). Fang claims, "iNACOL president Susan Patrick traverses right-leaning think tanks spreading the gospel of virtual schools. In the past year, she has addressed the Atlas Economic Research Foundation, a group dedicated to setting up laissez-faire nonprofits all over the world, as well as the American Enterprise Institute in Washington." Patrick's relationship to conservative foundations and think tanks is logical since, as we will discuss in chapter 5. it is these organizations that have been promoting both a free market in education and the use of for-profit education companies by public schools.

The policies of the International Association for K-12 Online Learning highlight the interconnections between education businesses and government. First is the importance of the trade association's support of changing government laws to expand the market for the products of the virtual school industry. Second, the International Association for K-12 Online Learning supports local school policies that use taxpayer money to purchase these virtual school products. And the lasting impact of these policies, something that the trade association advocates, is shifting local public school money from the hiring of teachers to the purchase of virtual instruction from for-profit industries.

Global Governance: The World Economic Forum

Flexians network through the World Economic Forum to influence global education policies. The organization provides this official history of its development (2011a): "The World Economic Forum was first conceived in January 1971 when a group of European business leaders met under the patronage of the European Commission and European industrial associations.... The Forum is perhaps most widely known for its Annual Meeting in Davos-Klosters" (World Economic Forum, 2011a). Illustrating the organization's role in networking world leaders in government, business, and civil society leaders its official history states: "Through the years, numerous business, government and civil society leaders have made their way to the Swiss Alpine resort to consider the major global issues of the day and to brainstorm on solutions to address these challenges" (World Economic Forum, 2011a).

Social networking at the World Economic Forum's annual meetings at Davos involves face-to-face encounters. *New York Times* columnist Andrew Ross Sorkin (2011) offered this description of networking at Davos: "Of course, much of the week is really about one thing: networking. As the 'Black Swan' author Nassim N. Taleb described it to Tom Keene of Bloomberg Television, the event is 'chasing successful people who want to be seen with other successful people. That's the game'" (Sorkin, 2011). The Economic Policy Institute's Jeff Faux agrees with Sorkin but recognizes the economic and political impact of networking at Davos: "It is more like a political convention, where elites get to sniff one another out, *identify which ideas and people are 'sound'* [emphasis added] and come away with increased chances that their phone calls will be returned by those one notch above them in the global pecking order" (cited by Rothkopf, 2008, p. 266).

In other words, networking at Davos plays an important role in legitimizing ideas among the global elite as captured in Faux's phrase: "identify which ideas and people are 'sound'." Of course, Faux's statement is a generalization that might not apply to all ideas approved by different attendees at Davos. However, the World Economic Forum does issue reports including those covering educational policy. These reports might be considered a reflection of network discussions about education that are "sound" and acceptable to the global elite.

What are the major educational ideas that floated through the World Economic Forum network? In 2003 the World Economic Forum created a Global Education Initiative (GEI) designed to network business, government, the academia, international organizations, civil society, and nongovernmental organizations "to effect positive, sustainable and scalable changes in education at global and regional levels with a focus on innovation, quality and relevance" (World Economic Forum–Education, 2011b). The stated goal was to improve global education by increasing the "engagement of the private sector" (World Economic Forum–Education, 2011b).

The World Economic Forum's Global Education Initiative promotes the interests of global business by emphasizing Entrepreneurship Education as "a tremendous force that can have a big impact in growth, recovery, and societal progress by fuelling innovation, employment generation and social empowerment" (World Economic Forum–Education, 2011b). Highlighting the networking of the Global Education Initiative with the for-profit education and financial industries is its Strategic Partners and Board Members which include Abraaj Capital, Cisco, Deloitte, Edelman, EMC, HCL, Heidrick & Struggles, Intel, Juniper Networks, Lenovo, ManpowerGroup, McGraw-Hill, and Microsoft (World Economic Forum–Education, 2011b).

The World Economic Forum's Roundtable on Entrepreneurship Education in the Middle East and North Africa (MENA) met in Marrakech, Morocco on October 24, 2010 and issued a "Manifesto for Creating Jobs and Economic Growth in MENA through Entrepreneurship and 21st Century." The Manifesto reflected the World Economic Forum's push to align national education systems with the needs of the global economy and to have a business agenda influence national curricula. The Manifesto states:

Transform the Education System by Integrating 21st Century Skills and Entrepreneurship

Educational institutions, from the earliest levels up, need to adopt 21st century methods and tools to develop the appropriate learning environment for encouraging creativity, innovation and the ability to think "out of the box" to solve problems. Entrepreneurship enables the development of leadership and life skills and has become increasingly recognized as a key competency.... Embedding entrepreneurship and innovation, cross-disciplinary approaches and interactive teaching methods in education requires new models, frameworks and paradigms. Changes in the educational system are needed across all levels and should address the lifelong learning process as well as critical links and interactions between levels (primary, secondary, higher and vocational education).

(World Economic Forum MENA, 2010).

In addition to aligning national education systems with business needs, the World Economic Forum continues to advocate increasing the role of the private sector, in other words, expanding the education networks of the shadow elite. At the World Economic Forum's 2011 Annual Meeting of its organizational subgroup the New Champions at the Summer Davos in Dalian, China one topic was "New Solutions: Closing the Educational Gap (World Economic Forum New Champions, 2011c). For both national education systems in developed and developing nations, the meeting asserted: "The private sector has proved to be the most dynamic actor in pursuing innovative approaches to education. One of the best forms of collaboration between government and the private sector is the contribution of funds by high net worth funds, working in collaboration with foundations that have public accountability" (World Economic Forum, 2011c).

World Economic Forum: ICT Companies and Education

Reflecting efforts to increase involvement of the private sector in national education systems, World Economic Forum reports advocate increasing ICT in education. This agenda is supported by a global network of for-profit ICT companies. In the World Economic Forum's *Global Information Technology Report 2010–2011: Transformations 2.0* global ICT leader César Alierta, Executive Chairman and Chief Executive Officer of Telefónica and member of the Boards of Directors of China Unicom and Telecom Italia, summarized the general attitude about "The Promise of Technology": "The contribution of ICT to both social fields—education and health—is not only obvious, but is also one of the areas where the implementation of technology has enormous potential" (Dutta, 2011). Among ICT's contributions to education, he states, are instant access to knowledge, opportunities to improve teaching methods, and distance and lifelong learning.

The Global Information Technology Report 2010–2011 advocates the application of what it calls the "Transformation 2.0 agenda" to education and other social services (Dutta, Mia, & Geiger, 2011, p. 3). What is transformation 2.0? It is the application and analysis of data related to school management, operations, student assessment scores, and instructional materials. Data collected on students, in this paradigm, could be used to match instructional materials with student abilities and predict the student's educational future. The person chosen to write the Report's section on "Transformation 2.0 for an Effective Social Strategy" was Mikael Hagström, the Executive Vice President of Europe, the Middle East, Africa and Asia Pacific at SAS which as described on its website "is the leader in business analytics software and services, and the largest independent vendor in the business intelligence market" (SAS, 2011a). Given this corporate background it is not surprising that Hagström believes that the use of analytic software, of the type produced by his firm to interpret data is at the heart of Transformation 2.0.

Hagström argues that the use of data-driven decision making has evolved through three stages; stages that can be used to frame its application to education. The first stage of data management occurred in business which used ICT to collect data and subject it to quantitative analysis. The second stage, and this encompasses public education, involved applying these methods developed in the private sector to government operations, including schools.

Today, Hagström argues, the world is embarking on the third stage: "investing heavily in analytic capabilities and driving the development of new techniques and technologies, including high-performance computing, data integration, and complex event processing" (Hagström, 2011, p. 92). He compares the first two stages to looking in the rearview mirror while driving. Quantitative analysis involves looking at data collected on past events, such as the results of student test scores.

The third stage uses "analytics," which he defines as the software and processes that convert data in "actionable insights" (Hagström, 2011, p. 92). In this third stage, one is looking through the front windshield at potential future circumstances: "we can use analytics to spot patterns and predict future trends with far greater accuracy than ever before.... Analytics gives you the ability to see forward, peek into the future and make meaningful judgments that result in better outcomes" (Hagström, 2011, p. 92).

Hagström's article on Transformation 2.0 reflects the business objectives of his own company SAS which is part of the global network of ICT companies. The company uses the concept of "analytics" to sell its software products: "SAS Analytics provide an integrated environment for predictive and descriptive modeling, data mining, text analytics, forecasting, optimization, simulation, experimental design and more" (SAS, 2011b). SAS targets the education market along many other markets including casinos. The company claims to have worked for over 30 years in the education field with its products now being used in 3,000 educational institutions worldwide. Under "education" on its website, SAS states that it offers a range of educational products "from online curriculum resources that enhance student achievement and teacher effectiveness to on-site or hosted administrative offerings that supply SAS customers with the accurate and reliable information and analysis they need to make the best data-driven decisions possible" (SAS Education, 2011c). One SAS product Education Value-Added Assessment System designed to measure academic growth using data from standardized tests is used in the United States by the Metropolitan Nashville Public Schools, Hershey Intermediate in Pennsylvania, and the High Point Central High School North Carolina. The Education Value-Added Assessment System does not involve the sale of software but has states and school districts sending their "electronic data directly to SAS, where the data is cleaned and analyzed. SAS transmits the results via a secure Web application that is a powerful, but user-friendly, diagnostic tool for any user with security privileges to access" (SAS EVASS, 2011a).

SAS's Education Value-Added Assessment System exemplifies the Transformation 2.0 championed by the World Economic Forum. Its website stresses the use of this product will provide a basis for future decision making.

> As the most comprehensive reporting package of value-added metrics available in the educational market, SAS EVAAS for K-12 provides valuable diagnostic information about past practices and reports on students' predicted success probabilities at numerous academic milestones. By identifying which students are at risk, educators can be proactive, making sound instructional choices and using their resources more strategically to ensure that every student has the chance to succeed.
>
> (SAS EVAAS for K-12, 2011a)

SAS promises that, "Effectively implemented, SAS EVAAS for K-12 allows educators to recognize progress and growth over time, and provides a clear path to achieve the US goal to lead the world in college completion by the year 2020" (SAS EVAAS for K-12, 2011a).

Reflecting its advocacy of applying analytics to educational data, World Economic Forum's (2011c) report *Empowering People and Transforming Society: The World Economic Forum's Technology Pioneers 2011* identified Knewton as one of its three pioneers of Information Technology and New Media for 2011. Knewton is bringing analytical tools to teachers and students as textbooks become digital and are delivered through e-readers (World Economic Forum Empowering People, 2011c, p. 20). Their analytical tools will identify parts of the e-textbooks by structure and level of difficulty and link them to the digital profile of each student. Knewton's website provides the following description of its pioneering work (2011):

> Knewton is developing the industry's most powerful Adaptive Learning Platform, customizing educational content to meet the needs of each student. Whereas traditional classrooms and textbooks provide the same material to every student, Knewton will dynamically match lessons, videos, and practice problems to each student's ideal learning arc.
>
> Knewton works by tagging all content down to the atomic concept level. The system further tags the resulting content by structure, difficulty level, and media format. Then we can dynamically generate for each student, each day, the perfect bundle of content based on exactly which concepts she knows and how she learns best.
>
> (Knewton, 2011)

Knewton also provides Web-based test preparation courses for GMAT, LSAT, and SAT test preparation courses.

In summary, the Global Economic Forum's advocacy of more private sector and ICT involvement in national education systems supports Janine Wedel's contention that pressure is being put on governments to privatize their services with more government contracts being issued to private companies to provide services and manage schools. In turn, the growth of private sector involvement expands Wedel's shadow elite involvement in educational governance.

Conclusion: Shadow Elite and ICT

The evolution of Wedel's new governing system and the growing importance of ICT in education is occurring during the same time period. Consequently, promoters of ICT usage in schools and for-profit educational technology companies can use these shadow networks to ensure government laws favoring educational technology in the classroom and to ensure the purchase and integration of ICT companies' products into school instruction. A key factor in this new governing system that favors the business sector is the privatization of government services. The privatization of government services, including educational services, creates Swiss-cheese governments lacking sufficient regulators to oversee privatized government services. Also, the private sector is motivated by financial gain to intensive it's lobbying efforts to enact laws that privatize more government services and to increase funding of these privatized services.

Within the networks created by privatization flexians move between government, foundations, and private industry selling the idea that ICT is a panacea for schools. It is not our purpose to criticize educational technology but to point out how the new leverages of power can be used to the financial benefit of ICT companies. Within these networks, Wedel argues, is a coincidence of interests that can be primarily professional, financial or a combination or both. We illustrated the coincidence of interests in the networks created around the Gates Foundation with its funds and personnel moving between government, other foundations, and private companies. These networks, as discussed in this chapter, often result in a personalized bureaucracy where those seeking favorable regulations and laws along with more money can approach government bureaucrats on a first name basis.

What will this mean for the future? It is difficult to predict the future because events and conditions can change so swiftly. However, what if Jeb Bush's Foundation for Excellence is successful in convincing state and local officials that budget gaps can best be handled by utilizing less expensive online courses sold by companies like Pearson and by changing state laws to allow students to take most of their courses online? Will this mean schools of the future will have fewer teachers and more ICT? Will brick and mortar schools with age graded classrooms be replaced by community centers where students drop by for assistance with online instruction done at home or will they travel to the community center to do their online lessons?

Consider the example of Westwood Cyber School in Michigan included in the previously discussed National Education Technology Plan. Based on the British model of "Not School" it is functioning as a dropout recovery and prevention program with students doing most of their work at home using the Internet and reporting to a brick and mortar school 2 hours a week (U.S. Department of Education, 2010, p. 69). Or consider one of the scenarios provided by researchers for the Organization for Economic Cooperation and Development (OECD), which they label "deschooling." In the deschooling scenario school systems would be replaced by universal networking where: "There is no longer reliance on particular professionals called 'teachers': the demarcations between teacher and student, parent and teacher, education and community, break down. New learning professionals emerge, whether employed locally to teach or act as consultants" (OECD, n.d., p. 10).

The possibility of Not School or deschooling indicates that ICT is prompting new ways of thinking about the organization of national education systems at the very time that governments are increasing their privatization of services. This new governance system could result in ICT companies gaining a greater foothold in education resulting in major transformations in the organization of school systems. Of course, other factors will temper the final outcome of the role of ICT in education, such as the reaction of teachers and administrator unions, public response to the possible demise of the traditional brick and mortar school and age-graded classroom, and the concerns of parents' organizations and a host of other civil society groups. We will have to wait to see how the shadow elite in ICT networks are able to influence the ultimate impact of ICT and governing structures on national school systems.

References

Bill and Melinda Gates Foundation. (2011, April 27). Gates foundation announces portfolio of innovative grants to develop new teaching and learning tools that support teachers and help students. Retrieved May 1, 2011, from Bill and Melinda Gates Foundation: http://www.gatesfoundation.org/press-releases/Pages/common-core-tools-110427.aspxBroad Center. (2011). *Record number of Broad Residents take on local, state, federal roles.* Retrieved from http://broadresidency.org/asset/0-tbr%20national%20press%20release.pdf

Broad Foundation. (2011). *About us.* Retrieved from http://www.broadfoundation.org/about_broads.html

Cisco. (2011, September). Welcome to the human network. Retrieved from http://www.cisco.com/web/IN/thehumannetwork/index.html

Digital Youth Network. (2011). *About us.* Retrieved from http://www.digitalyouthnetwork.org/1-about/pages/1-overview

Dillon, S. (2011, May 21). Behind grass-roots advocacy, Bill Gates. *New York Times*, p. 1.

Dutta, S. a. (2011). *The global information technology report 2010–2011.* Geneva, Switzerland: World Economic Forum.

Dutta, S., Mia, I., & Geiger, T. (2011). The network readiness index 2010. In S. a. Dutta, *The information technology report 2010–2011* (p. 3). Geneva, Switzerland: World Economic Forum.

Fang, L. (2011, November 16). How online learning companies bought American schools. Retrieved from http://www.thenation.com/print/article/164651/how-online-learning-companies-bought-americas-schools

Florida Virtual School. (2011). *About us.* Retrieved from http://www.flvs.net/areas/aboutus/Pages/default.aspx

Forbes. (2010). The world's billionaires #132 Eli Broad. Retrieved from http://www.forbes.com/lists/2010/10/billionaires-2010_Eli-Broad_599L.html

Foundation for Excellence in Education. (2011a). *Digital learning now.* Retrieved from http://www.excelined.org/DOCS/Digital%20Learning%20Learning%Now%20Report%20For%Governors.pdf

Foundation for Excellence in Education. (2011b). *Meet the sponsors.* Retrieved from http://www.excelined.org/Pages/Programs/Excellence_in_Action/Meet_the_Sponsors.aspx

Gates Foundation. (2011, April 27*). Gates foundation announces portfolio of innovative grants to develop new teaching and learning tools that support teachers and help students.* Retrieved from http://www.gatesfoundation.org/press-releases/Pages/common-core-tools-110427.aspx

Hagström, M. (2011). Transformation 2.0 for an effective social strategy. In S. a. Dutta, *The global information technology report 2010–2011* (pp. 91–99). Geneva, Switzerland: World Economic Forum.

iNACOL. (2009a, July). *Advocacy: K-12 online learning: A smart investment NOW more than ever.* Retrieved from http://www.inacol.org/advocacy/

iNACOL. (2009b, August). *Advocacy: What can Congress and the federal government do to promote quality online learning opportunity for all students?* Retrieved from http://www.inacol.org/advocacy/

iNACOL. (2011a). *iNACOL President and CEO .* Retrieved from http://www.inacol.org/about/president.php

iNACOL. (2011b). *Members.* Retrieved from http://www.inacol.org/membership/members.php

Institute of Play. (2011). *About us.* Retrieved from http://www.instituteofplay.org/about/

IQuity. (2011). *Welcome to IQuity.* Retrieved from IQuity: http://www.iq-ity.com/index.aspx

Knewton. (2011). *About Knewton.* Retrieved from Knewton: http://www.knewton.com/about

No Child Left Behind Act of 2001. Retrieved from http://www.ed.gov/policy/elsec/leg/esea02/107-110.pdf

OECD. (n.d.). *The starter pack: Futures thinking in action.* Retrieved from http://www.oecd.org/document/33/0,3343,en_2649_35845581_38981601_1_1_1_1,00.html

Pearson. (2011a). *Education: Around the business.* Retrieved from http://www.pearson.com/about-us/education/around-the-business

Pearson. (2011b). *Pearson at a glance.* Retrieved from http://www.pearson.com/about-us/pearson-at-a-glance

Pearson Education. (2011c). *Pearson education.* Retrieved from http://www.pearson.com/about-us/education

Pearson Foundation. (2011a). *Home.* Retrieved from http://www.pearsonfoundation.org

Pearson Foundation. (2011b, April 27). *Pearson foundation partners with Bill and Melinda Gates Foundation to create digitial learning programs.* Retrieved from http://www.pearsonfoundation.org/pr/20110427-pf-partners-with-gates-foundation-to-create-digital-learning-programs.html

Quest Atlantis. (2011). *Welcome.* Retrieved from http://atlantis.crlt.indiana.edu/site/view/Researchers#58

Reasoning Mind. (2011). *About us.* Retrieved from http://www.reasoningmind.org/?mv=5

Reasoning Mind Technology Sponsors. (2011). *Technology sponsors.* Retrieved from http://www.reasoningmind.org/?mv=5

Rothkopf, D. (2008). *Superclass: The global power elite and the world they are making.* New York: Farrar, Straus & Giroux.

SAS.(2011a). *About.* Retrieved from http://www.sas.com

SAS. (2011b). *Analytics.* Retrieved from http://www.sas.com/technologies/analytics

SAS.. (2011c). *Education.* Retrieved from http://www.sas.com/industry/education/index.html

SAS EVAAS. (2011a). *SAS EVAAS for K-12.* Retrieved from http://www.sas.com/govedu/edu/k12/evaas/index.html#s1=1

SAS EVASS. (2011b). *SAS EVAAS for k-12: System Requirements.* Retrieved from http://www.sas.com/govedu/edu/k12/evaas/index.html#s1=4

Smith, E. (2009, January 8). *Florida Department of Education: Florida virtual school as school choice.* Retrieved from http://info.fldoe.org/docushare/dsweb/Get/Document-5250/dps-2009-07.pdf.

Software & Information Industry Association. (2011a). *About SIIA.* Retrieved from http://www.siia.net/index.php?option=com_content&view=article&id=159&Itemid=6

Software & Information Industry Association. (2011b). *SIIA member programs & resources.* Retrieved from http://www.siia.net/index.php?option=com_content&view=article&id=64&Itemid=23

Software & Information Industry Association-Education. (2011). *Education and the workforce.* Retrieved from http://siia.net/index.php?option=com_content&view=article&id=641:education-a-workforce-development&catid=66:public-policy-overview&Itemid=710

Sorkin, A. (2011, January 24). A hefty price for entry to Davos. Retrieved from http://dealbook.nytimes.com/2011/01/24/a-hefty-price-for-entry-to-davos/?hp

Spring, J. (2011a). *The American school: A global context from the Puritans to the Obama era* (8th ed.). (chapters 6, 10, 13, 15). New York: McGraw-Hill.

Spring, J. (2011b). *The politics of American education.* New York: Routledge.

SRI. (2011). *About us.* Retrieved from http://www.sri.com/about/

Stanford Center for Innovations in Learning. (2011). Roy Pea. Retrieved from http://scil.stanford.edu/about/staff/bios/pea.html

Teachscape. (2011). Board of directors. Retrieved from http://www.teachscape.com/html/ts/nps/board_of_directors.html

Trip, G. (2011, April 26). Jeb Bush leads broad push for educational change with "Florida Formula." Retrieved from http://www.nytimes.com/2011/04/27/education/27bush.html?ref=todayspaper

U.S. Department of Education. (2010). *National education technology plan 2010: Transforming American education: Learning powered by technology.* Washington, DC: Author.

U.S. Department of Education. (2011a). *James H. Shelton III, Assistant Deputy Secretary for Innovation and Placement—biography.* Retrieved from http://www2.ed.gov/news/staff/bios/shelton.html

U.S. Department of Education. (2011b, May). *Karen Cator, Director of the Office of Educational Technology—biography.* Retrieved from http://www2.ed.gov/news/staff/bios/cator.html

VIP Tone. (2011). *About.* Retrieved from http://www.viptone.com/about.html

Walton Foundation. (2011). K-12 Education reform. Retrieved from http://www.waltonfamilyfoundation.org/educationreform/index.asp

Wedel, J. (2009). *Shadow elite: How the world's new power brokers undermine democracy.* New York: Basic Books.

Winerip, M. (2011, September 19). When free trips overlap with commercial purposes. *New York Times,* p. A15.

World Economic Forum. (2011a). *About us: History.* Retrieved from http://www.weforum.org/history

World Economic Forum. (2011b). *Education.* Retrieved from http://www.weforum.org/issues/education

World Economic Forum. (2011c). *Empowering people and transforming society: The world economic forum's technology pioneers 2011.* Geneva, Switzerland: World Economic Forum.

World Economic Forum MENA. (2010). *Global education initiative: MENA roundtable on entrepreneurship education Marrakech, Morocco.* Geneva, Switzerland: World Economic Forum.

World Economic Forum New Champions. (2011). *New solutions: Closing the education gap.* Retrieved from http://www.weforum.org/sessions/summary/new-solutions-closing-education-gap.pdf

3

TECHNOLOGY IN AMERICAN EDUCATION

Lewis Perelman authored a provocative book in 1992. The title was *School's Out: Hyperlearning, the New Technology, and the End of Education,* it called for policy makers to seize an opportunity that was then presenting itself in American education. He saw classroom teachers approaching "rapid obsolescence" and believed that their jobs could be done better by technology. He called for a major overhaul of the nation's schools that would transform teaching and learning from the traditional, human-intensive activity we know into a machine-intensive one. He claimed that teachers could be replaced by computers and the only reason this had not yet occurred was that the academic establishment and the "educrats" were not allowing it to happen (Perelman, 1992). The major overhaul of education to turn it into the technology-centric activity that Perelman called for did not occur but it doesn't mean that it isn't still on the horizon.

In 2008, Clayton Christensen, Michael Horn, and Curtis Johnson published *Disrupting Class: How Innovation Will Change the Way the World Learns.* Christensen is a professor at the Harvard Business School and the best-selling author of *The Innovator's Dilemma* (2011). In *Disrupting Class* Christensen, Horn, and Johnson presented a compelling rationale for changing education in a way that makes far greater use of online technology, providing more student-centered and individualized instruction. Among the most interesting aspects of this book was the prediction that by the year 2019 about one-half of all high school courses would be taught online.

Perelman and Christensen et al. represent the view that technology is beneficial to education and the more that is done with technology the better our public schools will be. They are not alone. Over the past century there have been several calls to make extensive uses of technology in education and to take advantage of "teaching machines" that could replace teachers.

In the 1920s, Sidney Pressey, and later B. F. Skinner, developed rudimentary teaching machines that were not at all suitable for mass production or introduction into public schools. However, they did demonstrate actual "programmed instruction" which would gain popularity with the development of digital technology in the latter part of the 20th century. In the 1960s, Patrick Suppes and Richard Atkinson designed several computer-assisted instruction programs using digital technology based on programmed instruction. This work evolved into stand-alone integrated learning systems (ILS) that enjoyed popularity in the 1980s and 1990s. At the time, ILSs represented the most intensive use of technology in teaching and learning. They integrated hardware, software, and curriculum and usually provided sophisticated computer-managed instructional techniques that were able to customize or individualize material for each student using the system. They were not designed to be an adjunct to teaching but to perform the actual teaching function. Two examples of integrated learning systems are Computer Curriculum Corporation's SuccessMaker, which had several reading and writing applications, and the Waterford Early Reading Program, which focused specifically on young readers. With the advent of the Internet in the mid-1990s, these systems underwent significant changes as they joined the chorus of software programs that moved from stand-alone to Web-based network delivery. The online versions of these systems are seeing significant increased popularity and represent the type of online digital applications that Christensen et al. are promoting. Before continuing this discussion of teaching machines, programmed instruction, and fully online individualized courses, it would be beneficial to look at the evolution of technology in American education. It is important to understand that this review is done with the understanding that technology has evolved into a major aspect of the education-industrial complex and has facilitated its growth and operations. Billions of dollars each year are expended on educational technology while the conclusive benefits of its uses continue to be questioned.

The Evolution of Technology in American Education

The nature of technology in American society has been evolving since the nation's founding. For purposes of this discussion, the advance of digital computers in the mid-20th century will be the starting point. Figure 3.1 provides a brief generic technology timeline that illustrates the development and acquisition of technology over the past 70 years. What is especially important is that the nature of technology, and hence the acquisition pattern, started to change significantly in the 1990s as more and more people, organizations, and corporations came to rely on the Internet for many basic functions. Portable and mobile devices have advanced and will continue to determine how technology is accessed and used. To frame this evolution within education, it will help to separate higher education from K-12 education and to distinguish technology used for administrative, instructional, and research purposes.

	1940→	1950→	1960→	1970→	1980→	1990→	2000→	2015→

	Pre-mainframe	Mainframe	Minicomputer	Microcomputer	Post-microcomputer
Machine	Experimental machines such as ENIAC	IBM 700, 360, 4300 Series	Digital Equipment PDP Series	PC Macintosh	Digital information appliances
Cost	Unaffordable	Affordable to large businesses	Affordable to large and small businesses	Affordable to individuals	Inexpensive—individuals will own several
Size	Large room	Room	Large desk	Desktop laptop	Palm-size
Distribution	One in existence	Thousands sold	Hundreds of thousands sold	Hundreds of millions sold	Billions will be sold

FIGURE 3.1 Technology Time Line (1940–2015)

Pre-Internet (1960–1990s)

Prior to the 1990s and the arrival of the Internet, which changed the entire concept of technology not just for education but for all aspects of American society, technology was evolving at a steady pace in education. Higher education in particular was at the forefront of using large mainframe computers and later minicomputers to support university activities and especially research in the 1960s and 1970s. Large mainframe computer manufacturers such as IBM, Univac, and Control Data Corporation partnered with research faculty in engineering, science, and other fields to assist in the development of the new digital technology. These manufacturers also made acquisition of the technology attractive to colleges and universities by offering substantial discounts—in excess of 30 to 40%—to purchase or lease products. It is fair to say that there was a symbiotic relationship between computer manufacturers and higher education in the use and development of new hardware and software. Beyond research, computer technology found its way into other college and university activities, namely administrative and instructional applications.

It wasn't long before computers were used for student record-keeping, financial accounting, personnel, and payroll processing. New academic programs in computer science resulted in the use of technology to teach software programming and systems design. New management information systems, databases, and statistical analysis software further fueled the use of instructional computing in the social sciences, business administration, and other professional programs. In the 1980s with the large-scale migration of digital technology to microcomputers, higher education was again in the forefront of moving its administrative and instructional applications to the smaller devices as computer laboratories and media centers expanded and grew throughout college campuses. Administrative offices replaced typewriters with word-processing enabled microcomputers. Data-communications networks, designed to integrate computing throughout a university and beyond, appeared and expanded significantly. In the 1980s and 1990s, academic programs began to require that all students regardless of their majors be computer literate and fluent in order to insure that students were prepared for careers or graduate study. Academic departments introduced courses with technology components unique to their disciplines or subject areas. Simulations in the sciences, statistical software analysis in the social sciences, synthesizers in music, and graphics programs in art became commonplace.

In K-12 education, the evolution was different. In the early years K-12 education was not seen as a partner in the development of technology by the large computer manufacturers. While many school districts, especially some of the larger ones, began to use technology for administrative applications, little was being done in instruction. In the 1980s, this began to change with the arrival of microcomputers and new companies such as Apple began to market their products to primary and secondary schools. Several interesting software products such as *The Oregon Trail, Reader Rabbit,* and *Where in the World is Carmen Sandiego* were developed in the 1980s to supplement instruction. The children's programming language, Logo, developed by Seymour Papert at the Massachusetts Institute of Technology, enjoyed a certain amount of use and application. By the late 1980s and early 1990s, new fully integrated learning systems designed to replace instruction enjoyed a certain appeal but were never fully embraced by the K-12 world. Educators were surely interested in the potential of the technology but expressed reservations about its implementation and appropriateness.

In June 1997, the journal *Technological Horizons in Education* celebrated its 25th anniversary with a special edition that looked back at educational technology milestones over the preceding 25 years. Articles by major contributors to the field of educational technology celebrated achievements and lamented obstacles. Technology luminaries such as Andrew Molnar, Director for Applications of Advanced Technologies, National Science Foundation; Seymour Papert, Developer of Logo and Professor, The Media Laboratory, Massachusetts Institute of Technology; and Alfred Bork, Professor Emeritus, Information and Computer Science, University of California, Irvine, all agreed that technology in education had grown since the 1970s from an object of study to an indispensable tool. However, they also agreed that the potential had yet to be realized and that education, especially K-12, was not as far along as other sectors in its use of technology. This was to change in the 1990s as the Internet began to make itself felt in all aspects of society.

The Internet (Mid-1990s to Present)

With the advent of the Internet, the power of a global network had significant ramifications on educational activities. Faculty engaged in research applications in colleges and universities were able to extend their work and collaborate more gracefully with colleagues around the country and around the world. Administrative applications were redesigned to make use of the World Wide Web, which was the common networking platform. This greatly enhanced the ease with which data could be shared among individuals and offices across buildings, campuses, or administrative departments that might be hundreds of miles apart. Database management systems were developed that allow administrators to maintain accurate information on students, faculty, curriculum, and finances as well as to integrate and analyze these data to make operations more efficient and effective. Colleges and universities created or expanded offices of institutional research to study the operational and instructional activities and provide senior administration with the data necessary to manage budgets, develop new academic programs, and serve more students. The most significant development that the new Internet technology provided, however, was the ability to offer courses and academic programs online. Students no longer needed to attend a physical classroom but could participate wherever they had access to the Internet through the availability of affordable portable devices at any time and in any place. While a certain amount of distance learning had developed earlier in higher education using radio and television, the Internet provided a new level of interaction and immediate communication that the earlier technologies did not. As a result, online learning replaced the older distance learning technologies, adding a whole dimension embraced by many colleges and universities for students who lived at a distance as well as for students who lived in close proximity. Allen and Seaman (2011) have conducted national studies on the nature and extent of online learning in higher education for 9 years. In their latest study, based on survey results from a national sample of chief academic officers, they found that:

- Over 6 million students were taking at least one online course during the fall 2010 term, an increase of 10% (560,000 students) over the previous year.
- Nearly 31% of higher education students now take at least one course online.
- Sixty-five percent of all reporting institutions said that online learning was a critical part of their institution's long term strategy, a small increase from 59% in 2009. (Allen & Seaman, 2011, p. 4)

Figure 3.2 illustrates that the growth in online learning is not only substantial but is outpacing the overall growth in higher education enrollments. Online learning has also spurred the growth of the for-profit higher education industry that enrolled approximately 2 million students in 2010. As late as 2000–2001, enrollments in for-profit institutions were no more than several hundred thousand students.

	Total Enrollment	Annual Growth Rate of Total Enrollment	Students Taking at Least One Online Course	Online Enrollment over Previous Year	Annual Growth Rate of Online Enrollment	Online Enrollment as a Percent of Total Enrollment
Fall 2002	16,611,710	NA	1,602,970	NA	NA	9.6%
Fall 2003	16,911,481	1.8%	1,971,397	368,427	23.0%	11.7%
Fall 2004	17,272,043	2.1%	2,329,783	358,386	18.2%	13.5%
Fall 2005	17,487,481	1.2%	3,180,050	850,267	36.5%	18.2%
Fall 2006	17,758,872	1.6%	3,488,381	308,331	9.7%	19.6%
Fall 2007	18,248,133	2.8%	3,938,111	449,730	12.9%	21.6%
Fall 2008	19,102,811	4.7%	4,606,353	668,242	16.9%	24.1%
Fall 2009	19,524,750	2.2%	5,579,022	972,669	21.1%	28.6%
Fall 2010	19,641,140	0.6%	6,142,280	563,258	10.1%	31.3%

FIGURE 3.2 Total and Online Enrollment in Degree-granting Postsecondary Institutions – Fall 2002 through Fall 2010. *Source:* Allen, I. E. & Seaman, J. (2011). *Going the distance: Online education in the United States, 2011.* Babson College Survey Research Group and The Sloan Consortium. http://www.babson.edu/Academics/centers/blank-center/global-research/Pages/babson-survey-research-group.aspx

As impressive as the enrollment figures above are, they do not tell the full story since they only report students enrolled in fully online courses. There is another side to online learning that "blends" with traditional face-to-face learning. These blended programs and courses that include some face-to-face and some online activities, may enroll as many if not more students than fully online courses. Unfortunately there is little hard data available on blended courses in higher education because of the absence of a single definition and the lack of reporting mechanisms at many colleges. Nevertheless, the greatest growth in online learning applications might be occurring within this blended modality of learning. Using a broad definition of blended learning, it would not be rash to estimate that probably half of all students in higher education now take a fully online or blended course in any given year. Most of these students are enrolled in not-for-profit public 4-year, not-for-profit public 2-year, and for-profit colleges and universities.

Since the late 1990s, social networking and media such as Facebook, You-Tube, and Twitter have been embraced by large segments of society. These facilities are being used in higher education as well. In addition to being integrated into instruction, many colleges use them for communication, counseling, advisement, and other ways of assisting students.

In K-12, the Internet has had significant impact on how primary and secondary schools operate. On the administrative side, Internet technology has fueled a significant increase in data gathering applications. Because of the assessment requirements imposed through national and statewide funding programs such as the No Child Left Behind Act, primary and secondary schools have been inundated with demands for data demonstrating the effectiveness of their academic programs. "Data-driven decision making" has become the catchphrase that practically all K-12 schools have adopted. "School" report cards generally provided publicly on websites, use data-driven decision-making techniques and are now required in most school districts to demonstrate a school's overall performance and to monitor student academic progress. The cost for these data-driven decision making systems can be quite expensive, especially for large school districts and statewide assessment efforts. In New York City, for instance, the development of the Achievement Reporting and Innovation System (ARIS) cost in excess of $80 million when first installed in 2008. This type of system, which integrates the data from more than a thousand schools, would be extremely difficult, if not impossible, to develop without the availability of the Internet and the World Wide Web as a common data communications network.

Another major change for K-12 schools with the advent of the Internet was in online learning. While much slower than in higher education, K-12 schools are now adopting more online learning applications that promise to mushroom in the years to come. Estimates of online learning in K-12 are approximately several million students, with projections exceeding 5 million students by 2016 (Picciano & Seaman, 2010). Christensen et al. (2008), referenced earlier, estimated that more than half of all high school courses will have an online component by 2019. Both estimates may be low, especially if online learning proceeds in the same manner as it did in higher education where growth was not at a steady rate but accelerated as a percentage of total enrollments. In addition, new online applications derived from integrated learning systems mentioned earlier in this chapter are making significant inroads at the high school level. These online ILSs are being used extensively for "credit-recovery" or for students who have failed to complete a course needed for graduation. These applications are being seen as panaceas for moving students through to graduation and at the same time saving money by reducing or eliminating other credit-recovery techniques such as offering make-up summer school programs.

A Look to the Future—Will Technology Transform Education?

The term transformation has been used to characterize the potential impact of technology on education. For example, the U.S. Department of Education's National Technology Plan (2010) is titled, "Transforming American Education: Learning Powered by Technology." According to Webster's Third New International Dictionary as well as the Free Online Dictionary, the word transform has two basic meanings:

1. to change completely or essentially in composition or structure and
2. to change the outward form or appearance.

Surely there has been a significant investment in technology throughout education but has it actually transformed what goes on schools and colleges and will it do so in the future? Let's look first at the K–12 schools. A useful indicator of technology integration is the student per microcomputer ratio. In 1983, the student-per-microcomputer ratio in all K–12 public schools was approximately 125:1; by 2004 it was 4:1. In 2012 it is closer to 3:1 and schools are now adopting "one laptop per child" programs. Based on the number of machines purchased and the dollars invested over the past 50 years, one might assume that computer technology has become an integral part of instruction in our nation's schools and revolutionized K–12 education. This is debatable. Larry Cuban (2000, 2001), a professor of education at Stanford University, claimed that computers were "oversold and underused" and that many teachers at all levels remained occasional users or nonusers. Furthermore, those who were regular users seldom integrated the machines into core curricular or instructional tasks. In a national survey conducted for *Education Week* in 2004, many teachers considered themselves beginners in the use of technology in their classes and only 63% of the fourth grade students surveyed reported using a computer at least once a week in school (Park & Starazina, 2004).

Beyond the issue of usage, the basic question remains whether or not technology improves learning. In 2007, the National Center for Education Statistics issued a report, based on a series of experimental and quasi-experimental studies, on a number of different reading and mathematics educational software products across 33 districts, 132 schools, and involving 439 teachers. The major findings indicated that test scores in treatment classrooms that were randomly assigned to use the software products did not differ from test scores in control classrooms that used traditional instructional methods (Dynarski et al. 2007). This study was followed up in 2009 and resulted in the same findings (Campuzan, Dynarski, Agodini, & Rall, 2009). In 2010, The U.S. Department of Education completed a long-awaited meta-analysis of 45 studies comparing the effectiveness of face-to-face, fully online, and blended learning environments. The major conclusions were as follows.

> In recent experimental and quasi-experimental studies contrasting blends of online and face-to-face instruction with conventional face-to-face classes, blended instruction has been more effective, providing a rationale for the effort required to design and implement blended approaches. When used by itself, online learning appears to be as effective as conventional classroom instruction, but not more so.
>
> However, several caveats are in order: Despite what appears to be strong support for blended learning applications, the studies in this meta-analysis do not demonstrate that online learning is superior as a *medium*. In many of the studies showing an advantage for blended learning, *the online and classroom conditions differed in terms of time spent, curriculum and pedagogy*. It was the *combination* of elements in the treatment conditions

(which was likely to have included additional learning time and materials as well as additional opportunities for collaboration) that produced the observed learning advantages. At the same time, one should note that online learning is much more conducive to the expansion of learning time than is face-to-face instruction.

In addition, although the types of research designs used by the studies in the meta-analysis were strong (i.e., experimental or controlled quasi-experimental), many of the studies suffered from weaknesses such as small sample sizes; failure to report retention rates for students in the conditions being contrasted; and, in many cases, potential bias stemming from the authors' dual roles as experimenters and instructors.

Finally, the great majority of estimated effect sizes in the meta-analysis are for undergraduate and older students, not elementary or secondary learners. Although this meta-analysis did not find a significant effect by learner type, when learners' age groups are considered separately, the mean effect size is significantly positive for undergraduate and other older learners but not for K-12 students.

Another consideration is that various online learning implementation practices may have differing effectiveness for K-12 learners than they do for older students. It is certainly possible that younger online students could benefit from practices (such as embedding feedback, for example) that did not have a positive impact for college students and older learners. Without new random assignment or controlled quasi-experimental studies of the effects of online learning options for K–12 students, policymakers will lack scientific evidence of the effectiveness of these emerging alternatives to face-to-face instruction.

(U.S. Department of Education, 2010, p. xviii)

The differences among the three modalities were modest at best with other factors such as time engagement influencing the results. Even the modest positive effects reported may be more appropriate for adult undergraduates rather than for primary and secondary school students. In response to a question on the benefits of commercial online learning courses and modules in K-12 schools in Illinois, Samantha Dolen, Assistant Superintendent of Student Services at Palatine School District 211 stated: "We have yet to see a vendor who has made the case that students who lack the motivation to do homework, to engage in class, to manage their time efficiently…will be more successful in online learning" (cited in Keilman, 2011). It would appear that although schools continue to invest significant resources in technology, educators remain cautious and concerned about its impact and much instruction continues to rely heavily on traditional face-to-face modes.

Online learning in colleges and universities started earlier than in K-12 environments and is more established with more than 6 million college and university students enrolled in at least one fully online course and several million more in blended courses. These enrollment figures are celebrated by some as indicative of the "transformation" that is occurring in higher education (Florida, Kaimal, Oblinger, & Blessing, 2003; Graham & Robinson, 2007; Rogers, Oblinger, & Hartman, 2007). Practically all American colleges and universities have acquired some form of course management system (CMS) or learning management system (LMS) needed to teach online. But are the millions of students enrolled in online courses really experiencing new pedagogical approaches afforded by the new technology, or have the traditional face-to-face pedagogies simply been transferred? The answer depends upon the teaching model being used in online and blended courses. Here are examples of three common models. In the first case, a school decides to use a commercially available programmed instruction course to deliver a fully online course that allows students to participate at their own pace without a teacher being directly involved. In the second case, in a fully online teacher led course, the instructor makes extensive use of collaborative learning techniques that involve the entire class using blogs, wikis, discussion boards, and social media. In the third case, an instructor puts a lecture online via a podcast and then has students respond as they would in a regular classroom. The first case can be considered transformative and is totally different from what normally goes on in a typical course. The second case may be incrementally transformative. The third case is probably not transformative, changing instruction on the surface but not in its essence. A transformation may be in the offing but has not yet occurred.

To conclude, several observations based on the research literature can be made. First, online learning in K-12 schools is in its beginning stages and it is too early to make a definitive judgment. Blended approaches that combine online with face-to-face instruction whether at the program, course, or module level will likely be more readily accepted in the future than fully online programs.

Second, in American higher education, a foundation has been established upon which a transformation could occur. However, much of this foundation exists in specific segments of the higher education enterprise, namely publicly funded university systems, community colleges, and select for-profit institutions addressing a specific subset of students. A sizable minority of higher education institutions especially highly-selective 4-year private liberal arts schools, continue to either ignore online education, or relegate it to the peripheral of their activities. These institutions show little sign of embracing online learning in the future. For a true transformation to occur, online education will need to be embraced by the full range of American higher education institutions.

Third, issues regarding the quality of online learning and the level of effect required to develop and teach online courses continue to be of concern at all levels of education. It appears that more developmental work needs to be done. As Christensen et al. (2008) and others have stated, there needs to be a cultural shift in pedagogical approaches that takes advantage of the newer online technologies.

Lastly, regardless of the pedagogy and instructional effectiveness of online learning, all levels of education are, in fact, taking greater advantage of this technology to deliver instruction. For adults who are geographically dispersed or because of time are not able to enroll in traditional face-to-face programs, online learning is increasingly seen as a viable option. High school students in budget-strapped school districts are able to take online courses that are too expensive for their schools to offer face-to-face. It might be that greater access to course material and increased communication among teachers and students is sufficient to warrant large-scale investment in online technology. If so, American education at all levels will be relying increasingly on online technology to deliver instruction and every indication is that this will increase in the years to come.

Technology and the Education-Industrial Complex

A key question for discussion in this chapter is: Why the emphasis on technology in the education-industrial complex? Isn't it the case that since technology is growing rapidly in all aspects of human endeavor, the same would apply to education? Perhaps, but education unlike other endeavors, has always been characterized as a high-touch human activity based largely on teacher–student relationships that extend over time. It has rarely been characterized as an automated production of goods or services. In K-12 education, helping to nurture young people in social and emotional development is as important as their academic development. In colleges and universities, faculty advise and counsel students on academic, career, and personal matters. Good teachers at all levels seek to inspire their students to seek knowledge, to grow personally, and to contribute to society. Fundamental to these views is a sense that students, as a result of education, will come away with a desire to learn more about themselves, others, and the world about them. Drawing from experiential theories, a basic assumption is that people are born with a natural curiosity about the world, and the main function of an education is to stimulate that curiosity. Once the desire to learn has been instilled, students will learn a great deal on their own. Education succeeds when we begin to learn through experiences, and by learning are motivated to experience more, so that a cycle of lifelong learning and experiencing evolves. Seymour Sarason (1995), psychologist and school reformer, described this concept succinctly:

> If when a child is motivated to learn more about self and the world, then I would say that schooling has achieved its overarching purpose....The student knows that the more you know the more you need to know.... To want to continue to explore, to find answers to personally meaningful questions, issues, and possibilities is the most important purpose of schooling.

(p. 135)

This emphasis in American education may be changing, especially in publicly supported schools and colleges. But why?

Technology and Ideology

Since the federal government's report, *A Nation at Risk* (National Commission on Excellence in Education, 1983), there has been a marked emphasis on student productivity, which in turn relates to teacher productivity, which in turn relates to school and college productivity. Student outcomes as measured by standardized tests and assessments have become the norm for much of American K-12 education and they are becoming increasingly important in higher education. Furthermore, there is emphasis on rational, data-driven assessments of student performance at all levels of the education system (student, teacher, school, school district, state). This approach moves public education toward a production line process for developing student skills and reduces the affective side of schooling. Technology has always been seen as an efficient tool for supporting production processes requiring speed and accuracy. As American education continues to shift from the affective to the efficient, technology becomes more important and desirable. This view serves as one of the ideological foundations of the education–industrial complex and a main vehicle for its promotion.

Related to the use of technology for testing and assessment of outcomes is the belief that technology saves money and that private industry operates more efficiently than public agencies including schools. Privatization of other public services such as health and prison operations are much further along than education but the same "privatization principle" is being applied. The education–industrial complex seeks to promote greater reliance on "more efficient" private educational service providers including education management companies (EMOs), for-profit schools supported by vouchers, tutoring services, or online content providers. Many of these providers of educational services make extensive use of technology in their operations. For example, fully online learning programs and courses such as K-12 Inc. or the University of Phoenix are technology-based. Tutoring-type courses and services at the high school level as provided by Aventa Learning and taken for credit-recovery are increasingly using technology-programmed-instruction software. EMOs such as Edison Schools and National Heritage Academies, pride themselves on the innovative uses of technology in their operations. Traditional textbook publishers such as Pearson Education and McGraw-Hill are integrating more online content into their traditional paperbound products.

Another view, beneficial to the education–industrial complex, is the belief that private industry, driven by competition, is always more cost beneficial than government-operated agencies. This belief is based on the concept that efficiency drives down costs thereby generating competition among actors and providing the most product for the dollar. Since public agencies including schools operate as monopolies that have little if any competition, they do not necessarily operate in cost-beneficial ways. Parents should have choices as to where their children are educated including privately operated schools. If public schools are to improve and become more cost-beneficial, competition and parental choice in the form of vouchers and charter schools are necessary and desirable. To measure, monitor, and manage this competition, assessments as provided by standardized tests, merit pay for teachers, and school report cards need technology. The sheer volume of data generated cannot be handled and analyzed in any other fashion. The relationship therefore between technology and competition, privatization, and school choice is direct and strong.

While there are advocates for greater efficiency, competition, and school choice, there are also detractors. Perhaps the most vocal and powerful are teachers unions. Frequently these unions are at odds with organizations and corporations that promulgate policies that promote efficiencies and competition. The unions are seen as standing in the way of many of the proposals and positions generated by the players in the education-industrial complex and as a result have become targets of criticism as part of its overall policy platform. All unions operate in political policy making spheres. Teachers unions such as the National Education Association (NEA) and the United Federation of Teachers (UFT) have a strong presence at the local, state, and federal levels wherever policy related to education is developed. So much of education is people intensive, and major savings are difficult without reducing costs for personnel. These savings can only be realized by reducing staff or significantly reducing the salaries of existing staff, either of which are generally unacceptable to the teachers' unions. But how would a public school continue to educate students with fewer teachers? The answer is through technology. The more instruction that could be delivered via online programmed instruction, the fewer teachers would be needed or the full-time teacher role would be reduced to that of a part-time tutor helping students manage their way through an online course. Teachers' unions understand this well and have been cautious if not in full opposition to large-scale integration of technology into instructional activities. The result is a vying for influence in the education policy arena where major players in the education-industrial complex compete with the teachers' unions over a number of issues including efficiency measures, assessments, data-driven decision making, and the use of technology.

Technology and the For-Profit Sector

The relationship of technology to the for-profit sector of the education-industrial complex is fairly obvious. Technology is not free and in fact can be quite expensive. Furthermore the investment of American education in technology is growing substantially. It is difficult to pinpoint the overall expenditures for technology because while some expenditures are directly related to teaching and learning such as purchasing computer equipment or rewiring a building for high-speed Internet access, some technology expenditures support other activities such as paying for students to enroll in an online course at a virtual school or subscribing to online providers to augment library, advisement, and counseling services. Private market research agencies put the expenditure for information technology (IT) in American K–12 and higher education at approximately $60 billion per year (Nagel, 2008, 2010). The actual amount has probably been underestimated for the difficulties mentioned above. Regardless, $60 billion per year is a sizable market and one in which many for-profit providers of technology goods and services are very interested. While all schools are investing substantial funds in technology, large urban school systems, in particular, because of their size and record keeping requirements have major yearly expenditures just to maintain services to keep up with technological advances.

In New York City, for instance, even in the midst of major cutbacks in 2011–2012 requiring elimination of thousands of positions, expenditures for educational technology were expected to grow to $547 million (Otterman, 2011). While much of the funding for these expenditures comes from states, individual school districts, and colleges, the federal government through a number of programs, directly or indirectly, funds educational technology. The Elementary and Secondary Education Act, reauthorized as No Child Left Behind and Race to the Top, has a number of provisions that assist schools in acquiring technology. The E-Rate is a federally managed program that provides significant discounts on telecommunications technologies to schools in low-income areas. Discounts of as much as 90% are available based on the percentage of students in a school who participate in the federal school lunch program. The E-Rate is administered through the Universal Service Fund, maintained by fees charged to all telephone users. Federal financial aid in the form of Pell grants provided to individual college students is used extensively for enrollment in online academic programs. The Apollo Group, the largest operator of for-profit online colleges including the University of Phoenix, received over $1 billion in 2009–2010 from students using Pell grant funds.

While the present expenditures for educational technology are substantial, significant growth (as much as 8% per year) is projected as major aspects of education are converted into technology-based activities (Nagel, 2008, 2010). Successful virtual schools such as the Florida Virtual School and the Kentucky Virtual School while relatively new, already enroll more than 100,000 students per year. State legislatures in Michigan, Alabama, and Idaho have recently passed legislation requiring all high school students to enroll in at least one online course in order to receive a diploma. As more and more states adopt or otherwise support virtual schooling, there will be substantial increases in enrollments and hence the need to acquire more technology to support it. The textbook which has been the staple for providing educational content is undergoing rapid change as more states and school districts move to digital content in the form of e-book, laptop per child, and open-source online content approaches. California, the largest textbook market in the country is hoping to save almost $400 million as part of an initiative to convert all paperbound textbooks to digital content. However, developing, organizing, and making this content available to teachers and students will require substantial new additional investments in technology.

Data-driven decision making using large-scale database management systems has seen a growing interest among education policy makers at all levels. These systems can easily cost tens of millions of dollars to develop and maintain depending upon the size of a school district or state. The federal government gave these systems a major boost by establishing eligibility requirements in the major federal K-12 education aid program Race to the Top, stipulating that applicants for these funds must provide assurance that areas such as "Standards and Assessment" and "Data Systems to Support Instruction" will be addressed. States that were awarded these funds had to focus on increasing, acquiring, or adopting instructional improvement systems based on statewide assessment and common longitudinal data systems. To meet these requirements and be eligible for funding, states had to develop or otherwise acquire new data systems that were capable of supporting school districts in collecting and submitting data to statewide systems for subsequent analysis and school district comparison reviews. These systems will require substantive new spending on technology with much of the initial funding coming from the federal government and subsequent funding being provided by states and school districts.

In sum, education in the United States is moving from a teacher–student intensive activity to a machine–student activity. Funding this transition will be substantial with many private enterprises poised to make significant profits. What was once a negligible market of no more than several billion dollars in the 1990s has grown considerably in the 21st century. Educational technology will represent more than $100 billion yearly in education spending in the not-too-distant future.

Case Studies: How Technology Acquisition is Promulgated in the Education-Industrial Complex

Technology Infusion in the K-12 Schools

This chapter started with a reference to Lewis Perelman, the author of *School's Out: Hyperlearning, the New Technology, and the End of Education,* who called for policy makers to seize an opportunity that was presenting itself to infuse technology into American education. Perelman is respected for his knowledge, interest in, and contributions to technology issues. He was qualified to write his book. However, Perelman's book was the outcome of his 3-year association with the Hudson Institute where he was paid as a senior research fellow (Raney, 1997) The Hudson Institute has gained most of its financial support from many of the foundations and corporations that have also bankrolled the conservative movement. Major funders of the Hudson Institute have included: .Castle Rock Foundation; Koch Family Foundations (David H. Koch Foundation);.John M. Olin Foundation; Lynde and Harry Bradley Foundation; Scaife Foundation. All of these foundations support right-of-center and neoconservative positions (Sourcewatch, 2010). In addition, two of its six senior administrators, namely, John P. Walters, the Chief Operating Officer and Executive Vice President, and Lewis "Scooter" Libby, Senior Vice President, were high-ranking members of the George W. Bush administration. From December 2001 to January 2009, Walters was director of the White House Office of National Drug Control Policy (ONDCP) and a cabinet member during the Bush Administration. From 2001 to 2005, Libby was Chief of Staff to Vice President Richard B. Cheney, Assistant to the Vice President for National Security Affairs, and Assistant to the President (Hudson Institute, 2011). Libby was convicted in 2007 of lying and obstructing a leak investigation that reached into the highest levels of the Bush administration. The verdict was the culmination of a nearly 4-year investigation into how CIA official Valerie Plame's name was leaked to reporters in 2003. The trial revealed that top members of the administration were eager to discredit Plame's husband, former Ambassador Joseph Wilson, who had accused the administration of doctoring prewar intelligence on Iraq. Perelman's association with the Hudson Institute begs the question of how much its ideology drove his writing and conclusion. The support he received allowed him to promulgate his and the education-industrial complex's beliefs that technology in education is good, it is needed for efficiency, and that teachers can and should be replaced by computers. This was at best a premature position and at worst an example of unbridled enthusiasm for the use of technology. The instructional software needed to implement large-scale replacement of teachers was not sufficiently developed at the time of his publication. Keep in mind that the Internet as we understand it today was not developed or available. The available technology included dedicated hardware, software, and curriculum content systems that minimally would cost hundreds of thousands of dollars to implement in small school systems and millions of dollars in larger school systems. The integrated learning systems (ILS) epitomized this technology.

The Educational Products Information Exchange (EPIE) Institute conducted one of the most extensive studies of ILSs (Sherry, 1990). Field visits were made to 24 schools using these systems, and eight different ILSs were evaluated. Overwhelmingly, administrators, teachers, and students supported the use of these systems. Ninety-six percent of the teachers and administrators interviewed in these schools recommended that other schools install similar systems, and 99% of the students interviewed indicated that they too would recommend these systems for other schools. The major benefits of ILSs most often cited by teachers and administrators in this study were the individualization of instruction, the extensive reporting capabilities, and the completeness of content. Should all schools have acquired such systems, and should schools with these systems have expanded their use? Because technology was good, was more technology better? The answer to both these questions was no. In addition to careful planning, EPIE recommended caution in investing in ILSs. Administrators, teachers, and students all endorsed their use, but their enthusiasm for such systems would not likely have endured if ILSs were the primary (or only) teaching delivery system employed in their schools (Sherry, 1990). Lewis Perelman represented the proponents of an ideology, that technology is the means to a more efficient public school system. However, his recommendations represented an ardor and eagerness beyond the realities of the technology. The lesson in this case study was important in the 1990s and is just as important today. Present-day proponents who see technology-infused schools as panaceas for "transforming education" should look at the experience at the Kyrene School District in Arizona. In 2005, the school district infused all its classrooms with technology with a $33 million initiative. Classrooms were equipped so that each child had a laptop, overhead projectors and Smartboards were abundant, curricula materials reviewed and redesigned, and teachers trained to use the new technologies. While students have been using the technology more for multimedia presentations, blogging, and Internet-based research, there has not been any appreciable change in student achievement in the past 6 years. In a comprehensive report by the *New York Times* in 2011 on the Kyrene School District and its use of technology, parents, teachers, and administrators were divided as to its benefits and costs. However, the article concluded: "Clearly, the push for technology is to the benefit of one group: technology companies" (Richtel, 2011). In a new initiative to upgrade the technology in the Kyrene schools, a $47 million referendum was voted down by the residents in 2011.

Wireless Generation

Another case study mirrors a well-known segment of the military-industrial complex, in which a number of high-ranking retired generals became consultants and representatives of defense contractors. *The Boston Globe* did an investigative report on this matter in 2010:

> Dozens of retired generals employed by defense firms maintain Pentagon advisory roles, giving them unparalleled levels of influence and access to inside information on Department of Defense procurement plans....
>
> The generals are, in many cases, recruited for private sector roles well before they retire, raising questions about their independence and judgment while still in uniform. The Pentagon is aware and even supports this practice....

The feeder system from some commands to certain defense firms is so powerful that successive generations of commanders have been hired by the same firms or into the same field. For example, the last seven generals and admirals who worked as Department of Defense gatekeepers for international arms sales are now helping military contractors sell weapons and defense technology overseas....

When a general-turned-businessman arrives at the Pentagon, he is often treated with extraordinary deference—as if still in uniform—which can greatly increase his effectiveness as a rainmaker for industry. The military even has name for it—the "bobblehead effect."

"We are changing the perception and maybe the reality of what it means to be a general," said retired General Robert "Doc" Foglesong, who retired as the second-ranking Air Force officer in 2006....

"The fundamental question," he said, "is whether this is shaping the acquisition system and influencing what the Pentagon buys. I think the answer is yes."

(Bender, 2010)

Similar situations exist in the education–industrial complex. Joel Klein was chancellor of the New York City public school system, the largest in the country, from 2002 to 2011. Prior to this, he served as Deputy Counsel to President Bill Clinton and as Assistant Attorney General in the U.S. Department of Justice. In 2008, while chancellor he proposed and implemented the Achievement Reporting and Innovation System (ARIS), an $80 million plus project led by IBM with several subcontractors including Wireless Generation. Eventually IBM pulled out as the lead contractor for the program and was replaced by Wireless Generation. In early November 2010, Klein indicated that he would be stepping down as chancellor at the end of the year to join News Corporation, the large media conglomerate owned by Rupert Murdoch, as an executive vice president for educational services. On November 22, 2010, 2 weeks after Klein's announced resignation, News Corporation announced that it would be buying 90% of Wireless Generation and it would come under his [Klein's] direction. Gene Russianoff, a spokesman for the New York Public Interest Research Group, a good-government organization, in reference to this appointment stated "it goes to the heart of the public concern that there's a revolving door between government and the private sector" (cited by Santos, 2010).

The benefits of the ARIS system have been questioned by many people both inside and outside the New York public school system. NY1, a 24-hour Internet-based news service, reported that 30% of New York City's high school principals refused to use the ARIS system and opted instead for a much less expensive data system more attuned to their needs. A similar ARIS contract in the state of North Carolina was canceled because it was "taking too long and not being user-friendly" (Christ, 2011). The New York Public School Parents (2011) website referred to ARIS as a "boondagle" and a "supermugging." Betsy

Gotbaum, the then Public Advocate of the City of New York, issued a report in August 2009 entitled, *ARIS on the Side of Caution: A Survey of New York City Principals on the City's Accountability Computer System*. Its conclusions were:

- The majority of principals believe that the DOE overpaid for the ARIS System.
- While the majority of principals do not believe that ARIS interferes with their ability to be instructional leaders at their schools, a significant number believe it does.
- While the majority of principals surveyed believe that ARIS will improve teaching and learning at their schools, more than a third do not.
- While the majority of principals believe that ARIS is a good use of their time, more than a quarter do not.
- While the majority of principals believe that ARIS is a good use of their staff's time, nearly a quarter do not.
- While the majority of principals use/will use ARIS's networking components, more than a third do not/will not use networking.
- While the majority of principals believe their staff uses/will use ARIS's networking components, nearly a third believe they do not/will not use networking.
- While the majority of principals believe that ARIS provides them with information they were unable to get in the past, nearly half believe it provides information that was already available before the implementation of ARIS. (Gotbaum, 2009)

In June 2011, the New York State awarded a no-bid contract to Wireless Communication for $27 million to build a system similar to ARIS across the state which raised conflict of interest issues involving Joel Klein and his relationship with the New York State Education Department (Kain, 2011). The New York Public School Parents website commented:

> New York is well aware of the risks of large-scale technology projects that tend to run over budget, behind schedule and be under-whelming when delivered. Which is a perfect description of ARIS.
> It is surprising that NY State Comptroller Di Napoli would provide this waiver after his *2009 audit*, exposing DOE's abuse of the no-bid contract process. These are precious funds that should be used to benefit children, rather than line the pockets of Joel Klein and Rupert Murdoch.
> (New York Public School Parents, 2011)

In August, 2011, New York State Controller Thomas DiNapoli, canceled the $27 million contract citing an "incomplete record" about Wireless Communications for the contract (Lovett, 2011). In early 2012, the New York State Education Department citing a possible loss of federal Race to the Top funding was still requesting that Wireless Generation be awarded a no-bid contract. In

January 2012, John Liu, the New York City Comptroller, conducted an audit of ARIS in the New York City public school system and found that:

> Many New York City teachers and principals are not using the city's $80 million student information database.... About 42 percent of teachers, assistant principals and principals did not log on to the program last year or the year before, according to the city's usage data.
>
> (Philips, 2012)

The Klein/Wireless Generation/News Corporation episode exemplifies the education-industrial complex. It is a network of individuals and private and public organizations that seek to push an ideological agenda while reaping profits for products of marginal value through means and influences that bend if not in fact attempt to bypass approved government acquisition policy.

References

Allen, I. E., & Seaman, J. (2011). *Going the distance: Online education in the United States, 2011.* Babson College Survey Research Group and The Sloan Consortium. Retrieved from http://www.babson.edu/Academics/centers/blank-center/global-research/Pages/babson-survey-research-group.aspx

Bender, B. (December 26, 2010). In large numbers, and with few rules, retiring generals are taking lucrative defense-firm jobs. *The Boston Globe.* Retrieved from http://articles.boston.com/2010-12-26/news/29319170_1_generals-defense-firms-private-sector

Campuzano, L., Dynarski, M., Agodini, R., & Rall, K. (2009). *Effectiveness of reading and mathematics software products: Findings from two cohorts* (NCEE 2009-4041). Washington, DC: U.S. Department of Education, Institute of Education Sciences.

Christ, L. (March 16, 2011). More schools passing up DOE database. NY1. Retrieved from http://www.ny1.com/content/news_beats/education/135696/more-schools-passing-up-doe-database-part-1

Christensen, C. (2011). *The innovator's dilemma: The revolutionary book that will change the way you do iBusiness.* New York: HarperBusines.

Christensen, C. M., Horn, M. B., & Johnson, C. W. (2008). *Disrupting class: How innovation will change the way the world learns.* New York: McGraw-Hill.

Cuban, L. (2000, February 23). Is spending money on technology worth it? *Education Week, 19*(24), 42.

Cuban, L. (2001). *Oversold and underused.* Cambridge, MA: Harvard University Press.

Dynarski, M., Agodini, R., Heaviside, S., Novak, T., Carey, T., Campuzano, L., ... Sussex, W. (2007). *Effectiveness of reading and mathematics software products: Findings from the first student cohort* (NCEE 2007-4005). Washington, DC: U.S. Department of Education, Institute of Education Sciences.

Florida, R., Kaimal, G., Oblinger, D., & Blessing. L. (2003). How generations X and Y (Millennials) will reshape higher education. Society for College and University Planning, Virtual Seminar. Retrieved from http://www.scup.org/profdev/archive_cds/gen_x-y.html

Gotbaum, B. (2009). ARIS on the side of caution: A survey of New York City principals on the city's accountability computer system. Retrieved from http://publicadvocategotbaum.com/pages/documents/ARISFINAL.pdf

Graham, C., & Robinson, R. (2007). Realizing the transformational potential of blended learning: Comparing cases of transforming blends and enhancing blends in higher education. In A. G. Picciano & C. Dzuiban (Eds.), *Blended learning: Research perspectives.* Needham, MA: The Sloan Consortium.

Hudson Institute. (2011). Leadership. Retrieved from http://www.hudson.org/learn/index.cfm?fuseaction=hudson_leadership

Kain, E. D. (2011). New York State Dept. of Education awards $27M no-bid contract to Murdoch-owned Wireless Generation. *Forbes.* Retrieved from http://blogs.forbes.com/erik-kain/2011/06/09/new-york-state-dept-of-education-awards-27m-no-bid-contract-to-news-corp-company/

Keilman, J. (April 24, 2011). Online learning for Illinois high schoolers inspires praise, suspicion. *Chicago Tribune.* Retrieved from http://articles.chicagotribune.com/2011-04-24/news/ct-met-onlineclass-20110424_1_effectiveness-of-online-courses-innosight-institute-online-classes

Lovett, K. (August 27, 2011). State hacks ed contract with Murdoch firm. *The New York Daily News,* p. 21.

Nagel, D. (May 19, 2010). Education IT to grow $2.5 billion. *Campus Technology.* Retrieved from http://campustechnology.com/articles/2010/05/19/education-it-to-grow-2.5-billion.aspx

Nagel, D. (September 18, 2008). Education technology spending to top $56 billion by 2012. *T.H.E. Journal.* Retrieved from http://www.thejournal.com/articles/23299

National Commission on Excellence in Education. (1983). *A nation at risk.* Washington, DC: Author.

New York Public School Parents. (June 2011). Another super-mugging? NY State Education Department to award $27 no-bid contract to Joel Klein and Rupert Murdoch. Retrieved from http://nycpublicschoolparents.blogspot.com/2011/06/another-super-mugging-ny-state.html

Otterman, S. (2011, March 29). In City schools, tech spending to rise despite cuts. *New York Times.* Retrieved from http://www.nytimes.com/2011/03/30/nyregion/30schools.html

Park, J., & Staresina, L. (2004, May 6). Tracking U.S. trends. *Education Week, 23*(35), 64–67.

Perelman, L. (1992). *School's out: Hyperlearning, the new technology, and the end of education.* New York: Morrow.

Phillips, A. M. (2012, January 23). Audit finds limited use of City's data system. *New York Times.* Retrieved from http://www.nytimes.com/schoolbook/2012/01/23/citys-data-system-is-being-underused-liu-audit-finds/?scp=1&sq=john%20liu%20ARIS&st=cse

Picciano, A. G., & Seaman, J. (2010). *Class connections: High school reform and the role of online learning.* Needham, MA: Babson College Survey Research Group. Retrieved from http://www3.babson.edu/ESHIP/research-publications/upload/Class_connections.pdf

Raney, M. J. (1997, Fall). Interview with Lewis Perelman. *Technos Quarterly, 6*(3). Retrieved from http://www.ait.net/technos/tq_06/3perelman.php

Richtel, M. (September 3, 2011). In classroom of the future, stagnant scores. *New York Times.* Retrieved from http://www.nytimes.com/2011/09/04/technology/technology-in-schools-faces-questions-on-value.html?pagewanted=6&nl=todaysheadlines&emc=tha2

Rogers, M., Oblinger, D., & Hartman, J. (2007). Education in exponential times: How technology-enabled change is reshaping higher education. Society for College and University Planning Webcast. Retrieved from www.lib.washington.edu/about/vision2010/2007initiativesupdates/Vision2010Undergraduates.ppt

Santos, F. (2010, November 23). News Corp., after hiring Klein, buys technology partner in a city schools project. *New York Times.* Retrieved from http://www.nytimes.com/2010/11/24/nyregion/24newscorp.html

Sarason, S. (1995). *Parental involvement and the political principle: Why the existing governance structure of schools should be abolished.* San Francisco, CA: Jossey-Bass.

Sherry, M. (1990). An EPIE Institute report: Integrated instructional systems. *Technological Horizons in Education, 18*(2), 86–89.

Sourcewatch. (2010, December 1,). Hudson Institute. Retrieved from http://www.sourcewatch.org/index.php?title=Hudson_Institute

U.S. Department of Education, Office of Educational Technology. (2010). *Transforming American education: Learning powered by technology.* Washington, DC: Author.

U.S. Department of Education, Office of Planning, Evaluation, and Policy Development. (2010). *Evaluation of evidence-based practices in online learning: A meta-analysis and review of Online learning studies,* Washington, DC: Author.

4

CORPORATE INFLUENCES

No Child Left Behind, Privatization, and Commercialization

The expanding educational-industrial complex received a boost with passage of the federal legislation No Child Left Behind Act (NCLB; 2002). The words *for-profit* appear throughout the legislation. The lobbying organization Education Industry Association, whose membership reaps profits from providing supplemental education services under NCLB, announced in 2011:

> The education industry is poised for explosive growth in all of its segments from preK–12 through post-secondary education. In fact, education is rapidly becoming a $1 trillion industry, second in size only to the health care industry, and represents 10 percent of America's GNP. Federal, state and local expenditures on education exceed $750 billion
>
> (Education Industry Association, 2011f).

The legislation supported the development of charter schools and, consequently, for-profit charter school management companies. NCLB authorized the spending of public money to purchase supplementary education services from for-profit companies to help students in failing schools. By emphasizing testing students, the legislation gave test publishers an opportunity to reap increased profits.

Providers of supplemental services represent one aspect of selling to schools. In *School Commercialism: From Democratic Ideal to Market Commodity*, Alex Molnar identifies three forms of commercial activities in schools: "Selling *to* schools (vending), selling *in* schools (advertising and public relations), and selling *of* schools (privatization)" (Molnar, 2005).

Supplementary education services are not the only vendors who benefit from NCLB. The most important part of the law calls for scheduled testing of students to create public report cards on schools and to identify failing schools. This aspect of the law benefits for-profit test makers, such as Pearson and McGraw-Hill. In the past, teachers created their own tests to evaluate students or used tests provided for in textbook supplements. Some schools periodically gave standardized tests but these tests were not required by federal law and they were not used to identify failing schools. In addition to NCLB, Barack Obama's presidency championed using student test scores to evaluate teachers and principals. As we discuss later in this chapter, for-profit companies that make and score standardized tests have an economic interest in expanding the use of these assessments.

Another aspect of NCLB that proved a boon to the privatization of school services was its support of public charter schools which benefited for-profit school management companies. A pioneer in this field is the for-profit Edison-Learning which claims: "We pioneered the concept of charter schools in the U.S." and now claims that it "is a leading international educational solutions provider with nearly 20 years of experience partnering with schools, districts, governments, organizations, charter authorizers, and boards" (2011a,b). Later we will discuss the pioneering role of Edison-Learning in for-profit education and its instrumental role in expanding the educational-industrial complex.

A growing commercial influence on public education is selling *in* schools involving advertising, product placement, and providing free educational materials to schools by special interest groups and corporations. This is an important aspect of the expansion of the educational-industrial complex.

Behind these trends in school corporatization is an ideology emerging after World War II which dismissed government bureaucracies as being inefficient and called for the privatization of government services and supported a free market approach to schooling. Free market arguments support school choice including the development of charter schools. An assumption of those advocating a free market approach to schooling is that American public schools are failing; this argument began in the 1950s and continues to this day.

In this chapter, we begin by reviewing the role of NCLB in opening the door to government support of for-profit companies and privatization of schools and school services. Next we will discuss the Edison Project, which foreshadowed NCLB's support of for-profits and charter schools. Then we will discuss NCLB's support of for-profit supplementary education services; and the expansion of the testing industry. And finally, we will explore the promotion of consumer products in schools and the freebies given to schools by corporations and special interest groups.

No Child Left Behind

NCLB was born of a complex set of legislative attempts to aid students from low income families that began with the passage of the 1965 Elementary and Secondary Education Act (ESEA; 1968). NCLB is a reauthorization of Title I of ESEA. Title I was a major component of the War on Poverty designed to provide supplementary funds to schools to provide supplementary education programs for children from low income families. NCLB opened the door to rapid expansion of the educational industrial complex by recognizing throughout the legislation the use of for-profit education companies. Scattered throughout NCLB are references to the use of for-profit education services. For instance, the supplementary educational services section of the legislation states that "the term 'provider' means a non-profit entity, a *for-profit entity* [emphasis added], or a local educational agency." As we will explain later in this chapter, supplemental education services such as tutoring are provided at government expense to children that are in schools labeled as failing under this legislation. The for-profit companies that benefit from this provision, such as Sylvan Learning Centers and Kumon Learning Centers, have an obvious interest in ensuring continued and expanded funding of the educational services provided for under the law. As discussed in chapter 2, the provision that allows for the hiring of for-profits to provide supplemental services results in "Swiss-cheese" government. Companies receiving benefits under NCLB are organized into a lobbying group seeking to increase their government benefits.

The legislation's support of charter schools contributed to the growth of for-profit charter school management companies. Despite the NCLB's support of public charter schools, in contrast to private charter schools, for-profit charter school management companies can be used to establish public charters or be hired to operate public charters. Also, NCLB helped to support the growth of the virtual charter school industry.

The legislation's emphasis on testing helped boost the profits of companies like McGraw-Hill and Pearson. It also resulted in the growth of test preparation companies like Kaplan and the Princeton Review. As we will discuss, supplementary education services became a growth industry after the passage of NCLB. The legislation also specified that failing schools should be restructured which created a new educational industry sector offering restructuring plans.

In this chapter, we will discuss each relevant section of NCLB as it is related to the growth of the educational-industrial complex. Behind the growth of the for-profit education sector was an ideology that maintained that for-profit companies, in contrast to government operated public schools, were more efficient and could better meet the needs and desires of parents and students.

Free Market Ideology

By the time of NCLB's enactment, free market ideologies, emphasizing the outsourcing of government programs to for-profit companies supported greater privatization of education. In addition, free market ideology justified school choice, including the development of charter schools, and privatization as improving the educational chances of children from low-income families. Applying the concept of free markets and for-profit schools to education can be traced to the work of Friedrich Hayek, an Austrian economist and Nobel Prize winner, who moved to the United States to teach at the University of Chicago from 1950 to 1962. Without government interference, he argued, marketplace competition would create ideal institutions. Applied to schooling, this meant no government provision or control of education. Instead, entrepreneurs would establish schools and compete for students while the "invisible hand" of the marketplace determined what forms of schooling were best (Spring, 2010, pp. 123–127).

In *The Road to Serfdom* (1962), Hayek argued that free market competition results in the production of goods wanted by the public. Also, competition would be the best way assuring the lowest consumer price (Hayek, 1962). Applied to the monopolistic world of public schooling competition between schools supposedly would be between schools that people wanted and at a lower cost. Milton Friedman in the 1960s, a colleague of Hayek's at the University of Chicago and 1976 Nobel Prize winner, advocated applying the principles of the free market to education by allowing parents free choice to choose a school for their children. Friedman proposed a government-financed voucher that parents could redeem "for a specified maximum sum per child per year if spent on 'approved' educational services" (Friedman, 1962, p. 89). Friedman argued that vouchers would overcome the class stratification embodied in the existence of rich and poor school districts. He suggested, "Under present arrangements, stratification of residential areas effectively restricts the intermingling of children from decidedly different backgrounds" (Friedman, 1962, p. 92). In general, free market ideologists argue that competition in the education market will result in improving the quality of education available to the American public. An unusual aspect of this argument is the support given to for-profit education. It is argued that a school operating for a profit will be more attuned to balancing costs with quality school instruction and appeal to parents. A for-profit education institution will want to market a good product to attract customers and control costs to ensure a profit. The argument that for-profit schooling will be more cost efficient and improve the quality of education underlay the creation of the first major for-profit alternative to public schools, namely Chris Whittle's Edison Project which foreshadowed NCLB's support of for-profit companies and charter schools.

The Edison Project: A New Dimension to the Educational Industrial Complex

The Edison Project illustrates the interrelationship between government financing and for-profit schooling. In many ways, the Edison Project, later called Edison Schools and EdisonLearning, pioneered two important parts of the growing educational-industrial complex. One part is the hiring by public school districts of for-profit companies to manage their schools. The idea of a for-profit company managing public schools received support in the NCLB legislation. NCLB requires schools identified as failing based on low test scores, tests often purchased or scored by for-profit companies, to restructure. Restructuring could involve replacing the school staff or "Reopening the school as a public charter school" (NCLB, 2002, p. 61). NCLB requires that restructuring a failing school include the implementation of a plan for alternative governance: "the local educational agency shall implement one of the following alternative governance arrangements for the school consistent with State law" (2002, p. 61). Important for school management organizations is the restructuring of failing schools by "Entering into a contract with an entity, such as a private management company, with a demonstrated record of effectiveness, to operate the public school" (2002, p. 61).

In the 1980s, Chris Whittle, the entrepreneur behind the Edison Project, marketed to public schools Channel One, a classroom news program that included commercial advertising. Channel One represents both the privatization of a school service and the commercialization of schools by advertising products to students products such as "Snickers, Levis, and Head & Shoulders shampoo" (Saltman, 2005, p. 23). Channel One was a privatization of teachers' roles in informing students of current events; for instance one of the authors worked with a public school teacher who daily recorded news for free from a public radio station without commercials to play to his students. With Channel One, schools bought a product from a for-profit company, which in turn was used by it to market products to students.

In 1991, under the name the Edison Project, Whittle envisioned franchising 200 for-profit schools over a 5-year period. At first, Whittle hoped that the franchised schools would receive support from a national voucher plan supported by the administration of President George H. W. Bush. But that plan never materialized and Whittle turned to marketing Edison schools as charter schools (Saltman, 2005, pp. 31–34). In 2011, EdisonLearning, the most recent name for the enterprise, claimed, "We pioneered the concept of charter schools in the U.S. and our tradition of innovation is at the core of what we do" (EdisonLearning, 2011a).

In 1993, the Edison Project began managing public schools, which by 1997 included 25 schools. Later, Edison would sign a contract with the Philadelphia school system to manage 60 of their 240 schools. Through the years Edison

Schools received financial support from a variety of investors with up and down swings in its financial status. In 1992, Whittle hired Benno Schmidt, Jr., President of Yale University, to head the Edison Project. Schmidt had a background in both education and investment with his father, Benno Schmidt, being a wealthy venture capitalist (Saltman, 2005, pp. 33–47).

In 2011, EdisonLearning offered restructuring services under the brand name Alliance. This restructuring service could be used for turning around schools identified as failing under the provisions of NCLB. The Alliance is described as:

> a comprehensive school turnaround program in which EdisonLearning partners with underperforming schools to make sustained and ongoing improvement on achievement. The *Alliance* program is a change management program that sends a team of education professionals directly to the partnering school to work closely with educators and administrators to develop site capacity. The program operates with a whole school approach, combining leadership development, curriculum improvements and a proven assessment system to target all components of the learning process.
>
> (EdisonLearning Alliance, 2011b)

Also, EdisonLearning now offers education services that can be bought by school districts to help improve the test scores of low achieving students. The company brands this product Learning Force which it advertises as:

> Learning Force is targeted for students who are low performing or who have learning gaps on some foundation skills. In addition to well-designed lesson plans, pre- and post-assessments and progress monitoring, *Learning Force* comes with a full support team to help your school or district put an effective intervention plan in place.
>
> *Learning Force* is delivered for Grades 3–8 through two complementary modules, *Reading Force*™ *and Math Force*™.
>
> (EdisonLearning, 2011c)

As mentioned previously, EdisonLearning claims to have pioneered the idea of charter schools. In 2011, EdisonLearning advertised the following charter school services:

- School Management Services
- Brick and Mortar Charter Schools
  - Secondary School Design
  - Elementary School Design
- Educational Services for Charter Schools
- Online and Blended Learning (EdisonLearning, 2011d)

In summary, the Edison Project and its later brand name EdisonLearning pioneered many of the for-profit education services that would later find their way into NCLB. Channel One, as we will discuss later, expanded the idea of commercializing public schools by introducing direct advertising of products into the school classroom.

NCLB: Charter Schools and For-Profit Educational Management Companies (EMOs)

NCLB provided extensive support to the expansion of charter schools. While NCLB treats charter schools as public schools there is the option for for-profit educational management companies or EMOs to operate publicly chartered schools. NCLB specifically supports public charter schools that are chartered by state education agencies. NCLB defines a public charter as being authorized by the state and "exempt from significant State or local rules that inhibit the flexible operation and management of public schools"; "is created by a developer as a public school, or is adapted by a developer from an existing public school"; "is operated under public supervision and direction"; and "is a school to which parents choose to send their children, and that admits students on the basis of a lottery, if more students apply for admission than can be accommodated" (NCLB, 2002, pp. 374–375). NCLB promotes the expansion of charter schools by "providing financial assistance for the planning, program design, and initial implementation of charter schools"; "expanding the number of high-quality charter schools available to students across the Nation"; and "encouraging the States to provide support to charter schools" (NCLB, 2002, p. 364). For-profit companies are involved in public charter schools as managers or by a charter school adopting their school designs.

According to the National Center for Education Statistics' *Condition of Education 2010* there was a rapid growth of charter schools from 1,500 in 1999–2000 to 4,400 in 2007–2008 with the number of students enrolling in U.S. charter schools tripling from 340,000 in 1999–2000 to 1.3 million in 2007–2008 (National Center for Education Statistics, 2010, p. 98). Obviously, EMOs have an economic stake in expanding the number of charter schools allowed by state laws. In 2011, K12, Inc., one of the more successful EMOs, estimated its potential market to be worth $15 billion including revenues from the operation of charter schools and through virtual schools created as part of state and public school districts. For instance, K12's Agora Cyber Charter School alone was expecting a 2011 income of $72 million based on an enrollment of 8,836 students.

In addition to managing schools, several states and school districts buy virtual curriculums from EMOs such as K12. As an example, the Tennessee Virtual Academy (2011) advertises its program as follows:

> ## Who We Are
>
> ### *Our School at a Glance*
>
> The Tennessee Virtual Academy uses the K12 curriculum to offer Tennessee students in grades K–8 an innovative learning experience. With individualized learning approaches, Tennessee Virtual Academy and K12 provide the tools kids need to succeed—in school and beyond. Tennessee Virtual Academy is the premiere statewide K12 education program in Tennessee (Tennessee Virtual Academy, 2011).

K12, Inc. boasts, "Kindergarten through 12th grade students in most states are enrolled in online public schools or "virtual schools" that partner with K12, and the number of students is growing rapidly every year. In fact, with over one million courses delivered to date, K12 is the leader—by a wide margin—in providing learning programs to public schools in the U.S." (K12, 2011).

Supplementary Education Services

As previously mentioned, NCLB specifies that for-profit providers can be hired to provide supplemental educational services to failing schools. As explained by the U.S. Department of Education:

> Supplemental educational services (SES) are additional academic instruction designed to increase the academic achievement of students in schools in the second year of improvement, corrective action, or restructuring. These services, which are in addition to instruction provided during the school day, may include academic assistance such as tutoring, remediation and other supplemental academic enrichment services failing schools.
>
> (U.S. Department of Education, 2010)

Supplemental education services are offered to parents and students in schools identified as failing. NCLB states, "the local educational agency serving such school shall, subject to this subsection, arrange for the provision of supplemental educational services to eligible children in the school from a provider with a demonstrated record of effectiveness that is selected by the parents and approved for that purpose by the State educational agency" (NCLB, 2002, p. 67).

Providers of supplemental education services, along with charter school management organizations and school restructuring services are organized as a government lobbying group in the Education Industry Association (EIA). EIA asserts that its mission in keeping with free market ideology is to promote "market-based drivers" to improve schools.

EIA seeks to expand educational opportunities and improve educational achievement for learners of all ages by infusing American education with market-based drivers of high-quality service, innovation, and accountability. We promote increased public awareness of the education industry's contributions to better teaching and learning.

EIA works to foster the development of a vibrant preK-12 education industry by:

- Promoting public policies that ensure equitable and fair access to the education marketplace
- Creating high standards of program and business practices, while enhancing accountability
- Educating the public about the contributions of the education industry for better teaching and learning
- Supporting entrepreneurs to achieve scale.

(Education Industry Association, 2011b)

The lobbying goals of the SES Coalition of the Education Industry Association are clearly stated by the organization: "The Coalition represents the interests of providers when it engages local school officials, States, the US Department of Education and the Congress. By working together, organizations can amplify their voices with these stakeholder groups so that the special interests of SES providers will be better understood" (Education Industry Association, 2010).

In 2011, EIA along with the for-profit Mosaica Education and the Turkish Uğur Test Preparation Centers and Educational Institutions met in Istanbul, Turkey to form the International Consortium of Education Entrepreneurs. EIA announced to its membership that, "By attending the Istanbul planning meeting, you will help shape the governance and organizational structure of this emerging international consortium, learn more about business opportunities in major and emerging markets world-wide and meet your colleagues that operate preK-12 private schools" (Education Industry Association, 2011a).

Hoping to expand the reach of supplemental education services beyond students in failing schools, EIA lobbied the U.S. Congress "to increase access by middle-class families for after-school supplemental education" by creating savings plans similar to a 401-K which would allow families to save for the purchase of these services. In the words of EIA, "households could save $5000–10,000 per year as a salary reduction, and deposit addition funds that may build up tax free, coupled with employer contributions. This translates into almost a 30%–40% effective discount on the costs of tutoring services, making it more accessible and affordable to the middle class" (Education Industry Association, 2010).

The EIA considers federal monies for supplementary education services so important to its membership that it created a special subgroup in 2004 called the Supplemental Education Services (SES) Coalition. The SES Coalition claims that "through the media, [it] regularly promotes the success stories of providers in helping to close the achievement gap of hard to serve children" (Education Industry Association, 2011c). The EIA claims that, "By joining the EIA SES Coalition, you directly support our Campaign to save and improve after-school tutoring for low-income/low-achieving students" (Education Industry Association, 2011c).

So important was the reauthorization of NCLB to members of the Education Industry Association, the organization drafted templates for parents and teachers to send to their Congressional representatives. The instructions for parents are presented with the imperative:

Make Your Voice Heard

Tell President Obama and Congress to Keep SES Free Tutoring for Your Children

As the parent or guardian of a child enrolled in free after-school tutoring known as Supplemental Educational Services (SES), you know better than anyone just how the tutoring has helped improve his or her grades and boosted self-confidence. But the federal government and U.S. Congress may take away this service and with it, your power to choose the right program for your child.

If your child's experience in this after-school tutoring program has been successful, it is important to make your voice heard by officials in Washington, DC. Sign the petition below, and tell President Obama and Members of Congress that you and your child value the after-school tutoring program, and that you want the freedom to choose the educational services that work best for your family.

The statement parents were to sign explained: "By signing the petition below, I certify that my child participated in the SES after-school tutoring program named above, that I have found it helpful, and that I call on President Obama and Congress to keep the program and to give me the educational choices my child and I want and deserve." Teachers were instructed to write: "As a teacher. I continue my commitment to education by providing *after-school* Supplemental Educational Services (SES) to low-income children in my community. Over the past [number of years or months], I have worked with about [number] young people through the after-school tutoring program offered by *[name of SES provider who employs you]*, one of the private-sector companies that provide SES."

The staging of Education Industry Days from February 24 to 25, 2011 in Washington, DC launched a major EIA lobbying effort to increase funding for SES in the reauthorization of NCLB. The announcement of Education

Industry Days referred to the political controversy in Congress and wondered: "But how will the drama play out for education entrepreneurs and companies, SES providers, and other organizations seeking federal funding, as Congress and the Administration finally take up, as is expected, the reauthorization of the Elementary and Secondary Education Act (ESEA)" (Education Industry Association, 2011a)?

The speakers from the K-12 education industry at the Education Industry Days included Joseph Olchefske, Educate Online; Barbara Dreyer, Connections Academy; Chris Blue, EduVation; Scott Drossos, Pearson K-12 Solutions; Michael Connelly, Mosaica Education. Joseph Olchefske, president of Educate Online and a newly appointed member of EIA's Board of Directors, is a flexian who has networked through the investment industry, public schools, and the government. Educate Online operates as a virtual tutoring program using assessment tools and online instruction (Educate Online, 2011). His EIA biography states: "Joseph Olchefske joined Educate Online in 2010 after distinguished careers in both the K-12 public education arena and the investment banking industry. As EO's President, he is responsible for leadership of the vision and strategy for expanding EO and the impact of its tutoring services for students throughout the country" (Education Industry Association, 2011d). Olchefske commented about Educate Online's role through EIA, "I want Educate Online to play, through EIA, a more significant role in the public policy issues surrounding education in general and online/tutoring specifically" (Education Industry Association, 2011d).

While Olchefske is primarily interested in NCLB's funding of supplemental education, another speaker at EIA's education days and also a newly appointed member of EIA's Board of Directors, Michael Connelly, CEO of Mosaica Education, Inc., is interested in the legislation's provisions for charter schools. The reader will recall that Mosaica teamed up with EIA to organize the International Consortium of Education Entrepreneurs. EIA's newsletter states, "Mosaica Education manages 90 charter schools, serving 18,000 students in eight states, the District of Columbia, and the Persian Gulf countries of Qatar and United Arab Emirates" (Education Industry Association, 2011d). Similar to Olchefske, Michael Connelly comes from the world of investment banking and his statement in the EIA newsletter captures the concern about government funding of for-profit education: "I have long supported EIA's mission and believe that the political challenges to for-profit education companies are greater today than they've ever been" (Education Industry Association, 2011d).

Another major player in EIA is the publishing and testing giant Pearson which has a stake in selling online courses, as discussed in chapter 2, and ensuring a heavy testing agenda for schools to ensure sales of its products. The newly appointed Board Member of EIA, Scott Drossos, President of Pearson K-12 Solutions, joined Pearson after spending 5 years at EdisonLearning as Chief Development Officer. While Olchefske has a stake in supplemental education services and Connelly in charter schools, Pearson K–12 Solutions makes money selling turn–around packages to schools labeled as failing under NCLB. The Pearson website explains, "A division of Pearson, the world's leading education services and technology company, Pearson K–12 Solutions engages in multi-year state and district partnerships to foster school improvement, create innovative new models and custom solutions, and to help turn around struggling schools" (Pearson, 2010).

Also, Pearson was represented at Education Industry Days by one of the scheduled speakers, Barbara Dreyer of Connections Academy (2011) which was recently purchased by Pearson. Connections Education is the second largest company after K12 in the online for-profit education industry. As an example of the amount of money earned by these companies, Connections Education's estimated revenues are $190 million and Pearson bought the company for $400 million (Saul, 2011). Connections Academy posted the following announcement of the Pearson purchase on its website.

Pearson Acquires Connections Education

Gains Leading Position in Fast-Growing Market for Virtual Schools

September 15, 2011. Pearson, the world's leading learning company, is announcing today the acquisition of Connections Education from an investor group led by Apollo Management, L.P.

Through its Connections Academy business, the company operates online or 'virtual' public schools in 21 states in the US—serving more than 40,000 students in the current school year (Connections Academy, 2011).

For-Profit Supplemental Education Services: Sylvan and Kumon

Returning to the issue of EIA's lobbying for federal money for supplemental education services, several important companies are identified as major beneficiaries of this funding, such as Sylvan Learning and Kumon Learning Centers. One of the signatories of the Education Industry Association's Code of Ethics, Sylvan Learning, provides tutorial services and test preparation for state tests and college entrance exams. The company entices customers with the following Web advertisement: "Sylvan's individualized approach to learning builds the exact skills your child needs to succeed at school and at life. If you're ready to give your child a brighter future, contact us to learn more about our programs today" (Sylvan Learning, 2011).

Illustrating its corporate reach and work, Sylvan Learning advertises the sale of franchises with the following list of the corporate benefits and recognitions. Sylvan Learning's promotion of its franchises highlights the political stake it has in the continued government funding of for-profit supplementary education services. It functions like any corporation trying to expand its reach and profits. Sylvan Learning boasts to potential buyers of its franchises:

Industry Leadership

With more than two million students served since 1979, Sylvan is proud of our industry leadership. Our recognition includes:

- Ranked 24 times in *Entrepreneur* magazine's "Franchise 500 Ranking," the industry's premier franchise ranking. Ranked number 61 overall in its 2009 "Franchise 500 Ranking" and number 52 in the publication's "Top Global Franchises" ranking.
- Ranked number 57 in the *2008 Franchise Times'* "Top 200 Systems" based on number of total units.
- Recognized by *PODER Enterprise* magazine as one of the "Top 25 Franchises for Hispanics" in April 2009.
- Ranked in *Bond's Top 100 Franchises*.

(Sylvan Learning, 2011a)

Another signatory to EIA's ethics code is Kumon Learning Centers which operates a vast number of global franchises. In the United States, where it is partly dependent on government support and therefore joins the Education Industry Association in its lobbying efforts, in 2009 it had 1,204 franchises. In addition, the company has over 25,000 franchises in other countries (*Entrepreneur* Magazine, 2010). In 2011, Entrepreneur Magazine listed Kumon Learning Centers as the number 1 franchise for tutoring services and number 14 in a list of the top 500 franchises, while Forbes listed Kumon Learning Centers as number 3 in 2011 among the top franchises for the money (Kumon Learning Centers, 2011).

Reaping the Profits of Testing

Profits can be made from the NCLB's emphasis on testing through the selling and scoring of tests and through test preparation paid for by students, parents, or local school districts. One of the most important parts of NCLB that stimulated the growth of for-profit test producers and test preparation companies was the requirement that each state implement a statewide assessment system. NCLB states "Each State plan shall demonstrate that the State educational agency, in consultation with local educational agencies, has implemented a set of high quality, yearly student academic assessments that include, at a minimum, academic assessments in mathematics, reading or language arts, and science that will be used as the primary means of determining the yearly performance of the State and of each local educational agency" (NCLB, 2002, p. 25).

Pearson, a United Kingdom based corporation, reaped major profits from the boom in assessment requirements included in NCLB. As noted in chapter

2, Pearson is also a major player in providing online courses based on common core standards. The importance of changes in U.S. educational policies for Pearson's profits is revealed in the company's 2010 financial report. In 1999, according to the 2010 financial report, the company's operating profit, not revenues, was £449 million ($694.19 million at December 14, 2011 currency rates) with "Education" representing 35% of this profit. In 2010, operating profits increased to £857 million ($1.32 billion at December 14, 2011 currency rates) with 81% coming from "North American Education" and "International Education." Again, we want to stress that these figures are profits and not revenue (Pearson, 2010, p. 8). Pearson "learning materials, technologies, assessments and services to teachers and students" in North America resulted in 2010 revenues of £2,640 million ($4,065 at December 14, 2011 currency rates) with an adjusted operating profit of £433.92 million ($668.23 at December 14, 2011 currency rates) (Pearson, 2010b, p. 2).

In 2010, the growth of Pearson's testing business gained new importance with a decrease in school publishing revenue resulting from declining educational budgets. The Pearson 2010 financial report stated: "In North America, we see growth in ... assessment more than offsetting a slower year for the school publishing industry (the result of the lower new adoption opportunity and pressure on state budgets)" (Pearson, 2010b, p. 17). An important source of assessment revenue came from administering the SAT college entrance examination. The 2010 report proudly announced, "We renewed two important contracts, extending our long-standing relationships with the College Board to administer the SATs and with the Texas Education Agency to administer statewide student assessments" (Pearson, 2010b, p. 20).

Politically, Pearson is concerned with maintaining the profits it receives from government education budgets and policies. Their dependence on government revenues highlights the growth of educational industrial complex. The 2010 Pearson report warned that "Our US educational solutions and assessment businesses may be adversely affected by changes in state and local educational funding resulting from either general economic conditions, changes in *government educational funding, programs, policy decisions, legislation at both at the federal and state level* [emphasis added]" (Pearson, 2010b, p. 36).

Consequently, Pearson engages in lobbying efforts for government policies that will ensure a steady profit. The company monitors government education policies as acknowledged in their 2010 reports, "We actively monitor changes through participation in advisory boards and representation on standard setting committees. Our customer relationship teams have detailed knowledge of each state market" (Pearson, 2010b, p 36). The 2010 report gives this description of their lobbying efforts: "We work through our own government relations team and our industry trade associations including the Association of American Publishers. We are also monitoring municipal funding and the impact on our education receivables" (Pearson, 2010b, p. 36).

In its 2010 report, Pearson Chairman Glen Moreno stated regarding the company's future strategy and purchase of educational companies: "I am convinced that this steady reallocation of resources into learning companies that are heavily oriented towards developing markets and new technologies is an excellent strategy for Pearson to pursue. Our return on capital from all acquired companies from 2002–2010 is 12%, well above our average cost of capital" (Pearson, 2010b, p. 8). This investment strategy reflects the reports opening claim: "Pearson is the world's leading learning company. We have 36,000 people in more than 70 countries, helping people of all ages to make progress in their lives through all kinds of learning" (Pearson, 2010, p. 2).

The other assessment powerhouse that benefits from NCLB is CTB/McGraw-Hill (2011). CTB, originally called Research Service Company, was founded in 1926 by Ethel Clark, the wife of Willis Clark who was Assistant Director of Research for the Los Angeles school district and one of the developers of the successful *Los Angeles Diagnostic Tests in the Fundamentals of Arithmetic*. In an early example of the educational-industrial complex and flexian activities, Ethel Clark bought the publishing rights to the test and sent postcard advertisements to school districts. The first customer, the Kansas City, Missouri school district, purchased 20,000 copies of the test. Between the founding of the company and its purchase by McGraw-Hill in 1965, CTB developed and marketed a variety of tests including the California Achievement Tests, the California Test of Mental Maturity, and the Personnel Selection and Classification Test (CTB/McGraw-Hill, 2011). In 1948 CTB began establishing branch offices around the country. In 1959 CTB developed an answer sheet that could be mechanically scored using the Electronic Scoring Punch machine which made practical testing large numbers of students. On August 31, 1965 McGraw-Hill purchased CTB, and Ethel Clark announced the purchase in a radio interview, "With the kind of financial, technical, and promotional assistance McGraw-Hill can furnish, we [CTB] think we can go far" (CTB/McGraw-Hill, 2011). Between 1965 and passage of NCLB, CTB/McGraw-Hill developed and marketed a variety of tests including the Criterion Referenced Tests (CRTs), the Diagnostics Math Inventory, updated versions of the California Achievement Tests and Comprehensive Tests of Basic Skills, Language Assessment Scales in Spanish and English, and the Spanish Assessment of Basic Education. In 1997, CTB/McGraw-Hill set the stage for the massive testing required by NCLB by introducing electronic imaging for computerized scoring (CTB/McGraw-Hill, 2011).

By the time of the passage of NCLB, CTB/McGraw-Hill had already established itself as an important part of the growing educational-industrial complex. Its growth depended on purchases by public school systems particularly products like the California Achievement Tests and the Comprehensive Test of Basic Skills. Recognition of the financial importance of NCLB is given on its website, "With No Child Left Behind enacted, CTB was prepared to offer customized testing solutions for state-specific needs that met federal requirements. CTB was also able to provide enhanced NCLB-complaint student achievement reporting systems" (CTB/McGraw-Hill, 2011).

Seeking profits from the NCLB requirement that failing schools be restructured, McGraw-Hill Education created a Center for Comprehensive School Improvement "to help districts turn around failing schools" (McGraw-Hill Companies, 2011, p. 13). In 2010 revenues for McGraw-Hill School Education Group serving elementary and high school markets totaled about $1 billion (McGraw-Hill Companies, 2011, p. 29). In 2010, CTB/McGraw-Hill sold products to 18 million students in 46 countries (McGraw-Hill Companies, 2010, p. 19).

In summary, both Pearson and CTB/McGraw-Hill financially benefited from the enactment of NCLB. These two companies represent the reliance of the educational-industrial complex on government funding and policies.

Test Preparation: Kaplan and Princeton Review

Despite the increased emphasis on testing for college admission and to meet the requirements of NCLB, profits for test preparation companies such as Kaplan and the Princeton have recently been declining. Test preparation companies earn most profits from the direct sale of their products, including test guides and actual test preparation courses, to consumers. Consumer demand for test preparation services is directly dependent on government and college policies. NCLB stimulates consumer demand for test preparation and tutoring services sold by for-profit companies. Entrance examinations required for college admission stimulate consumer demand for test preparation. Without the requirements of NCLB and college admissions there would be a sharp decline in consumer demand for test preparation courses and publications. This section will review the activities of two major test preparation for-profit companies Kaplan and the Princeton Review.

Kaplan, with its origins in test preparation, was ideally suited to benefit from the testing provisions of NCLB. A pioneer in test preparation for college entrance examinations, Stanley Kaplan in 1928 began tutoring students in his parents' basement in Brooklyn. After World War II his company began preparing students for standardized college entrance examinations. In 1984, Kaplan was purchased by the Washington Post Company and by 2004 Kaplan's revenues exceeded $1 billion (Kaplan, 2009). In 2000, Kaplan entered the higher education market by acquiring Quest Education Corporation. According to the official Kaplan company history, with this acquisition "Higher education becomes Kaplan's biggest business" (Kaplan, 2009). In 2010, Kaplan reported revenue for Test Preparation $415.7 million and for Kaplan Higher Education about $1.8 billion with education making up 62% of the total revenue for the Washington Post Company (2010). The company's experience in test preparation logically led to preparing students for state tests required under NCLB.

In 2011, Kaplan K12 Learning Services announced that it was partnering with the previously discussed K12 Inc., "to offer a complete portfolio of college preparation solutions" (Kaplan, 2011). Kaplan K12 Learning is a unit of Kaplan Test Prep which is a division of Kaplan Inc., a subsidiary of The Washington Post Company. Kaplan K12 is offering "state test readiness programs to help students meet and exceed state standards, and college preparation solutions that support students as they prepare for college entrance exams and the admissions process" (Kaplan, 2011).

The 2010 Annual Report of Kaplan's parent company the Washington Post opened with concerns about Congressional criticism of its online Kaplan University for its recruitment practices and loan defaults. The Annual Report expressed concern about the possible decline in revenues from Kaplan Higher Education. However, between 2008 and 2010 the net revenue from Kaplan Higher Education actually increased from $1.1 billion to $1.7 billion. During the same period the net revenue for Kaplan Test Preparation declined from $511 million to $415 million. For the parent company, as noted above, education represented 62% of its total revenue with other revenues from cable television (16%), newspaper publishing (14%), television broadcasting (7%), and other businesses (1%) (*Washington Post*, 2011).

Founded in 1981 as a test preparation company, the Princeton Review provides test preparation for a wide variety of standardized examinations including the Scholastic Aptitude Test, Advance Placement Examinations, Graduate Record Examination, and other major college and professional tests. The company offers classroom courses in 41 states and 21 countries, online and school-based courses, one-on-one tutoring and small-group instruction, and publishes a series of test preparation books including the its best-selling *Cracking the SAT* (Princeton Review, 2012).

Unlike Kaplan, the Princeton Review does not rely on government money for support except in cases where local schools offer their courses. The Princeton Review primarily earns its income directly from consumers who purchase their products and training courses in order to gain admission to colleges and graduate and professional schools. The fact that the cost of test preparation is born by the student does not exempt institutions from helping ensure the company's profits. The majority of these tests are required by colleges and graduate and professional schools for admission which raises the question of why the institution does not pay for the cost of the exam. If the institutions were required to pay for the tests then they might hesitate to require them. So the student must bear the cost of the exam and the cost of test preparation.

Recognizing the financial burden of test preparation for low-income students, the company created the Princeton Review Foundation in 1987. The Foundation focuses on high school students from low-income families by providing reduced-fee test preparation programs. It also provides test preparation for high school exit examinations (Princeton Review Foundation, 2011).

The Princeton Review's revenue has been increasing rapidly. In 2006 its total revenue was a little over $97 million and by 2010 it had increased to a little over $214 million more than double the 2006 revenue. However over the same period of time operating expenses exceeded revenue resulting in a net loss (Princeton Review, 2011, p. 28). The company is listed on the NASDAQ.

The increasing emphasis on standardized tests created a market for test preparation courses and publications. While Kaplan Test Preparation and the Princeton Review are having financial problems, they still remain an important part of the educational-industrial complex. Their businesses are dependent on government and college policies that emphasize high-stakes examination for success in elementary, middle, and high school and for admission to colleges and graduate and professional programs.

Commercialization of School Life

Commercialization of schools extends the educational-industrial complex into the daily lives of students through the sale of products and advertising and the use of public relations to promote business interests. Alex Molnar argues that budget concerns often prompt the sale of naming rights to school athletic facilities, the signing of contracts for placing vending machines in schools, the use of corporate sponsored education materials and activities, and the placing of advertising on school buses and school facilities. However, he argues the actual revenue from this commercial invasion of student life is "often very modest" (Molnar, 2005, p. 39).

The commercialization of schools is not new but it is increasing. For instance, Molnar concluded that between 1990 and 2004 commercial sponsorship of school activities increased by 146%; the signing of exclusive contracts with corporations to supply products or services increased by 858%; the buying of naming rights to athletic facilities, school buildings, and even classrooms increased by 394%; and the use of corporate sponsored educational materials bearing the sponsor's name increased by 1,038% (Molnar, 2005, pp. 21–25).

The direct relationship between student's lives and the commercialization of schools is illustrated by the controversial in-school sale of soft drinks. Concern about childhood obesity prompted calls to limit soft drinks in schools by the World Heart Association and other international health groups concerned about children's nutrition (Popovich, 2010). Bruce Silverglade, legal affairs director for the Center for Science in the Public Interest stated: "Our original goal was to get both Coke and Pepsi and the smaller soft drink companies to sign on to a standard, uniform policy that would remove carbonated soft drinks and sugary beverages from all schools—primary and secondary. And that didn't quite happen. The industry couldn't agree with itself " (Popovich,

2010). However PepsiCo did issue a global policy to restrict the sale of soft drinks in school (2011).

Soft drink companies like PepsiCo often sign exclusive agreements to sell their products in schools, such as the 2003 contract between the Hillsborough County (Florida) and the Pepsi Bottling group for a 12-year, $50 million right to ensure that the county's 62 middle and high schools only sold Pepsi products (Molnar, 2005, p. 22). Exemplifying the importance of these exclusive contracts was the infamous 1998 Colorado Springs situation reported in national newspapers. The school district signed an exclusive contract with Coca-Cola which required students to drink 70,000 cases of the product for the district to receive full financial payments from the soft drink company. When it looked like this quota would not be reached John Bushey executive director of school leadership sent a memo to school principals to "Allow students to purchase and consume vended products throughout the day" and "locate machines where they are accessible to students all day" (Molnar, 2005, p. 40).

The impact of these exclusive soft drink contracts is on student health as recognized by the 2011–2012 national and global guidelines on school sales agreed to by PepsiCo. The guidelines state:

> PepsiCo will encourage our bottlers, vending companies and third-party distributors to work closely with parents, community leaders and school officials to ensure that only products that meet the following guidelines are offered to schools for sale to students through vending machines, the cafeteria and school stores in primary and secondary schools as such schools are defined in the local markets.
>
> (PepsiCo, 2011)

PepsiCo's guidelines limit the sale of their high caloric drinks but not their bottled water Aquafina or its juices sold under the Tropicana and Dole brand names. For instance, the companies guidelines for stocking primary school vending machines includes water, 100% juices, juice/water beverages with no added sugar, milk, and products nutritionally equivalent to milk. Secondary school guidelines require the in-school vending of the same products as primary schools but allows for the sale "of juice/fat-free or low fat dairy or nutritionally equivalent milk alternatives with no more than 10% kcal from added sugar" and "beverages containing no more than 40 kcal per 240 ml" (Pepsico, 2011). Under these guidelines PepsiCo would still be able to make a profit from in-school sales through the vending of water, juices, and juice mixtures.

Building brand loyalty is one purpose for selling products in schools and distributing educational materials labeled with corporate names and logos. A child represents a lifetime of consumption. In tackling criticisms of in-school sales PepsiCo hit upon the idea of making their school vending machines convey a sense of healthy activities and, consequently, building a positive brand image for its products. The company's global guidelines states:

Vending Machines

PepsiCo will encourage our bottlers, vending companies, and third-party distributors to provide vending machines in a variety of graphic designs, including activity-based and non-commercial imagery and to provide only activity-based and non-commercial imagery on vendors placed in primary schools. We also recommend the use of nutritional information panels that can be attached to vending machines.

(Pepsico, 2011)

Another example of attempting to gain brand name loyalty is Pizza Hut's BOOK IT! program (2012). The program was started in 1985 and by 2012 Pizza Hut claimed it was reaching 10 million students annually (BOOK IT!, 2012). The program is operated through schools from October to March. Teachers set reading goals for each child in their classes. Pizza Hut supplies teachers with tracking charts to measure student progress to meeting reading goals. "As soon as a child meets the monthly reading goal, the teacher gives him or her a Reading Award Certificate. Pizza Hut is proud of all BOOK IT! readers! The restaurant manager and team congratulate every child for meeting the monthly reading goal and reward them with a free, one-topping Personal Pan Pizza, BOOK IT! card and backpack clip" (BOOK IT!, 2012). Conveniently the BOOK IT! website provides a store locater so that students can easily get their personal pan pizzas.

The BOOK IT! program is a win-win marketing tool for Pizza Hut. First it promotes brand loyalty between the student and Pizza Hut products. Second, it creates a positive public image for the company as a supporter of learning and schools. And lastly, it can mean a profit for Pizza Hut if families accompanying their children when they get their free personal pizza order and pay for their own pizzas and drinks. Does the child also purchase a drink?

Provision of free materials to schools can be used to persuade students to adopt certain ideologies and to promote corporate images. This method of corporate persuasion through free school materials has been going on for years. An important example of the attempt to influence student thinking in favor of corporations over labor unions was the American Way campaign of the 1930s. Launched in 1936, the "American Way" public relations campaign was designed to counter the growth of antibusiness attitudes. The National Association of Manufacturers (NAM) spearheaded this public relations effort. The NAM suggested the introduction of probusiness ideas into schools through the medium of printed materials, movies, and slides for school libraries and classrooms. In 1937, Lewis H. Brown, president of Johns-Manville Corporation, declared, "We must with moving pictures and other educational material carry into the schools of the generation of tomorrow an interesting story of the part that science and industry have played in creating a more abundant life for those who are fortunate to live in this great country of ours" (Ewen, 1996, pp.

297–298). He warned that teachers knew more about Karl Marx than about the inner workings of local factories.

In the schools, the National Association of Manufacturers conducted a public relations campaign to establish in the public mind the "inter-relation" and "inseparability" of free enterprise and democracy. On the surface, these two ideas are distinct: Free enterprise is an economic doctrine, and democracy is a political system. Many European countries, however, practice varying forms of democratic socialism; a democratic government might have a socialized economy and a totalitarian government might allow free enterprise. Believing that emotions rather than reason shaped public opinion in 1939 the NAM public relations committee announced that its goal was to "link free enterprise in the public consciousness with free speech, free press and free religion as integral parts of democracy" (Ewen, 1996, p. 306).

Eager to create positive opinions of American business and establish in the public mind a connection between free enterprise and democracy, corporations and the NAM flooded classrooms with printed material and movies. The NAM distributed to schools a series of booklets titled *You and Industry,* which were designed to evoke in the reader positive feelings about the American industrial system. In 1937, the NAM began distributing to 70,000 schools a newsweekly, *Young America,* containing articles such as "The Business of America's People Is Selling," "Building Better Americans," and "Your Local Bank" (Ewen, 1996, p. 314). A 10-minute film, *America Marching On,* was distributed to schools with the message, "America marching upward and onward to higher standards of living, greater income for her people, and more leisure to enjoy the good things of life as the greatest industrial system the world has ever seen began to develop" (Ewen, 1996, p. 315).

It would be difficult to determine whether or not the NAM school campaign was successful in getting students to spontaneously make the connection between democracy and capitalism. However the American Way campaign exemplifies the attempt by corporate America to directly influence student minds to have a favorable view of corporations and, consequently, reject ideas that are pro-union or critical of corporations.

A current example of attempts to influence student thinking and create brand loyalty is the Field Trip Factory which organizes school visits to sponsoring sites. The Field Trip Factory describes itself:

> As the undisputed leaders in experience-based education for all ages, Field Trip Factory brings lessons to life in a whole new way. By providing hands-on activities in real-world environments, Field Trip participants experience learning in a context that is relevant to daily life, and always close to home. Field Trip Factory experiences take place throughout the aisles of community-conscious retailers.
>
> (Field Trip Factory, 2010b)

As Alex Molnar points out retailers pay the Field Trip Factory to bring children to their stores. He quotes a Petco manager—children are taken to Petco stores to learn about animal welfare—"We are getting kids in at a young age so we can educate them and hopefully turn them into customers" (Molnar, 2005, p. 35). Students are taken to Ralphs grocery stores to study environmental issues. Field Trip Factory website explains: "*Speak Out. It's Your Earth!* (2010b) encourages children to find their voice and help make a positive impact on the environment. Students will explore the aisles of Ralphs while learning easy ways to make a difference" (Field Trip Factory Enviromental Programs, 2010c). Peapod, the online store for Stop and Shop groceries, sponsors an online field trip: "This online experience encourages discovery and interpretation of the nutritional value of the foods we eat using resources available at online food retailers such as Peapod.com" (Field Trip Factory Nutrition Detective , 2010c).

Conclusion

The educational-industrial complex expanded and grew richer under the provisions of NCLB. Throughout the legislation the words *for-profit* appear. The emphasis on standardized testing to measure school and student failure and success was a boon to the testing industry and publishing giants like Pearson and CTB/McGraw-Hill along with test preparation companies. The legislation's requirements that parents in failing schools be allowed to choose for-profit supplementary services to help their children with school work enlarged the industry and created a strong lobbying group, such as the Educational Industry Association, seeking for more government and policies favorable to the industry. NCLB's support of restructuring for failing schools opened the door to for-profit companies to offer these services to local school districts. Also, the support of charter schools aided the growth of for-profit educational management organizations. As public schools were consumed by the educational-industrial complex, they became more commercialized through in-school advertising and vending, and free curriculum materials from corporations.

What are the results of NCLB and the commercialization of schools? More for-profit education companies are lobbying for increasing amounts of public funds. Flexians move between government and the for-profit education sector. Money that might have gone directly to local schools to make decisions about how it should be spent are now funneled through for-profit companies. How much of the public funds spent through for-profits goes to company profits and administration? Is this the most efficient use of public money? Do students benefit? Will pressures from the education-industrial complex result in more schools services, including teaching and administration, being turned over to for-profit companies?

Case Study—Edison Schools

Edison Schools, now one of the largest EMOs in the country, was founded in 1991 by the media executive Christopher Whittle. While possessing an innovative and creative approach to education, its private, for-profit management model was not profitable in managing public schools. In the late 1990s and early 2000s, Edison started directing more of its energies to managing charter schools and offering software tools and online courses.

Christopher Cerf, is the past president of Edison Schools (name changed to EdisonLearning in 2008) and an attorney who worked as an associate counsel in the Clinton White House along with Joel Klein in the 1990s. Cerf served as legal counsel to the Edison Schools and became its president in 2001. During his tenure as president, Edison Schools became the largest provider of management services to public schools with 77,000 students in 150 schools. Cerf left Edison Schools as president in 2005. While continuing to serve on the Edison Board of Directors, he formed a consulting firm called the Public Private Strategy Group. He was subsequently hired as a full-time adviser to Joel Klein, Chancellor of the New York City school system and Cerf's former law colleague in Washington. A year later he was named Deputy Chancellor of the New York City public school system while still owning stock in Edison Schools. As Deputy Chancellor, he was in a position to establish new charter schools in New York City, a situation that raised ethical questions regarding his appointment.

> By the measure of the law, Cerf did nothing wrong regarding Edison. He had already disclosed his stake to education officials and recused himself from all matters involving the company. Moreover, at the time the meeting took place, a ruling from the city's Conflicts of Interests Board was pending on whether he could keep the shares.
>
> He [Cerf] said he deserved praise, not condemnation, for relinquishing the shares without compensation and that his actions were motivated by the desire to avoid any kind of distraction for the department and the chancellor....
>
> Despite his stance, the department's investigative arm, the Special Commissioner of Investigation, opened a probe into the matter. It found that when Cerf gave up his shares in Edison via e-mail, he asked that in return, a charitable contribution of $60,000 be made to the Darrow Foundation, a nonprofit group that runs a wilderness camp for disadvantaged children. Cerf serves on Darrow's board.
>
> After he was interviewed by the investigator, Richard Condon, Cerf rescinded the donation request, which had not yet been filled, according to Condon's report.
>
> Condon forwarded his findings to the conflicts board, which took no action against Cerf. The board's chairman, however, wrote to Cerf as a

"formal reminder of the importance of strict compliance with the city's conflicts of interests law," according to a New York Times account.

Cerf said he "absolutely rejects" any notion of impropriety, adding that he did not ask for the donation in his capacity as a public official and that he was recused from business involving Edison in any event."

(*Star-Ledger* Staff, 2011)

Cerf left the New York City public school system in 2009 to work on Mayor Michael Bloomberg's reelection campaign. Soon after, he took a position as President and Chief Executive Officer of Sangari Global Education, a private company that sells curricula to school districts, mainly overseas. It was in May of 2010, while still president of Sangari, that Cerf and a partner, Rajeev Bajaj, formed Global Education Advisors, a consulting company based at Cerf's home address in Montclair, New Jersey.

In late 2010, funded by a $500,000 grant from the Broad Foundation (Los Angeles), Cory Booker, mayor of Newark, New Jersey, hired Global Education Advisors to perform a comprehensive assessment of the Newark district's enrollment figures, test scores, and facilities. Global Education Advisors issued a set of recommendations to close a number of failing schools and, in their place, open 11 charter schools and five new district schools. Cerf was appointed Acting Commissioner of Education in the State of New Jersey in 2011. The Global Education Advisors report is still pending and Cerf, as acting education commissioner, would have final say over the proposal in the state-run Newark district (*Star-Ledger Staff*, 2011). At issue were a number of conflict of interest concerns related to Cerf's position as Acting Assistant Commissioner of Education and association with Global Education Advisors, as well as EdisonLearning, on whose board he continued to serve. Cerf is also a member of the board of directors of the KIPP charter schools in New Jersey (Hu, 2010).

Later in 2011 and 2012, Cerf was involved in another issue involving a gift of $100 million from Mark Zuckerberg, founder of Facebook. The American Civil Liberties Union filed a lawsuit against Newark on behalf of a parents group (Secondary Parent Council) who were denied access to records requested under New Jersey's Open Public Records Act. Specifically, access was requested to review correspondence and e-mails between Mark Zuckerberg, Newark Mayor Cory Booker, Governor Chris Christie, and Acting Education Commissioner Chris Cerf regarding whether there were any conditions established for the Zuckerman gift. The request was rejected by city officials in July 2011 (Wilwohl, 2011). *The Chronicle of Philanthropy* also reported that:

> The biggest individual recipients [of the Zuckerberg gift] are Global Education Advisors ($1.96-million), a consultancy established by Chris Cerf before he was named the state's acting education commissioner, and Tusk Strategies ($1.53-million), which managed the 2009 re-election

campaign of New York Mayor Michael Bloomberg, for whom Mr. Cerf previously worked as an adviser.

(*The Chronicle of Philanthropy*, 2012)

In January 2012, Essex County Superior Court Judge Rachel N. Davidson ordered Newark officials to hand over a list of e-mails related to the $100 million donation Facebook founder Mark Zuckerberg gave to Newark schools (Adarle, 2012).

At the time of this writing, the suit over the Facebook gift was still pending. New Jersey State Sen. Ronald Rice, a Democrat from Essex County, had also vowed to hold up Christopher Cerf's confirmation as Education Commissioner until the above matters involving the Newark schools and Global Education Advisors were resolved.

References

Adarle, S. (January 27, 2012). Judge orders Newark to release document list on Facebook donation. *NewarkPatch*. Retrieved from http://newarknj.patch.com/articles/judge-orders-newark-to-release-documents-on-facebook-donation.

BOOK IT! (2012). *You are your child's first reader.* Retrieved from http://www.bookitprogram.com/Parents/about.asp

Chronicle of Philanthropy (2012, January 29). Consultants top recipients so far of Newark Facebook money. Retrieved from http://philanthropy.com/blogs/philanthropytoday/consultants-top-recipients-so-far-of-newark-facebook-money/41537

Connections Academy. (2011, September 15). *Pearson acquires Connections Education.* Retrieved from http://www.connectionsacademy.com/news/pearson-acquisition.aspx

CTB/McGraw-Hill. (2011). *About us.* Retrieved from http://www.ctb.com/ctb.com/control/ourHeritageAction?p=aboutUs

EdisonLearning. (2011a, November 9). *About EdisonLearning.* Retrieved from http://edisonlearning.com/index.php?q=about-edisonlearning

EdisonLearning. (2011b, November 12). *Alliance-school turnaround service.* Retrieved from http://edisonlearning.com/alliance-school-turnaround-model

EdisonLearning. (2011c, November 12). *Learning force.* Retrieved from http://edisonlearning.com/learning-force

EdisonLearning. (2011d, November 12). *Products and services.* Retrieved from http://edisonlearning.com/products-services

Educate Online. (2011e, December 12). *Our programs.* Retrieved from http://www.educate-online.com/#/our_programs/k12_academic_intervention/how_educate_online_works

Education Industry Association. (2010a). *Middle class tax incentives for tutoring.* Retrieved from http://www.educationindustry.org/index.php?option=com_content&view=article&id=51:middle-class-tax-incentives-for-tutoring&catid=19:news-and-policy

Education Industry Association. (2010b, March 2). *SES/Public Policy.* Retrieved from http:www.educationindustry.org/tier.asp?sid=2

Education Industry Association. (2011a, January). EIA's 11th Annual Education Industry Days Legislative Conference. *Enterprising Educators: The Education Industry Association's Monthly Publication*, p. 3.

Education Industry Association. (2011b, December 5). *Make history on December 6, 2011 by helping launch global initiative for education entrepreneurs.* Retrieved from http://www.educationindustry.org/index.php?option=com_content&view=article&id=77:icee-meeting-istanbul-turkey&catid=19:news-and-policy&Itemid=158

Education Industry Association. (2011c, December 11). *Mission and goals*. Retrieved from http://www.educationindustry.org/mission-and-goals

Education Industry Association. (2011d, January). New faces at EIA. *Enterprising Educators: The Education Industry Association's Monthly Publication*, p. 5.

Education Industry Association. (2011e, December 5). *SES coalition*. Retrieved from http://www.educationindustry.org/ses-coalition

Education Industry Association. (2011f, December 5). *Who we are*. Retrieved from http://www.educationindustry.org/who-we-are

Elementary and Secondary Education Act of 1965. In S. B. Mosher (Ed.), *ESEA: The Office of Education administers a law* (pp. 235–266). Syracuse, NY: Syracuse University Press.

Entrepreneur Magazine. (2010, March 12). Kumon math and reading centers: Supplemental education. Retrieved from http://www.entrepreneur.com/franchises/kumonmathandreading-centers/282507-0.html

Ewen, S. (1996). *PR! A social history of sprin*. New York: Basic Books.

Field Trip Factory. (2010a). *Real learning meets real life at the Field Trip Factory*. Retrieved from http://www.fieldtripfactory.com/tour-factory/who-we-are

Field Trip Factory. (2010b). *Speak out. It's your earth*. Enviromental Programs. Retrieved from http://www.fieldtripfactory.com/ralphsearthday

Field Trip Factory. (2010c). *Nutrition detective*. Retrieved from http://www.fieldtripfactory.com/peapod

Friedman, M. (1962). *Capital and freedom*. Chicago, IL: University of Chicago Press.

Hayek, F. (1962). *The road to serfdom*. Chicago, IL: University of Chicago Press.

Hu, W. (December 17, 2010). Christie picks Klein ally for New Jersey Schools. *New York Times*. Retrieved from http://www.nytimes.com/2010/12/18/nyregion/18cerf.html

K12. Inc. (2011, December 12). *Online public schools*. Retrieved from http://www.k12.com/schools-programs/online-public-schools

Kaplan. (2009). *History*. Retrieved from http://www.kaplan.com/about-kaplan/history

Kaplan. (2011, November 15). *Kaplan K12 learning services and K^{12} partner to maximize college preparation*. Retrieved from http://www.kaplan.com/newsroom/Pressreleases/Pages/PressReleases.aspx?ID=647

Kumon Learning Centers. (2011, December 12). *Franchise home*. Retrieved from http://www.kumonfranchise.com/

McGraw-Hill Companies. (2010). *A smarter, better world: 2009 annual report*. New York: McGraw-Hill.

McGraw-Hill Companies. (2011). *What does it take to succeed in the knowledge economy?: 2010 annual report*. New York: McGraw-Hill.

Molnar, A. (2005). *School commercialization: From democratic ideal to market commodity*. New York: Routledge.

National Center for Education Statistics. (2010). *The condition of education 2010*. Washington, DC: U.S. Department of Education.

No Child Left Behind Act of 2001. (2002, January 8). Retrieved from http://www2.ed.gov/policy/elsec/leg/esea02/index.html

Pearson. (2010a, September 15). *Danville, Virginia School District chooses Pearson as school turnaround partner*. Retrieved from http://www.pearsoned.com/danville-virginia-school-district-chooses-pearson-as-school-turnaround-partner/

Pearson. (2010b). *Open to learn: Pearson annual report and accounts 2010*. London: Pearson.

PepsiCo. (2011). *PepsiCo global policy on the sale of beverages to schools*. Retrieved from http://www.pepsico.com/download/PepsiCo_Global_Policy_On_The_Sale_Of_Beverages_To_Schools.pdf

Popovich, N. (2010, March 18). *Pepsi to restrict caloric drinks in schools worldwide*. Retrieved from http://www.npr.org/blogs/health/2010/03/pepsi_global_school_soda_polic.html

Princeton Review. (2011). *2010 annual report*. Farmingham, MA: Author.

Princeton Review. (2012). *About the Princeton Review*. Retrieved from http://www.princetonreview.com/about-us.aspx

Princeton Review Foundation. (2011). *About us*. Retrieved from http://www.princetonreview. com/corporate/foundation.aspx

Saltman, K. (2005). *The Edison schools: Corporate schooling and the assault on public education*. New York: Routledge.

Saul, S. (2011, December 12). Profits and questions at online charter schools. *New York Times*, pp. A1, A24–25.

Spring, J. (2010). *Political agendas for education* (4th ed.).New York: Routledge.

Star-Ledger Staff (2011, March 13). N.J. acting schools chief faces questions about transparency, imperiling his confirmation. *Newark Star-Ledger*. Retrieved from http://www.nj.com/news/ index.ssf/2011/03/nj_acting_education_commission.html

Sylvan Learning. (2011a, December 12). *Sylvan builds the skills, habits and attitudes your child needs for lifelong success*. Retrieved from http://tutoring.sylvanlearning.com/tutoring_programs.cfm

Tennessee Virtual Academy. (2011, December 12). *Who we are*. Retrieved from http:// www.k12.com/tnva/who-we-are U.S. Department of Education. (2010, March 17). Retrieved from http://find.ed.gov/search?q=supplemental+education+services&client=d efault_frontend&output=xml_no_dtd&proxystylesheet=default_frontend&sa.x=18&sa.y =11&ie=UTF-8&ip=74.101.47.5&access=p&entqr=3&cntsp=a&oe=UTF-8& ud=1&sort=date%3AD%3AL%3Ad1

Washington Post. (2011). *2010 Annual Report*. Washington, DC: Author.

Wilwohl, J. (2011, August 24). ACLU sues Newark for details of $100M Facebook cash. *NewarkPatch*. Retrieved from http://newarknj.patch.com/articles/aclu-sues-newark-for-details-of-100m-facebook-cash

5

PROFITS, PRODUCTS, AND PRIVATIZATION

American education has always included the substantial involvement of private entities. Private K-12 schools, prep academies, and church and religious-affiliated elementary and high schools have been a part of the American education system since colonial times. It wasn't until the early 1800s that Horace Mann championed public or common schools to be funded by the states and localities. Higher education in the United States in its early years also started as a private system with the establishment of Harvard College in 1636. Today, American private colleges and universities enroll millions of students and are regarded as among the best in the world. These private schools whether K-12 or higher education have played and continue to play a significant role in American education. In the last 20 years, however, there has been a significant expansion of privatization in American education by profit-making entities. Education management companies (EMOs), private tutoring services, commercial software and online learning providers, and for-profit colleges and universities now play a much more significant role in American education than in the past. While some of these operate as private schools distinct and apart from public schools, others provide services that are integrated with public school operations. In this chapter, we look at the expansion of the role of these private entities in American education.

Privatization Movement in K-12 Education

Table 5.1 provides data from the U.S. Department of Education National Center on Education Statistics (NCES) illustrating that enrollment in private K-12 schools has steadily increased over the past 40 years to where it represents not quite 11% of the total elementary and secondary population or just over 6 million students. Every indication is that the modest increases in enrollments illustrated in this table will continue for the foreseeable future.

Originally, schools in the United States were founded as private entities that reflected the general interests and consensus of their communities. In 1632, Massachusetts with its Puritan traditions was among the first of the colonies to establish community schools that required parents "to see to it that their children could read and understand Congregational doctrine and the laws of the Commonwealth (Clabaugh & Rozycki, 1990). These schools evolved into privately run institutions funded by parents. Private Latin grammar schools

TABLE 5.1 Enrollment in Elementary and Secondary Schools, by Control and Level of Institution: Selected Years, Fall 1970 through Fall 2019 [In thousands]

Year	Total	Public			Private[1]		
		Total	Grades PreK-8	Grades 9-12	Total	Grades PreK-8	Grades 9-12
1970	51,257	45,894	32,558	13,336	5,363	4,052	1,311
1980	46,208	40,877	27,647	13,231	5,331	3,992	1,339
1985	44,979	39,422	27,034	12,388	5,557	4,195	1,362
1990	46,864	41,217	29,876	11,341	5,648[2]	4,512[2]	1,136[2]
1995	50,759	44,840	32,338	12,502	5,918	4,756	1,163
2000	53,373	47,204	33,686	13,517	6,169[2]	4,906[2]	1,264[2]
2005	55,187	49,113	34,204	14,909	6,073	4,724	1,349
2006	55,307	49,316	34,235	15,081	5,991[2]	4,631[2]	1,360[2]
2007	55,203	49,293	34,205	15,087	5,910	4,546	1,364
2008	55,235	49,266	34,286	14,980	5,969[2]	4,574[2]	1,395[2]
2009[3]	55,282	49,312	34,505	14,807	5,970	4,580	1,389
2010[3]	55,350	49,386	34,730	14,657	5,964	4,582	1,382
2015[3]	56,859	50,827	35,881	14,946	6,031	4,757	1,275
2016[3]	57,273	51,198	36,205	14,993	6,075	4,801	1,274
2017[3]	57,709	51,583	36,526	15,058	6,126	4,844	1,282
2018[3]	58,129	51,946	36,838	15,108	6,184	4,885	1,298
2019[3]	58,590	52,342	37,156	15,186	6,248	4,927	1,321

[1] Beginning in fall 1980, data include estimates for an expanded universe of private schools. Therefore, direct comparisons with earlier years should be avoided.

[2] Estimated.

[3] Projected.

Note: Elementary and secondary enrollment includes students in local public school systems and in most private schools (religiously affiliated and nonsectarian), but generally excludes homeschooled children and students in subcollegiate departments of colleges and in federal schools. Based on the National Household Education Survey, the homeschooled children numbered approximately 1.5 million in 2007. Excludes preprimary pupils in private schools that do not offer kindergarten or above. Detail may not sum to totals because of rounding.

Source: U.S. Department of Education, National Center for Education Statistics (2011). *Digest of Education Statistics, 2010* (NCES 2011-015), Table 3.

and secondary academies designed to prepare upper-class children for college came on the scene in the 1700s. In the 1840s, with large waves of immigrants arriving from Europe, private Catholic or parochial schools were created in the large urban areas such as New York, Chicago, and Boston. These parochial school systems, some of which received public funds, flourished well into the latter part of the 20th century. While receiving modest public funding, most of the private schools described above were nonprofit entities that were not interested in large-scale growth or providing an education to the masses. They were interested in their own constituencies based on class, religion, or cultural considerations. Their major requirement of federal, state, or local governmental authorities was to be left alone and free from public regulation or interference.

Privatization of public schools in the 21st century has a distinctly different character that focuses on providing for-profit education and services to primary and secondary schools. EMOs, tutoring services, educational software and online course providers now make up a sizable portion of the privatization element of K-12 education, all of which invest significantly in technology as a critical element of the services and products they provide. In 1999, to attract private investors to education, Merrill Lynch published *The Book of Knowledge,* a report on the "$740 billion education and training market" in the United States. Five "Big Ideas" were identified that would transform the education and training industry in the near future (Moe, Bailey, & Lau 1999):

1. **Distributed Learning.** "Democratization" of education by the application of Internet and PC technology.
2. **Education Portals.** Education-focused gateways to the Internet for the 55 million children in K-12 schools, the 14 million students in postsecondary institutions, and the 136 million working adults.
3. **Accountability and Assessments.** With graduation from high school becoming dependent on satisfactory test performance, there will be a growing demand for greatly improved information systems to track student performance on an ongoing basis.
4. **Private Management of Schools.** School choice, and the resulting greater competition for students, will increase the demand for private companies to manage traditional public schools as well as charter schools. This trend also will be driven by the push for greater accountability.
5. **Increased Teacher Training.** With computer literacy becoming an almost essential requirement in the new economy, K-12 teachers need to become proficient in the technology. This represents a significant opportunity since some 2 million new entrants are expected to boost teacher ranks to 3.5 million over the next ten years. (Moe et al., 1999)

Four of the five "big ideas" directly related to the use of technology, specifically 1, 2, 3, and 5. The one idea that does not have technology specifically mentioned is "private management of schools" or education management companies (EMOs). However, if one looks at the nature of many of these EMOs, technology is integral to their operations and generally incorporates the other four ideas.

EMOs

As introduced in chapter 4, education management companies came into existence in the 1990s and are now an important part of the privatization of K-12 education. While there were no more than a dozen or so by the 1990s, in 2010 EMOs numbered about 100, and were managing 758 schools and enrolling approximately 394,000 students. The vast majority (94%) of the managed schools are charter schools (Miron, Urschel, Aguilar, & Dailey, 2011). The number of fully online virtual schools operated by EMOs increased from 60 in 2009–2010 to 79 in 2010–2011. This represents 10% of all schools managed by for-profit EMOs. Table 5.2 provides summaries of the larger for-profit EMOs showing their location, number and types of schools, and student populations. Some such as K12, Inc. specialize in managing only virtual schools where all

TABLE 5.2 Ten Largest (Enrollment) EMOs

| EMO | Location | No. of Schools Managed | | | Enrollment |
		Charter	District	Total	
K12 Inc.	Herdon, VA	37	12	49	65,396
National Heritage Academies	Grand Rapids, MI	67	0	67	42,503
Imagine Schools, Inc.	Arlington, VA	83	0	83	38,656
EdisonLearning	New York, NY	33	16	49	28,863
Academica	Miami, FL	56	0	56	23,424
Connections Academy	Baltimore, MD	11	3	14	20,403
The Leona Group, LLC,	Phoenix, AZ	61	0	61	17,947
Charter Schools USA	Fort Lauderdale, FL	22	0	22	17,696
White Hat Management	Akron, OH	45	1	46	15,245
Mosaica Education, Inc.	New York, NY	32	1	33	10,520
Total		447	33	480	280,653

Source: Miron, G., Urschel, J.L., Yat Aguilar, M.A, & Dailey, B. (2011). *Profiles of for-profit and nonprofit education management organizations: Thirteenth annual report — 2010–2011.* Boulder, CO: National Education Policy Center. http://nepc.colorado.edu/publication/EMO-profiles-10

instruction is delivered online. One of the better known EMOs, EdisonLearning, integrates a full range of online courses into its management services.

The success of EMOs is a hotly debated topic. On the positive side, they have generally had to manage schools that were in difficult situations. After all, if a school or school district is doing well, there is little need for an education management company. In general, schools faired no worse after management was transferred to these companies. For example, in examining average yearly progress (AYP) in a large sample of schools (N = 677) managed by for-profit EMOs, almost half (48.2%) made AYP, while 51.8% of the schools did not (Miron et al., 2011).

In the past decade, most EMOs have moved toward managing charter schools rather than traditional public schools. With 394,000 students enrolled in 758 schools, EMOs do not represent a large segment of the K-12 market. As indicated earlier, the vast majority (94%) of EMO schools are charter schools. Hence their profits and viability lie with expansion of charter schools and to a degree with online schools and courses. EMOs have been and will continue to be among the most ardent supporters of these schools.

Most of the administrators and entrepreneurs associated with EMOs compete fairly in the marketplace. However, there are also people who rely on political influence and connections to secure contracts and profits for their companies. For example, William Bennett, former Secretary of Education during the Ronald Reagan presidency was the cofounder, former president, and chairman of the board of K12, Inc. He has many connections with Republican members of Congress and other officials. At the time of his resignation from K-12, Inc., the U.S. Government Accountability Office (GAO), the investigative arm of Congress, was looking into K-12, Inc.'s involvement in a project that received an improper multimillion-dollar grant from the U.S. Department of Education. Bennett resigned from K12, Inc. amid controversy over comments made during his radio show on September 28, 2005, when he stated: "it's true that if you wanted to reduce crime ... you could abort every black baby in this country, and your crime rate would go down" (Media Matters for America, 2006).

Educational Software Goes Online

In the past 30 years, a significant industry that provides software and online learning services to schools and school districts has evolved and is growing. In the 1980s and early 1990s, this industry essentially revolved around providing educational software used in schools to support teaching and learning. A wide variety of computer games and simulations such as *Oregon Trail* and *Where in the World Is Carmen San Diego?* were developed to supplement traditional classroom activities. As discussed in chapter 2, integrated learning systems (ILS) that were designed to replace the traditional classroom, were also developed.

While modestly popular in large urban school districts, the ILSs were never adopted on a large scale in K-12 education. By the 1990s with the coming of the Internet, much of this industry retooled its products and services to operate in online environments, resulting in a fairly robust industry that does tens of billions of dollars each year and includes software, tutoring services, online courses, and testing and assessment programs. In the following sections, some of these products and services will be reviewed.

Tutoring Services

For the most part, the educational software industry has grown because commerce and society in general have grown dependent on the Internet and online technology for providing goods and services. However, some of this growth can be attributed to promotion and government requirements and legislation. For example, a provision of the 2002 federal No Child Left Behind (NCLB) Act requires public schools that fail to make sufficient yearly progress to offer private supplemental educational services such as tutoring for children from low-income families. Under this bill, families are free to select a tutoring service of their choice while the school district must use its funds to pay for these services. Kaplan, a subsidiary of the Washington Post Company, is one of the major providers of tutoring services (Glod, 2008). While Kaplan provides one-on-one tutoring in certain parts of the country, it also relies extensively on *Smart Track* online software to assess student needs, to personalize instruction, and to provide ongoing reports to parents. The quality and benefits of the federal government's investment in tutoring has been mixed. A study by the Rand Corporation in 2007 concluded that tutoring improved test scores in several large urban school districts while studies in other areas and states such as Tennessee, Alabama, Georgia, Michigan, and Kentucky indicated that the mandated tutoring did not improve test scores. Although tutoring services may provide valuable assistance to students in need, there is concern that these services provide far more benefit to the for-profit providers than they do to students. Jack Jenkins, president of the Center on Education Policy in Washington, DC, stated: "This [tutoring] isn't helping poor kids.... All it's doing is taking money out of classrooms and putting it into the hands of private companies" (cited in Glod, 2008).

Credit-recovery is a specialized version of tutoring that provides instruction designed specifically to assist high school students to make up courses that they need to graduate. Typically these students have failed a course or in some cases, may have been taken ill during a course and need to complete it in order to have the requisite number of credits to earn a high school diploma. The vast majority of the companies that provide these programs do so in online environments, usually under the supervision of a teacher or tutor, but most of the instruction and monitoring is done under the control of the online software.

Companies such as Aventa Learning, Apex Learning, and Plato Learning are among the major providers of online credit recovery programs. Schools increasingly are turning to credit recovery because of pressure on the part of state and local governing bodies to improve graduation rates. In a national study of high school principals, credit recovery was found to be the most popular type of online course being offered at the secondary level. Urban high schools that historically have the lowest graduation rates of any schools in the country, are embracing online credit-recovery as a basic part of their academic program. At the same time, high school administrators have concerns about the quality of these programs and indicate that students need maturity, self-discipline, and a certain command of basic skills (reading and mathematics) in order to use them successfully. Regardless, these same administrators find it to be an important option for their students (Picciano & Seaman, 2010).

There have also been concerns that some school districts might be using credit-recovery as a quick, convenient way to move students through to graduation. As an example, questions have been raised by teachers and others that some New York City public schools were "taking shortcuts" and "gaming the system" to move students quickly through to graduation with questionable practices related to credit-recovery programs (Gootman & Coutts, 2010; Winerip, 2011a). Despite possible pitfalls, the students are happy because they graduate; principals are happy because they improve their graduation rates; and credit-recovery providers are happy because they have increased their profits. However, the students (and their parents) may have been duped into believing that their work was worthy of graduation. One New York City principal stated that: "I think that credit recovery and the related topic independent study is in lots of ways the dirty little secret of high schools. There's very little oversight and there are very few standards" (Gootman & Coutts, 2010). The issue was raised in 2010 and 2011 when nearly 80% of the students entering the City University of New York's (CUNY) community colleges failed at least one basic skills examination in reading, writing, or mathematics. Furthermore, the situation was getting worse with more high school graduates or 22.6% of CUNY entrants needing to take remedial coursework in all three basic skill areas, up from 15.4% in 2005. In October, 2011, the New York City Department of Education, using its own set of metrics concluded that 75% of its graduates in 2010 were not ready for college-level work (Winerip, 2011a). One observer blamed lax standards, the dumbing down of New York State Regents Examinations required for graduation, and an expansion of credit-recovery programs. David Bloomfield, a professor of education leadership at Brooklyn College, likened credit-recovery to "giving out credits like candy.... The graduation rate has increased, but without the subject mastery.... It amounts to social promotion" (Edelman, 2011). A local newspaper analysis concluded: "it does the failing kids no favors, either—turning them loose on the streets wholly unprepared for what they'll face" ("Cheaters Sometimes Win," 2011).

Virtual Schools

One of the fastest growing segments in K-12 educational software is the virtual school. Virtual schools offer entire programs and entire courses online. In recent years, they have also developed blended models (part online and part face-to-face) courses. Since 2002, enrollments in online courses have increased from practically zero to several million students with the majority of these students enrolled at the secondary level (Picciano & Seaman, 2010).

Publicly funded online learning programs in Florida, Kentucky, Michigan, and Idaho provide instruction to students mostly in their home states. The Florida Virtual School (FLVS), founded in 1997, enrolled 122,000 students in 2010–2011 and is considered one of the most successful K-12 virtual schools in the country. While it enrolls students from throughout the United States, FLVS is publicly funded and receives funds from the state of Florida. In addition to publicly funded K-12 virtual schools, there are a number of successful for-profit virtual schools. K12, Inc., mentioned earlier in this chapter, in addition to managing virtual charter schools, is also a for-profit online program provider that enrolled more than 65,000 students in 2010–2011. Data collected in a national survey indicated that for fully online courses, high schools reported using each of the following providers:

- Postsecondary schools (51%)
- State virtual schools (42%)
- Independent (For-Profit) vendors (36%)
- The home school district (25%). (Picciano & Seaman, 2010)

Southern high schools tend to use state-supported virtual schools more than other regions of the country. The reason for this is that southern states were among the earliest to establish virtual schools, some of which like FLVS enjoy excellent reputations. The rest of the country, however, mixes and matches online learning providers, and makes extensive use of postsecondary institutions as well as private, for-profit vendors. Large urban districts with low high-school graduation rates rely extensively on for-profit vendors, especially for credit-recovery type online courses. Because of the number of providers, monitoring and analyzing their growth and market can be difficult. School districts contract with multiple providers on a regular basis depending upon the type of courses needed. It is not unusual for one school district to contract out with a local public college for advanced or college-level courses, with a state virtual school for a basic American history course, and with the for-profit Aventa Learning for credit-recovery courses.

A major aspect of virtual school courses and programs is the infusion of media and more recently gaming into the online materials. As an example, FLVS has contracted with 360Ed, Inc. to develop *Conspiracy Code*, an American history course/game that creates an immersive environment for students. It uses a 360Ed,

Inc. learning management system Student/Teacher Interface (or SiTi) that allows students and teachers to communicate, review assignments and grades, and access course content outside the game environment. 360Ed is a developer and publisher of online education products, including game-based courses, rich media content, and advanced learning management systems. The 360Ed website has the major textbook publishers McGraw-Hill and Pearson as its partners and has worked with Microsoft and IBM on projects. The role of the teacher in *Conspiracy Code* is clearly as a facilitator and monitor of the course rather than as the prime mover or deliverer of the course. This type of course relegates the teacher to a secondary status, functioning as a tutor/monitor. In fact, a fully certified, full-time teacher is not needed to facilitate this type of course.

Course Management Software

Course management systems (CMS) go by several names including content management systems, learning management systems, and virtual learning environments. Essentially, a CMS is a software system that provides a database and web-based template for administering, conducting, and reporting on all or part of a course. These systems evolved from the authoring software that was used to develop computer-based courses and course modules prior to the Internet. CMSs have become essential components for offering courses online. Practically all colleges and most school districts have access to a CMS. The most popular CMS is Blackboard which maintains the lion's share of the market. This was not always the case. During most of the 1990s and early 2000s, there were several dozen CMS providers. Products such as Blackboard, WebCT, Sakai, Angel, and Desire2Learn, competed for the growing CMS market. Starting about 2004, Blackboard engaged in an aggressive acquisition policy and bought out much of its competition including WebCT and Angel. Blackboard also sued Desire2Learn in 2006 for patent infringement and settled out of court in 2010. In recent years, Blackboard also acquired other companies such as Eluminate and Wimba that provided web-based synchronous communication software tools.

In October 2010, Blackboard was acquired for $1.64 billion by Providence Equity which describes itself as the world's leading private equity firm focused on media, communications, information, and education investments. Providence Equity owns a number of for-profit, education-related companies including Archipelago Learning, Ascend Learning, and Education Management Corporation, each of which owns a number of other education for-profit schools and companies (Providence Equity, 2008). Blackboard has made every attempt to corner the market on CMS software and is in a critical position to dominate how online course materials are developed and delivered. While lucrative for Blackboard and Providence Equity, this could prove detrimental to schools, colleges, and other education providers. A key software product for developing online course materials is now controlled by a company that has significant investments in for-profit education. "Boycott Blackboard" movements (i.e., http://www.boycottblackboard.org/), especially in colleges and universities, have been emerging and are promoting open source CMS-like products such as Moodle. In addition to pricing and cost factors, there is also resentment and concern about having so much of education content including assessment and grading standardized on one particular software template.

Testing and Assessment Software and Services

Testing and assessment companies and organizations have existed in the United States for decades. Tests from Educational Testing Service, ACT, and the Iowa Tests of Basic Skills are regularly used by schools for a variety of instructional and assessment needs. However, in the past 10 years, as discussed in chapter 2, with the advent of No Child Left Behind testing and assessment has mushroomed as an industry. It is difficult to calculate the industry's overall revenue because while some costs are borne directly by school districts on a per student fee basis, others for consulting and development activities might be borne by school districts, state education departments, or federal agencies, and still others by individual students. In addition, charges for testing and assessment are sometimes built into other activities such as new curriculum development, implementation, and evaluation. Modest estimates put the revenue from school district spending at between $1.5 to 5.6 billion per year (Scher & Burchard, 2009; Topol, Olson, & Roeber, 2010; Tucker, 2011). Besides the three companies mentioned above, major providers of testing and assessment software and services are: McGraw-Hill, Houghton–Mifflin, Harcourt General, and Pearson Education. Since 2001, in order to comply with No Child Left Behind and subsequent Race to the Top federal funding, all 50 states have had to examine, redesign, and implement new testing and assessment systems thereby generating a plethora of new test instruments and services.

Technology is a critical aspect of testing and assessment as more states and school districts move away from paper tests to online tests and scoring services. This makes sense since online scoring accuracy is much higher and turnaround time is much quicker. Schools and schools districts must make sure that they have sufficient equipment for students to take the tests and many contract with private vendors to score, analyze, and store the test in a digitized form for subsequent processing by school personnel. The latter service can be quite expensive, especially for large urban school districts.

A major point of influence in the rise in testing and assessment requirements at the federal government level has been documented as emanating from the relationship of George W. Bush with Harold McGraw III, one of the principal owners of McGraw-Hill. Stephen Metcalf, writing for *The Nation*, in 2002, described the relationship as follows:

> The amount of cross-pollination and mutual admiration between the [George W. Bush] Administration and that [McGraw-Hill] empire is

striking: Harold McGraw Jr. sits on the national grant advisory and founding board of the Barbara Bush Foundation for Family Literacy. McGraw
in turn received the highest literacy award from President George H.W.
Bush in 1990, for his contributions to the cause of literacy. The McGraw
Foundation awarded President George W. Bush Education Secretary Rod
Paige its highest educator's award while Paige was Houston's school chief;
Paige, in turn, was the keynote speaker at McGraw-Hill's "government
initiatives" conference last spring. Harold McGraw III was selected as a
member of President George W. Bush's transition advisory team, along
with McGraw-Hill board member Edward Rust Jr., the CEO of State
Farm and an active member of the Business Roundtable on educational
issues. An ex-chief of staff for Barbara Bush is returning to work for Laura
Bush in the White House—after a stint with McGraw-Hill as a media
relations executive. John Negroponte left his position as McGraw-Hill's
executive vice president for global markets to become Bush's ambassador
to the United Nations.

(Metcalf, 2002)

McGraw-Hill has been one of the major beneficiaries of the expansion of
testing and assessment in this country. It provides dozens of testing and assessment products for all age groups and for all subjects. The initiatives started by
George W. Bush have been continued in the Barack Obama administration
even though there has been much discussion about the efficacy of existing tests
and assessments. Some of this discussion centers around the idea that typical
high-stakes standardized testing has not been successful in improving student
outcomes and achievement and in fact might be detrimental. A major 9-year
research project conducted by The National Academies–National Research
Council concluded that:

> Test-based incentive programs, as designed and implemented in the
> programs that have been carefully studied, have not increased student
> achievement enough to bring the United States close to the levels of the
> highest achieving countries. When evaluated using relevant low-stakes
> tests, which are less likely to be inflated by the incentives themselves, the
> overall effects on achievement tend to be small and are effectively zero
> for a number of programs.

(National Research Council, 2011, p. 4)

Among its recommendations were:

> To avoid having their results determined by the score inflation that occurs
> in the high-stakes tests attached to the incentives, researchers should use
> low-stakes tests that do not mimic the high-stakes tests to evaluate how
> test-based incentives affect achievement. Other outcomes, such as later
> performance in education or work and dispositions related to education,

are also important to study. To help explain why test-based incentives sometimes produce negative effects on achievement, researchers should collect data on changes in educational practice by the people who are affected by the incentives.

(National Research Council, 2011, p. 6)

It appears that the current U.S. Department of Education leadership is in agreement with the National Research Council report. As a result, there will likely be movement away from existing tests and assessments to more comprehensive and multiple forms of testing and assessment, which in turn, will again be lucrative for the providers of these services.

In addition to the federal government, there are also significant points of influence at the state and local level. State education departments and school districts, particularly large urban districts, are major procurers of testing and assessment services. State education commissioners, school district superintendents and chancellors and their staffs regularly evaluate contracts for these services. One example is the large contract awarded to Pearson Education in 2007 to develop a common Algebra II end-of-course high school examination. Nine states participated in the initial contract as part of the American Diploma Project (ADP). The cost per student to take this test was approximately $25 to $30 depending upon test options and total number of students participating (Pearson 2010). It was estimated that almost 200,000 students would be eligible to take this test from the ADP participating states yielding as much as $6 million in revenue annually to Pearson for just this one test for the nine ADP states. However, in the United States, there are almost 3.75 million high students per year who could take an Algebra II exam which potentially could mean in excess of $100 million per year in revenue for one test.

Most contracts such as the above follow state procurement and public bid procedures but that doesn't mean that the large test providers and their agents are not able to influence the bidding process. As mentioned in chapter 2, the *New York Times* reported that the Pearson Foundation (affiliated with Pearson Education) has routinely underwritten a number of international visits and meetings for members of the Council of Chief State School Officers (Winerip, 2011b). These international meetings involved destinations such as Rio de Janeiro, Helsinki, Singapore, and Seoul, South Korea. In addition to high-ranking education commissioners, these meetings are attended by counterparts in the visiting countries and by executives from Pearson Education. According to the article, since the passage of No Child Left Behind, the demand for standardized tests and packaged curriculums has exploded. Furthermore, Pearson is one of the companies that has dominated this expanding marketplace and is one of the leading providers of assessment and education data management services for states and school districts in North America. The article identifies the Illinois state superintendent, Christopher A. Koch, as having gone to Helsinki in 2009 and to Rio de Janeiro in 2011. The state of Illinois is currently paying Pearson $138 million to develop and administer its tests. Most of the participants in these trips declined to be interviewed for the article. Jack Jennings, president of the Center on Education Policy, compared the underwriting of these trips to pharmaceutical companies that run junkets for doctors or to lobbyists who fly members of Congress to vacation getaways. "If we want that kind of corruption in education, we're fools," he said (Winerip, 2011b).

Before ending this section on testing and assessment software and services, it is important to briefly revisit the case study in chapter 3. Wireless Generation is a company that builds databases to analyze student, teacher, and school performance, primarily based on tests and assessments, and participates with the New York State Education Department in its Race to the Top funding project. This case study exemplifies the influence of the federal government over state education departments and school districts, requiring them to comply with directives and guidelines. In order to access Race to the Top funding, states were required to establish statewide database systems in order to monitor schools and districts on a variety of measures including student and teacher performance. Failure to do so disqualified a state from receiving funds. These systems have opened up a whole new area of activity related to testing and assessment that will be quite costly for the federal government, the states, and school districts for many years to come. Initial outlays to establish these database systems, which typically will cost tens of millions of dollars for average size states, are just the beginning of the expenditures. Once established they will require ongoing maintenance, updates, and modifications which in turn will result in expenditures of anywhere from 15 to 20% of the original purchase price per year and a steady stream of revenue for companies like Wireless Generation. Lastly, many states and local school districts do not have the quality or quantity of personnel with the technical skills to manage highly sophisticated database systems. Once installed, the management and maybe even a certain amount of the day-to-day operations of these systems will likely be contracted out to the vendors who developed them. In fact, the operations of these types of systems will very likely be outsourced at least in part to the developers. The profit potential from these types of outsourced contracts will be quite substantial.

Privatization in American Higher Education: For-Profit Colleges and Universities

Enrollment in American higher education has been rising steadily for the past three decades and now stands at more than 20 million students (see Figure 5.1). While all sectors (public, private nonprofit, and private for-profit institutions) showed growth, over the recent past, the private for-profit sector has outpaced the other two. In the early 1990s, enrollment in private for-profit institutions was no more than a couple of hundred thousand students. It now represents close to 10% of the total postsecondary population and stands at just about 2 million students. To support this growth, the number of private for-profit

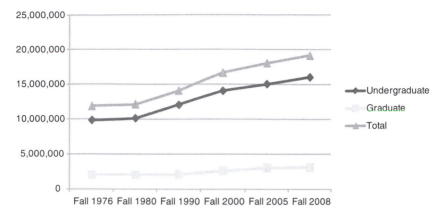

FIGURE 5.1 Postsecondary Enrollment Trends (Fall 1976–Fall 2008).

colleges and universities has increased significantly. Table 5.3 provides data on the growth of postsecondary institutions in the United States from 1998–1999 to 2008-2009. The data indicate that the number of public institutions has remained about the same; private nonprofits have decreased about 4%; and the number of private for-profits has increased more than 64%. While having started with a much lower base than the public or private nonprofit sectors, it is clear that for-profit higher education is now an important part of the American higher education landscape.

The Early Years

The beginnings of American for-profit higher education date back almost 200 years. Various types of for-profit entities offered specific courses such as penmanship, bookkeeping, or a foreign language such as French as early as the 1700s. Actual colleges that offered a more extensive program of study did not appear until the 1800s and these limited their offerings to practical or applied fields such as business, barbering, and cosmetology. Many were known as "proprietary" schools and were normally owned and operated by families or as limited partnerships. While some functioned as correspondence schools, most had physical facilities or a campus, a small faculty, and a director or manager. Many of these evolved into business colleges, some of which were quite successful. Of particularly note were the Bryant and Stratton colleges, which in the 1860s, operated a chain of 44 separate campuses in mostly large cities throughout the country. These colleges were owned by Henry B. Bryant and Henry D. Stratton. They had common curricula and common textbooks and students enrolled at one campus could take courses at any other campus. Fueled largely by these business colleges, growth in for-profit institutions was estimated to have reached 81,000 students in approximately 250 institutions by 1890 (Knepper, 1941). The traditional colleges at this time offered liberal arts and science

TABLE 5.3 Number of Institution Offering Postsecondary Education Programs (1998–2005)

Academic year	All Institutions			Public			Private								
										Non-profit			For-profit		
	Total	2-year	4-year	Total	2-year	4-year	Total	2-year	4-year	Total	2-year	4-year	Total	2-year	4-year
1998–99	4048	1713	2335	1681	1069	612	2367	644	1723	1695	164	1531	672	480	192
1999–00	4084	1721	2363	1682	1068	614	2402	653	1749	1681	150	1531	721	503	218
2000–01	4182	1732	2450	1698	1076	622	2484	656	1828	1695	144	1551	789	512	277
2001–02	4197	1710	2487	1713	1085	628	2484	625	1859	1676	135	1541	808	490	318
2002–03	4168	1702	2466	1712	1081	631	2456	621	1835	1665	127	1538	791	494	297
2003–04	4236	1706	2530	1720	1086	634	2516	620	1896	1664	118	1546	852	502	350
2004–05	4216	1683	2533	1700	1061	639	2516	622	1894	1637	112	1525	879	510	369
2005–06	4276	1694	2582	1693	1053	640	2583	641	1942	1647	113	1534	936	528	408
2006–07	4314	1685	2629	1688	1045	643	2626	640	1986	1640	107	1533	986	533	453
2007–08	4352	1677	2675	1685	1032	653	2667	645	2022	1624	92	1532	1043	553	490
2008–09	4409	1690	2719	1676	1024	652	2733	666	2067	1629	92	1537	1104	574	530

Source: U.S. Department of Education, National Center for Education Statistics. 1998–99 through 2008–09 Integrated Postsecondary Education Data System (IPEDS). *Institutional Characteristics Survey* (IPEDS-IC:'98–99) and Fall 2000 through Fall 2008.

programs focused largely on the humanities, Greek, Latin, science, and math-ematics. As a comparison to the enrollments in business colleges, in 1890, total enrollment in traditional colleges was 156,756 students.

In the late 1800s, the states and federal government began a significant expansion of public higher education. The federal "land grant" programs were particularly important in supporting the rise of the large public universities. In the early 1900s and especially during the Great Depression of the 1930s, enroll-ments in for-profit colleges declined and did not recover until after World War II with the emergence of the GI Bill. All of higher education enjoyed a renaissance of sorts in the 1950s and 1960s as millions of returning veterans took advantage of the opportunity to get a federally funded higher education. This period, however, was not without controversy for the for-profit sector as many of these institutions were involved with scandals, frauds, and abuse of federal funds (Kinser, 2006). Many schools were forced to close and those that remained open were subject to increased federal and state regulations and accreditation requirements. This continued well into the 1970s and 1980s when the public universities realized unprecedented growth.

The U.S. Department of Education Integrated Postsecondary Education System (IPEDS) data state that there are more than 1,100 for-profit colleges and universities currently operating in the United States. About 800 of these institutions are degree-granting (either 4-year or 2-year) and the remainder are nondegree, certificate granting (see Table 5.3). It should be mentioned that the IPEDS data, while good, is not perfect, especially for the for-profit sec-tor. IPEDS gathers information from every college, university, and technical and vocational institution that participates in the federal student financial aid programs. A number of for-profit private colleges do not participate in federal financial aid programs and therefore are not reflected in its data. A truer esti-mate of for-profit colleges puts their number at closer to 3,000, many of which are very small, local operations (Wilson, 2011).

As indicated earlier in this chapter, there have been significant increases in enrollments in the for-profit higher education sector. This has been due to a number of factors. First, the number of people seeking postsecondary education has increased substantially in the United States while the nonprofit and public sectors have not been able to keep up with the demand. Second, in the public sector, state funding on a per student basis has been decreasing. The funding dif-fers from state to state but some public universities are literally being "starved to death" (Cole, 2009, p. 471). Many public institutions have passed a greater por-tion of their costs on to students in the form of higher tuition, while others have simply begun to limit enrollments, which has served to drive many students to the for-profit sector. Third, the growth of the Internet and online learning has spawned a number of virtual colleges and has moved what were brick and mor-tar institutions to expand into online course and program offerings. Many new for-profit colleges have been able to start up with modest investments in Inter-net technology infrastructure rather than building or renting classroom, office, and support facilities. In fall 2010, it was estimated that 6 million students were enrolled in online courses in postsecondary education with approximately 40% or 2.5 million students at for-profit colleges. Fourth, there was a significant easing in federal regulations in 2006 that lifted the "50% Rule" which required colleges to deliver at least half their courses on a campus instead of online or at a distance to qualify for federal student aid. Colleges no longer had to offer any aspect of their programs in a traditional face-to-face mode, thus paving the way for fully online colleges. This will be discussed in greater detail later on in this chapter. Fifth, in the past 15 years there has been a significant investment of capital in large corporate owned, national and international shareholder, for-profit university chains. While many small and family-owned for-profit colleges have existed for decades, much of the increase in enrollments in the past decade has been in the large corporate universities. Kinser has termed this transformation of for-profit higher education as moving from *Main Street to Wall Street* (Kinser, 2006). Table 5.4 provides a list of 10 of the larger and better-known for-profit private colleges.

Who Do the For-Profit Colleges Serve and How Well Do They Serve Them?

To its credit, the for-profit sector provides educational opportunities to large numbers of adult learners, minority students, students who need flexible place and time schedules, online learners, and military personnel. Table 5.5 indicates that for-profit institutions enroll the largest percentage of minority students of any higher education sector. Approximately 48% of students in for-profit colleges are students of color. This is a full seven percentage points higher than the next highest sector, public 2-year colleges with 41%.

Many for-profit students seek certificate programs designed to prepare them for specific careers and trades. This is especially true in the 2-year for-profit

TABLE 5.4 Larger For-Profit Private Colleges

College	Enrollment
University of Phoenix (Apollo Group)	455,600
Education Management Corporation	136,000
Career Education Corporation	113,900
Kaplan Higher Education	103,800
Devry Inc.	101,600
Corinthian Colleges	93,000
American Public University	90,000
ITT Educational Services	79,200
Walden University	46,000
Capella University	35,000

TABLE 5.5 Percentage Distribution of Fall Enrollment in Degree-Granting Institutions, by Control and Type of Institutions and Race/Ethnicity: Fall 2008

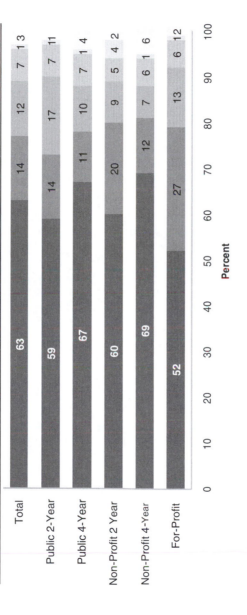

Percent

■ White ■ Black ■ Hispanic ■ Asian/Pacific Islander ■ Amer. Indian/Alaskan Native ■ Non-Resident Alien

Source: United States Department of Education. National Center for Educaton Statistics. 2008 Integrated Postsecondary Data System (IPEDS), Spring 2009.

schools. These programs typically require months rather than years to complete a degree. Adults who did not attend college, who dropped out of traditional degree college programs or who are looking to change careers are attracted to the more streamlined certificate program options that the for-profit colleges offer. Data (see Table 5.6) indicate that the 2-year for-profit colleges, with a 60.9% completion rate, have been successful for students in both certificate and degree program. It is important to note that the IPEDS data for purposes of completion do not distinguish between completing a certificate versus a degree program.

A number of for-profit colleges have also been successful in establishing flexible education and training collaborations with corporate partners. For example, in June 2010, the for-profit American Public University (APU), a member institution of the accredited American Public University System (APUS), announced an agreement with Wal-Mart Stores. The agreement enabled Wal-Mart and Sam's Club U.S. associates to earn a college degree at an affordable price through a combination of academic credit awarded for Wal-Mart job learning and experience, and online coursework. APU will serve as Wal-Mart's main education provider offering academic courses and degree programs to its associates. The APU website states that:

> According to a recent Wal-Mart survey, 72% of the 32,000 associates responding said they preferred an online university over other options. The breadth of 70 undergraduate and graduate degrees that APU offers in a flexible online format should make it an attractive option for Wal-Mart associates.
>
> (American Public University, 2010)

The APU–Wal-Mart partnership is indicative of the growing popularity of online learning for adults who must combine full-time work with earning a college degree. Many of the for-profit colleges have developed large portions of their programs for online delivery and have spearheaded the growth of this type of instruction, especially for adults who need to travel significant distances to attend a college. Military personnel find online programs desirable. State universities, community colleges, and private nonprofit colleges traditionally dominated this market by providing classes on bases under agreements with the military services. However, according to Defense Department and military data, for-profit colleges specializing in online degrees are making substantial inroads, particularly for military stationed overseas or in areas where on-ground education facilities are not available. The for-profit schools now account for 29% of college enrollments and 40% of the half-billion-dollar annual expenditure in federal tuition assistance for active-duty students. Larger and larger percentages of these students are enrolling in online programs (Golden, 2009).

While the for-profit sector is to be commended for providing higher education opportunities for nontraditional and minority students, the quality of the education has come under question. The Education Trust is an advocacy organization whose mission is:

TABLE 5.6 Higher Education Graduation Rates

Level and control of institution, gender, degree sought and degree completed	Total %	Amer. Indian or Alaska Native %	Asian or Pacific Islander %	Black %	Hispanic %	White %	Two or more races %	Race unknown %	Non-Resident Alien %
Bachelor's or equivalent degree seekers attending a 4–year institution and completing a degree.(Cohort year 2003)	57.4	38.3	68.0	39.1	48.7	60.8	40.3	53.7	53.3
Public	55.7	37.1	65.8	38.6	46.9	58.6	37.9	56.4	56.2
Men	52.9	34.9	62.7	32.9	42.3	55.9	38.1	53.8	53.3
Women	58.1	38.8	68.7	42.4	50.4	61.0	37.8	58.9	59.5
Private non–profit	65.1	47.6	75.9	45.0	59.4	67.7	48.8	63.7	69.1
Men	62.4	45.4	74.2	38.9	56.6	65.2	43.9	61.1	65.6
Women	67.1	49.2	77.2	49.2	61.2	69.7	53.3	65.8	73.0
Private for–profit	20.4	11.9	31.3	16.1	24.9	24.5	34.0	16.9	9.3
Men	22.7	16.0	33.6	16.6	25.2	26.7	35.6	20.6	9.3
Women	18.7	9.3	29.1	15.8	24.7	22.7	31.4	13.5	9.4
Total 2-year institutions (Cohort year 2006)	32.4	26.8	36.3	27.1	32.8	32.0	63.7	35.4	30.6
Public	22.1	19.8	26.6	14.6	17.0	24.7	35.4	19.7	24.9
Men	21.4	19.5	24.7	14.4	16.3	23.8	10.9	19.0	22.5
Women	22.7	20.0	28.6	14.7	17.7	25.6	41.5	20.4	27.3
Private non–profit	55.3	25.7	45.7	47.2	51.0	59.4	8.3	69.1	63.9
Men	53.7	27.0	52.2	44.2	53.8	56.9	12.5	66.3	63.7
Women	56.4	24.7	41.2	49.9	49.2	61.1	0.0	70.7	64.0
Private for–profit	60.9	57.7	73.1	48.9	63.7	64.8	67.2	57.5	65.1
Men	58.0	57.1	70.3	45.3	59.1	63.1	69.2	56.2	63.5
Women	61.4	58.0	74.9	50.5	65.9	65.6	66.3	58.3	66.5

Source: U.S. Department of Education, National Center for Education Statistics. *The Condition of Education 2011* (NCES 2011–033).

To promote high academic achievement for all students at all levels—pre-kindergarten through college. Our goal is to close the gaps in opportunity and achievement that consign far too many young people—especially those from low-income families or who are black, Latino, or American Indian—to lives on the margins of the American mainstream.

(Education Trust, 2009)

In 2010, the Trust issued a report that looked at the success of students in for-profit colleges. Using mostly data from the U.S. Education Department's National Center for Education Statistics, the report titled, *Subprime Opportunity: The Unfulfilled Promise of For-Profit Colleges and Universities*, found:

In the 2008-09 academic year, for-profit colleges received $4.3 billion in Pell Grants—quadruple the amount they received just ten years earlier—and approximately $20 billion in federal student loans. As a result of this large federal investment, the average for-profit school derives 66 percent of its revenues from federal student aid, and 15 percent of institutions receive 85 to 90 percent of their revenue from Title IV.11 The behemoth that is the University of Phoenix brought in over one billion dollars in Pell Grant funding alone in 2009-10 ... risks exceeding federal limits by deriving over 90 percent of revenues from federal financial aid. The rapid growth and record profit levels reported by these institutions might be acceptable if students were succeeding at record rates. But they are not.... Low-income students and students of color are getting access, but not much success.

(Lynch, Engle, & Cruz, 2010, p, 2)

This finding is especially true for students in the 4-year for-profit institutions where the data (see Table 5.6) indicate that only 20.4% of the students graduate within 6 years, whereas the graduation rates at the public 4-year and private nonprofit colleges are 55.7% and 65.1% respectively. The entire University of Phoenix system has a 6-year graduation rate of 9%. The University of Phoenix Online program has a graduation rate of 5% (Lynch et al., 2010). Furthermore, most of these low-income and minority students are incurring significant debt that will take them years to pay off. On average the median debt for students who graduate with a baccalaureate degree at a for-profit college is $31,190, while it is $7,960 for a public college, and $17,040 at a private, nonprofit college (Lynch et al., 2010, p. 6).

The report's conclusion was that:

For-profit colleges argue that they are models of access and efficiency in America's overburdened higher education system. But instead of providing a solid pathway to the middle class, they are paving a path into the subbasement of the American economy. They enroll students in high-cost degree programs ... that saddle the most vulnerable students with more debt than they could reasonably manage to pay off, even if they do graduate.

(Lynch et al., 2010, p. 7)

As the name suggests, the Education Trust report drew comparisons to the collapse of the housing market in this country in 2008 caused by unregulated subprime mortgage companies. It concluded that for-profit colleges provide access to higher education but deliver little more than crippling debt.

For-Profit Higher Education and the Education-Industrial Complex

For-profit higher education is a big player in the education-industrial complex. It has a major lobbying organization, the Association of Private Sector Colleges and Universities, as well as a number of smaller organizations and committees that pay and press government officials on behalf of its interests. In 2010, it was estimated that for-profit higher education spent more than $8 million dollars on lobbying federal government lawmakers and administrators. Among the highest lobbying payments made by the for-profit colleges for a 15-month period in 2010–2011 were:

Kaplan University—$1.7 million
Corinthian Colleges—$1.5 million
Career Education Corporation—$1.5 million
Education Management Company—$1.1 million
Apollo Group–University of Phoenix—$1 million. (Burd, 2011)

In addition, it contributed more than $2 million directly to political action committees. These campaign contributions were given to candidates from both parties and include congressional representatives and senators such as:

Harry Reid (Democrat, Senate majority leader),
George Miller (Democrat),
Barbara Mikulski (Democrat)
John Boehner (Republican, House majority leader)
Howard McKeon (Republican)
Lamar Alexander (Republican)
John Kline (Republican). (Kirkham, 2011a)

Furthermore, for-profit college representatives support, contribute, and are otherwise active in major political campaigns. In 2012, at the height of the Republican Party's presidential primaries, the *New York Times* reported that at a New Hampshire town hall meeting, Mitt Romney, in a response to a question about the cost of higher education, suggested that students should consider for-profit colleges like the Full Sail University in Florida. A week later in Iowa, Mr. Romney offered an unsolicited endorsement for:

"a place in Florida called Full Sail University." By increasing competition, for-profit institutions like Full Sail, which focuses on the entertainment field, "hold down the cost of education" and help students get jobs without saddling them with excessive debt, he said.

(Lictblau, 2012)

The article went on to comment on several issues associated with Romney's endorsement. First, at the time, the entire for-profit higher education industry was under government scrutiny involving fraudulent practices involving student financial aid, graduation rates, and gainful employment.

Second, the costs for most for-profits are far more expensive than public universities, especially community colleges. The cost of tuition at Full Sail for instance, can run as much as $81,000 for a 21-month program in "video game art." The *New York Times* article commented:

> The $81,000 video game art program ... graduated just 14 percent of its 272 students on time and only 38 percent at all, while the students carried a median debt load of nearly $59,000 in federal and private loans in 2008, according to data that the federal Education Department now requires for-profit colleges to disclose in response to criticism of their academic records.
>
> (Lictblau, 2012)

Third, Romney's connection to Full Sail is its chief executive, Bill Heavener, a major campaign donor and a cochairman of his state fund-raising team in Florida. That team, Mr. Romney said last fall when he appointed Mr. Heavener, "will be crucial to my efforts in Florida and across the country."

Fourth, it also appeared that Romney has received significant donations from other for-profit higher education entities including:

> Todd S. Nelson, chief executive at the Education Management Corporation ... gave the campaign $2,500. His company is the target of an $11 billion Justice Department lawsuit over accusations of fraudulent marketing and recruiting practices. Education Management is partly owned by Goldman Sachs, whose individual employees represent a bigger source of campaign revenue for Mr. Romney than any other single company.... Mr. Romney also just brought on Charlie Black, a prominent Washington lobbyist who has worked for for-profit colleges, as an informal campaign adviser.
>
> (Lictblau, 2012)

The lobby corps for for-profit higher education is comprised of a number of well-known, well-connected former members of Congress and presidential aides including former House Majority Leader Richard Gephardt, former special White House counsel Lanny J. Davis, and former Chief of Staff to President Bill Clinton, Tony Podesta.

Other individuals close to for-profit higher education who have held important government positions include Sally Stroup, Under Secretary for Higher Education in the U.S. Department of Education in the George W. Bush administration, who prior to being appointed was a lobbyist for the University of Phoenix. Former Governor of Maine, John McKernan, who after leaving the governorship in 1998, became the CEO of the for-profit Education Management Corporation. McKernan continues to serve as Chairman of its Board of Directors. He also is the husband of Senator Olympia Snowe (R-Maine). Mr. McKernan's company was the target of a major lawsuit brought by the U.S. Justice Department, 11 states, and the District of Columbia involving an employee whistleblower lawsuit. The complaint alleges that the for-profit college chain was illegally paying recruiters based on the number of students they could sign up.

It is likely that in the near future there will be calls for more regulation of these colleges, and possibly for all higher education in terms of financial aid and gainful employment upon graduation. At the same time, it appears that the for-profit institutions are serving a vital role in providing higher education opportunities for nontraditional students and are taking advantage of online learning technologies to do so. Given that every projection predicts growth in enrollments in higher education in general, these institutions have secured a role in meeting the increased demand.

Case Study—The U.S. Congress Deregulates Online Colleges

In 1992, the U.S. Congress enacted what became known as the "50% Rule" which required all colleges to deliver at least half their courses on a campus instead of online or via distance education in order to qualify for federal student aid. This rule was established after investigations showed that some for-profit trade schools were little more than diploma mills intended to harvest federal student loans (Dillon, 2006). In 2006, by adding eight lines of language buried in an 82,000-word budget bill, the U.S. Congress eliminated the "50% Rule" and allowed colleges, regardless of the number of courses held on campus or online, to qualify for federal student aid (Kirkham, 2011b). This rule could not have been changed without the enormous influence of players in the education-industrial complex. Sam Dillon, two-time Pulitzer prize-winning reporter for the *New York Times*, characterized the passage of this bill as follows:

> The Bush administration supported lifting the restriction on online education as a way to reach nontraditional students. Nonprofit universities and colleges opposed such a broad change, with some academics saying there was no proof that online education was effective. But for-profit colleges sought the rollback avidly.

"The power of the for-profits has grown tremendously," said Representative Michael N. Castle, Republican of Delaware, a member of the House Education and Workforce Committee who has expressed concerns about continuing reports of fraud. "They have a full-blown lobbying effort and give lots of money to campaigns. In 10 years, the power of this interest group has spiked as much as any you'll find."

Sally L. Stroup, the assistant secretary of education who is the top regulator overseeing higher education, is a former lobbyist for the University of Phoenix, the nation's largest for-profit college, with some 300,000 students.

Two of the industry's closest allies in Congress are Representative John Boehner of Ohio, who just became House majority leader, and Representative Howard P. McKeon, Republican of California, who is replacing Mr. Boehner as chairman of the House education committee.

And the industry has hired well-connected lobbyists like A. Bradford Card, the brother of the [George W. Bush] White House chief of staff, Andrew H. Card Jr.

(Dillon, 2006)

Ms. Stroup was in a pivotal position to support or not to support this legislation. She authored a series of reports outlining an imperative to lift the online learning restrictions—a major impetus for Congress to ultimately scrap the 50% rule (Kirkham, 2011b). Dillon characterized Stroup's evaluation as follows: "in a 2004 audit, the Education Department's inspector general said a 2003 report she provided to Congress on the program 'contained unsupported, incomplete and inaccurate statements'" (Dillon, 2006).

Most of Stroup's assertions were to the effect that online education was working as well or better than traditional methods, with little risk. The inspector general, citing the collapse of one participant in the program, the Masters Institute in California, chided the Education Department for reporting that it had found "no evidence" that the rule change could pose hazards. Ms. Stroup formally disagreed with the inspector general. In an interview, she said a subordinate had written the report, although she had signed off on it. In a later report to Congress, the department acknowledged "several possible risk factors" (Dillon, 2006).

Stroup represents the classic Washington flexian who started as a staffer on the House Education and Workforce Committee, then took a "$220,000-a-year job as a lobbyist for the Apollo Group, the parent company for the University of Phoenix and was then appointed by Bush as assistant secretary for post-secondary education ... overseeing the central interest of her previous employer" (Kirkham, 2011b).

While a number of U.S. representatives and senators, both Democrats and Republicans, received campaign funds from the for-profit lobby organizations, significant campaign donations were distributed to Boehner, Senator Mike

Enzi (R–Wyoming), and Rep. Howard "Buck" McKeon (R–Calif.), the men
who controlled the Education committees in the House and the Senate.

> McKeon held and sold stock for Corinthian Colleges Inc., ... during
> the time he was crafting policies for the industry on the House Educa-
> tion committee, according to his required personal financial disclosure
> forms.... For the three election cycles between 2002 and 2006, those
> three lawmakers and their political action committees alone took in
> nearly one-fifth of the money donated to federal candidates and commit-
> tees by the for-profit college industry.
>
> (Kirkham 2011b)

The result of the change in the 50% Rule has been dramatic (see Figure
5.2). Enrollments have soared at a number of for-profit colleges. For example,
Bridgeport, Inc. of San Diego purchased a small, failing college in Iowa and
grew enrollment from fewer than 350 students in 2005 to more than 76,000
students by the end of 2010. Grand Canyon Education, Inc. grew online enrollments from 3,000 in 2003 to more than 42,000 by the beginning of 2011. In
general, approximately 25% of the revenue accrued by the for-profit industry
from 2007 through 2011 was probably as a result of this change. "Most of the
large publicly traded institutions would not be able to exist the way they do
today if that rule had not been taken away," said Kevin Kinser, an associate professor at the University at Albany who studies the history of for-profit higher
education. "You have an entirely new revenue source that's been open to these
institutions.... The cost goes down, the revenue goes up, and that's a pretty
attractive investment vehicle" (cited in Kirkham, 2011b).

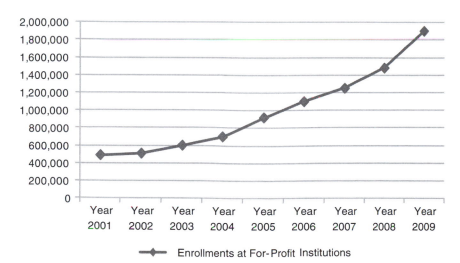

FIGURE 5.2 Enrollment at For-Profit Colleges (2000–2009). Source: U.S. Department of Education

In 2009, the federal government's General Accountability Office (GAO) conducted an undercover operation to gather information at 15 for-profit colleges. On August 4, 2010, Gregory D. Kutz, Managing Director of Forensics, Audits and Special Investigations, gave testimony before the Senate Committee on Health, Education, Labor, and Pensions. His testimony included the following summary:

> Undercover tests at 15 for-profit colleges found that 4 colleges encouraged fraudulent practices and that all 15 made deceptive or otherwise questionable statements to GAO's undercover applicants. Four undercover applicants were encouraged by college personnel to falsify their financial aid forms to qualify for federal aid—for example, one admissions representative told an applicant to fraudulently remove $250,000 in savings. Other college representatives exaggerated undercover applicants' potential salary after graduation and failed to provide clear information about the college's program duration, costs, or graduation rate despite federal regulations requiring them to do so. For example, staff commonly told GAO's applicants they would attend classes for 12 months a year, but stated the annual cost of attendance for 9 months of classes, misleading applicants about the total cost of tuition. Admissions staff used other deceptive practices, such as pressuring applicants to sign a contract for enrollment before allowing them to speak to a financial advisor about program cost and financing options. However, in some instances, undercover applicants were provided accurate and helpful information by college personnel, such as not to borrow more money than necessary.
>
> In addition, GAO's four fictitious prospective students received numerous, repetitive calls from for-profit colleges attempting to recruit the students when they registered with Web sites designed to link for-profit colleges with prospective students. Once registered, GAO's prospective students began receiving calls within 5 minutes. One fictitious prospective student received more than 180 phone calls in a month. Calls were received at all hours of the day, as late as 11 p.m.

Programs at the for-profit colleges GAO tested cost substantially more for associate's degrees and certificates than comparable degrees and certificates at public colleges nearby. A student interested in a massage therapy certificate costing $14,000 at a for-profit college was told that the program was a good value. However the same certificate from a local community college cost $520. Costs at private nonprofit colleges were more comparable when similar degrees were offered.

(Kutz, 2010)

This report and its subsequent testimony before a U.S. Senate committee touched off calls around the country for increased regulation of for-profit colleges. The names of the 15 colleges were not made public.

References

American Public University. (2010). American Public University to expand higher education opportunities for Wal-Mart Associates. Retrieved from http://www.apus.edu/news-events/news/2010/06-03-10-apu-walmart-partnership.htm

Burd, S. (2011, April 28). Democratic bigwigs cash in on for-profit college lobbying blitz. Higher Ed Watch Blog from the New American Higher Education Initiative. Retrieved from http://higheredwatch.newamerica.net/blogposts/2011/democratic_bigwigs_cash_in_on_for_profit_college_lobbying_blitz-49471

Cheaters sometimes win. (2011, October 15). [Editorial]. *New York Post*. Retrieved from http://www.nypost.com/p/news/opinion/editorials/cheaters_sometimes_win_LVQR6EVGE32UnyKKpQZ62L

Clabaugh, G. K., & Rozycki, E. G. (1990). *Understanding schools: The foundations of education*. New York: Harper & Row.

Cole, J. R. (2009). *The great American university*. New York: Public Affairs.

Dillon, S. (March 1, 2006). Online colleges receive a boost from Congress. *New York Times*. Retrieved from http://www.nytimes.com/2006/03/01/national/01educ.html?pagewanted=all

Edelman, S. (2011, October 22). "Remedial class" nightmare at CUNY. *New York Post*. Retrieved from http://www.nypost.com/p/news/local/remedial_class_nightmare_at_cuny_5JruiGppYWONCT1gE5xcyL

Education Trust. (2009). About the Education Trust. Retrieved from http://www.edtrust.org/dc/about

Glod, M. (2008, June 13). Mandated tutoring not helping MD, VA scores. *Washington Post*. Retrieved from http://www.washingtonpost.com/wp-dyn/content/article/2008/06/12/AR2008061203681.html

Golden, D. (2009, December 30). For-profit colleges target the military. *Bloomberg Business Newsweek*. Retrieved from http://www.businessweek.com/magazine/content/10_02/b4162036095366.ht

Gootman, E., & Coutts, S. (2008, April 11). Lacking credits, some students learn a shortcut. *New York Times*. Retrieved from http://www.nytimes.com/2008/04/11/education/11graduation.html

Kinser, K. (2006). *From Main Street to Wall Street: The transformation of for-profit higher education* (ASHE Higher Education Report, Vol. 31, no. 5). Hoboken, NJ: Association for the Study of Higher Education.

Kirkham, C. (2011a, April 25). For-profit colleges mount unprecedented battle for influence in Washington. *Huffington Post*. Retrieved from http://www.huffingtonpost.com/2011/04/25/for-profit-colleges_n_853363.html?page=1

Kirkham, C. (2011b, July 29) John Boehner backed deregulation of online learning, leading to explosive growth at for-profit colleges. *Huffington Post*. Retrieved from http://www.huffingtonpost.com/2011/07/29/john-boehner-for-profit-colleges_n_909589.html?page=1

Knepper, E. G. (1941). *History of business education in the United States*. Ann Arbor, MI: Edward Brothers.

Kutz. G. A. (2010, August 4). *Testimony before the Committee on Health, Education, Labor, and Pensions, U.S. Senate. Based on a report: For-Profit Colleges: Undercover Testing Finds Colleges Encouraged Fraud and Engaged in Deceptive and Questionable Marketing Practices*. Washington, DC: U.S. Government General Accountability Office. Retrieved from http://www.gao.gov/new.items/d10948t.pdf

Lictblau, E. (2012, January 15). Romney offers praise for a donor's business. *New York Times*. Retrieved from http://www.nytimes.com/2012/01/15/us/politics/mitt-romney-offers-praise-for-a-donors-business.html?_r=1&nl=todaysheadlines&emc=tha2

Lynch, M., Engle, J., & Cruz, J. L. (2010). *Subprime opportunity: The unfulfilled promise of for-profit colleges and universities*. Washington, DC: Education Trust. Retrieved from http://www.edtrust.org/dc/Subprime

Media Matters for America. (2006, January 5). Despite controversial comments and GAO investigation, Bill Bennett reportedly joining CNN as political analyst. *Media Matters*. Retrieved from http://mediamatters.org/research/200601050002

Metcalf, S. (2002). Reading between the lines. *The Nation*. Retrieved from http://www.thenation.com/article/reading-between-lines?page=0,0

Miron, G., Urschel, J. L., Yat Aguilar, M. A., & Dailey, B. (2011). *Profiles of for-profit and nonprofit education management organizations: Thirteenth annual report—2010–2011*.Boulder, CO: National Education Policy Center. Retrieved from http://nepc.colorado.edu/publication/EMO-profiles-10

Moe, M. T., Bailey, K., & Lau, R. (1999). *The book of knowledge*. San Francisco, CA: Merrill Lynch. Retrieved from http://news.heartland.org/newspaper-article/1999/10/01/book-knowledge

National Research Council. (2011). Incentives and test-based accountability in education. In M. Hout & S. W. Elliot (Eds.), *Committee and test-based accountability in public education, Board on Testing and Assessment, Division of Behavioral and Social Sciences and Education*. Washington, DC: The National Academies Press.

Pearson. (2010). Invitation to participate in the ADP Algebra II end-of-course exam—Spring 2010. Retrieved from http://www.nj.gov/education/assessment/hs/alg/NJAlgebraIISpring-2010Invitationletter.pdf

Picciano, A. G., & Seaman, J. (2010). *Class connections: High school reform and the role of online learning*. Needham, MA: Babson College Survey Research Group. Retrieved from http://www3.babson.edu/ESHIP/research-publications/upload/Class_connections.pdf

Providence Equity. (2008). Retrieved from http://www.provequity.com/about_us/index.asp?Section=1,0,0

Scher, A., & Burchard, S. (2009). Bush profiteers collect billions from No Child Left Behind. Retrieved from http://www.projectcensored.org/top-stories/articles/12-bush-profiteers-collect-billions-from-no-child-left-behind/

Topol, B., Olson, J., & Roeber, E. (2010). *The cost of new higher quality assessments: A comprehensive analysis of the potential costs for future state assessments*. Stanford, CA: Stanford University, Stanford Center for Opportunity Policy in Education.

Tucker, B. (2010, February 7). For-profit colleges change higher education's landscape. *Chronicle of Higher Education*. Retrieved from http://chronicle.com/article/For-Profit-Colleges-Change/64012/

U.S. Department of Education, National Center for Education Statistics. (1993).*120 years of American education: A statistical portrait*. Washington, DC: Author. Retrieved from http://nces.ed.gov/pubs93/93442.pdf

Wilson, R. (2011, October 11). The truth about testing costs. *Education Week*. Retrieved from http://www.edweek.org/ew/articles/2011/10/12/07tucker.h31.html?tkn=OQUF9Q%2Fq1Md5IMYEvUliV39KrQN8djmgSk%2B3&print=1

Winerip, M. (2011a, October 24). In college, working hard to learn high school material. *New York Times*. Retrieved from http://www.nytimes.com/2011/10/24/education/24winerip.html?ref=nyregion

Winerip, M. (2011b, September 18). When free trips overlap with commercial purposes. *New York Times*. Retrieved from http://www.nytimes.com/2011/09/19/education/19winerip.html?scp=1&sq=Pearson&st=cse

6

FOUNDATIONS AND THINK TANKS

Policies and Ideas Supporting the Educational-Industrial Complex

Foundations and think tanks helped expand the educational-industrial complex through the support and initiation of public and government policies and by influencing public thinking. It is sometimes hard to make a clear distinction between a foundation and a think tank. A basic difference is that foundations give financial support to actual working projects designed to bring about social change while think tanks support experts to do scholarly research and write policy statements designed to influence public thinking and legislative action. However, foundations also support policy reports designed to influence politicians and public opinion regarding school policies.

Funding for many initiatives in American education comes from private foundations that use their resources to "reform" education in accordance with their own views. In turn, the policies and programs of these foundations are in many cases, informed and supported by think tanks affiliated with ideologically compatible corporations and organizations. In recent decades, a number of these think tanks have become completely partisan in their views, the positions they take, and the studies that they publish. This chapter will specifically look at the role of several major foundations and think tanks that fund and promote the ideas of the players in the educational-industrial complex.

Foundations

Foundations have a long history in this country of doing good and contributing to the overall well-being of our society by benefitting institutions such as schools and colleges. In an essay, "The Gospel of Wealth," published in 1889, Andrew Carnegie called for people of means to use their wealth for the good of the many:

an ideal State in which the surplus wealth of the few will become, in the best sense, the property of the many, because administered for the common good; and this wealth, passing through the hands of the few, can be made a much more potent force for the elevation of our race.

(Carnegie, 1889, p. 3)

As a result, a number of "captains of industry" established foundations as the vehicles to use their surplus wealth to improve society. Education-related programs and activities were particularly popular. The Carnegie Foundation was a major funder and catalyst for the building and establishment of thousands of public libraries. The Rockefeller Foundation funded the work of Abraham Flexner who developed much-needed models and reforms for medical schools. The Julius Rosenwald Fund's "rural school building project" spurred the renovation and construction of over 5,000 new schools and shops in poor areas of the country largely populated by African Americans. The Ford Foundation was a major funder of the early childhood program Head Start as well as Public Broadcasting's first national educational television programs. These foundations generally received accolades for their generosity, and deservedly so. Arguments can be made, however, that this generosity also helped to improve the benefactors' personal or company public images and legacies. Upton Sinclair in *The Goose Step* (1922) and later *The Goslings* (1924) "mucked up" the reputations of a number of America's industrial leaders who as members of the "plutocratic empire" used their wealth, among other things, to control and direct American education. Specifically he observed that: "Our educational system is not a public service, but an instrument of special privilege; its purpose is not to further welfare of mankind, but merely to keep America capitalist" (Sinclair, 1922, p. 18).

Traditional philanthropy blossomed in the early 20th century because the industrial revolution in this country resulted in significant wealth being placed in the hands of a small number of entrepreneurs. In the latter half of the 20th century, a new group of entrepreneurs built incredible wealth, this time because of their acumen in the information, communications, finance, retail, and service industries. They too have become involved in philanthropy, but a new philanthropy different in style from the Carnegies, Rockefellers, and Rosenwalds.

Venture Philanthropy

The traditional philanthropy of the early 20th century has been joined by, and in some cases replaced by "venture philanthropy," also known as "philanthrocapitalism," in which a foundation's grant programs are developed along the lines of venture capitalism.

The phrase "venture philanthropy" was coined in the 1960s as an alternative strategy to merely having foundations write grant checks and hope the recipients (usually public charities) would use the money wisely. The concept is borrowed from venture capital and uses loans and equity investments along with ongoing management and strategic assistance as a way to help the recipient organizations become self-sufficient.

(Leibell, 2009)

While initially adopted by several foundations for specific grant programs, the concept grew in popularity in the late 1990s and the early part of 21st century. Writing in the *Harvard Business Review* (1997), Letts, Ryan, and Grossman, called for foundations to adopt a more venture capitalist approach to giving and to develop a new set of rules to play by. The essence of this approach was to look upon foundation funding as investments in nonprofit recipient organizations, in helping them to build the capacity to carry out their goals and objectives in a more effective manner. Also critical to this approach was ongoing management and partnering to insure that the elements of a grant are realized:

if foundations serve only as passive middlemen, as mere conduits for giving, then they fall far short of their potential and of society's high expectations.

Foundations can and should lead social progress. They have the potential to make more effective use of scarce resources than either individual donors or the government. Free from political pressures, foundations can explore new solutions to social problems with an independence that government can never have. And compared with individual donors, foundations have the scale, the time horizon, and the professional management to create benefits for society more effectively.

(Porter & Kramer, 1999)

This concept has been embraced by several major foundations including the largest in terms of financial assets, the Gates Foundation. (Leibell, 2009)

It may be true that "Free from political pressures, foundations can explore new solutions to social problems with an independence that government can never have" but when they get involved with publicly funded education, to whom are these foundations accountable if a program does not work or in fact does more harm than good? This issue was raised by a number of individuals including Diane Ravitch (2010) in her book *The Death and Life of the Great American School System*. In a chapter titled in "The Billionaires Boys Club," she commented that: "the foundations demand that public schools and teachers be held accountable but they themselves are accountable to no one" (p. 201). She went on to describe a Gates Foundation project in Denver, Colorado, in which

Manuel High School received a $1 million Gates Foundation grant in 2001. Manuel High School was a struggling school with a graduation rate of about 60%. The Gates Foundation proposed to restructure Manuel into three smaller schools; however, the implementation was questionable and rushed (Greene & Symonds, 2006). In an evaluation conducted in 2005 only 20% of the students entering in Fall 2001 graduated and the Denver Board of Education voted to close Manuel High School for a year. Does not the Gates Foundation share in the responsibility for why more students did not graduate and if so, what was their responsibility to these students? After much planning, redesign, and hard work, the Denver Board of Education reopened Manuel High School in 2006. Similar situations with Gates-funded small-school programs occurred in other parts of the country. In 2004, for example, Oregon launched its small-schools initiative with $25 million in grants from the Gates Foundation and the Meyer Memorial Trust. This initiative was heralded as "the best way to curb high dropout rates, forge connections to keep teenagers on track and prepare every graduate for college" (Hammond & Lednicer (2008). By 2008, the small schools failed to deliver on those promises. Instead, their statistics were basically the same as those of the high schools they were supposed to replace. Lots of students quit, and most of the graduates weren't ready for the rigors of college (Hammond & Lednicer, 2008). Perhaps the largest Gates investment in small schools occurred in New York City. Following grants made by the Annenberg Foundation in the 1990s, the Gates Foundation invested over $50 million to create 200 small schools in 2003. These schools were created by closing large comprehensive high schools that were common in New York City. Mayor Michael Bloomberg and Chancellor Joel Klein praised the movement to small schools as fundamental to reforming New York City high schools and made it a "centerpiece of the educational reform agenda" (Jennings & Pallis, 2010). Student performance in these schools was closely monitored and indications were that outcomes such as test scores on state examinations and graduation rates improved. However, these studies neglected to include an examination of the population of the new small schools. Eventually, the Annenberg Institute for School Reform, affiliated with Brown University, conducted a comprehensive study of the student characteristics of the New York City small high schools created with the funds provided by Gates and other foundations (Jennings & Pallis (2010). The conclusion was:

> In summary, we found that when compared with other schools in their borough over the period 2002–2003 to 2008–2009, new small schools enrolled students who were less likely to be proficient in mathematics, less likely to be male, more likely to qualify for free or reduced-price lunch, and less likely to be eligible for special education—especially full-time special education. When we limited these comparisons to schools serving all students, not solely ELL students, we also found that small schools were less likely to enroll ELL students.

But we saw a very different picture when we focused our attention on large comprehensive high schools that were closing or downsizing over time and the new small high schools that replaced them on the same campuses. These new small schools were very different than the large comprehensives they replaced; they enrolled students who were academically much better off than the students in the large comprehensives.

(p. 12)

In other words, the small-school programs had selected populations of students who were less likely to be full-time special education or English Language Learners and more likely to be academically better than the students in the remaining large comprehensive high schools. In sum, the small schools had not improved student performance but had segregated the better students from the students who needed additional educational services.

By 2008, the Gates Foundation ended its small school program. Ravitch and others have posed the question: Why doesn't the Gates Foundation bear the responsibility for the problems its grants programs have created in public schooling in this country?

The Major Foundations

School district budgets typically come under close scrutiny by taxpayers and government "watch-dog" organizations. In the vast majority of school districts in this country, budgets are presented to residents for approval on an annual basis and in most school districts have very limited discretionary money with which to start major initiatives or new programs. Grants from either public or private sources are part of the administrative culture for funding new programs. Table 6.1 provides a list of the major foundations that have programs devoted to education. It is obvious that the Gates Foundation is a dominant player in terms of its assets with almost $34 billion. While many of these foundations also use their funds for programs outside of education, in recent years, three of them (Gates, Broad, and Walton Family foundations) have been extensively involved in providing grants for education-related programs. In an article in *Dissent* magazine, foundation giving for education was summarized as follows:

> Hundreds of private philanthropies together spend almost $4 billion annually to support or transform K-12 education, most of it directed to schools that serve low-income children (only religious organizations receive more money). But three funders—the Bill and Melinda Gates Foundation, the Eli and Edythe Broad Foundation, and the Walton Family Foundation—working in sync, command the field. Whatever nuances differentiate the motivations of the Big Three, their market-based goals for overhauling public education coincide: choice, competition, deregulation, accountability, and data-based decision making. And they fund

the same vehicles to achieve their goals: charter schools, high-stakes standardized testing for students, merit pay for teachers whose students improve their test scores, firing teachers and closing schools when scores don't rise adequately, and longitudinal data collection on the performance of every student and teacher. Other foundations—Ford, Hewlett, Annenberg, Milken, to name just a few—often join in funding one project or another, but the education reform movement's success so far has depended on the size and clout of the Gates-Broad-Walton triumvirate.

(Barkan, 2011)

As the quote above indicates, foundations are collaborating with one another, the federal government, and private corporations on a number of programs, most of which center on student performance, database development projects, charter schools, school leadership, and teacher effectiveness. As an example, in 2010, 12 national foundations committed $500 million to leverage the U.S. Department of Education's $650 million Investing in Innovation (i3) Fund aimed at making more than $1 billion available to help expand promising innovations in education that support teachers, administrators, technology tools, and school design across all K-12 schools. More specifically, the i3 Fund seeks to support programs that revamp teacher and principal training, spur integrated technology tools for teaching and learning, and create capacity for alternative high quality schools (e.g., charter schools), as well as new models for school design. In 2010–2011, 600 proposals were submitted for this program.

TABLE 6.1 Major Private Foundations Sorted by Total Assets

1. Bill & Melinda Gates Foundation (WA) $33,912,320,600
2. Ford Foundation (NY) $10,881,598,073
3. The William and Flora Hewlett Foundation (CA) $7,377,414,000
4. W. K. Kellogg Foundation (MI) $7,238,160,845
5. The John D. and Catherine T. MacArthur Foundation (IL) $5,237,796,061
6. Lilly Endowment Inc. (IN) $5,184,625,647
7. The Andrew W. Mellon Foundation (NY) $5,051,530,000
8. The Annie E. Casey Foundation (MD) $2,564,720,003
9. The Duke Endowment (NC) $2,480,075,314
10. Carnegie Corporation of New York (NY) $2,432,582,536
11. Walton Family Foundation, Inc. (AR) $2,275,851,898
12. Charles Stewart Mott Foundation (MI) $2,080,000,000
13. Eli & Edythe Broad Foundation (CA) $1,689,097,000
14. The Annenberg Foundation (CA) $1,602,260,949
15. Lumina Foundation for Education, Inc. (IN) $1,098,556,458

The three major goals of the i3 Fund are typical of many of the funded grant programs involved with K–12 education.

Six hundred i3 proposals seems to indicate that many school districts are interested in this program, but given the approximately 15,000 school districts in the country, 600 represents a distinct minority. Nevertheless, given the amount of resources available, the partnership with the U.S. Department of Education, and the difficult economic times, many school districts could use additional funding and it is very difficult for some of them to resist the dollars that this and other foundation programs provide. At the American Education Research Association's annual meeting in 2011, this issue was presented from the floor during a plenary session titled, "Maintaining Public Education for the Public Good." Alfred Levine, president of the Woodrow Wilson Fellowship Foundation, responded that the only way to resist foundation funding and influence is to just say "no." This is easier said than done for financially strapped school districts (Levine, 2011).

Foundations and Higher Education

The relationship of foundations and colleges and universities is lengthy and extensive. In considering their relationship, it is important to remember that a large segment of American higher education is privately governed and to some degree independent of public oversight. These entities are free to enter into contracts as any private citizen or corporation might or does.

Higher education institutions, particularly those (public or private) engaged in large-scale research activities, have long been dependent upon foundations for a good deal of their financing. Corporate and individual grants and contracts are routinely solicited. Indeed the success of many college and university presidents is in part dependent upon their ability to raise private funds including major foundation grants. While presidents would prefer that grants and contracts were given unconditionally, it is commonly understood that they are given with expectations that certain programs or research endeavors will be carried out.

Many large-scale grant activities are not necessarily one-time agreements. To the contrary, it is very common for corporate funders to have developed ongoing relationships with large research universities to engage in research and development of new products, processes, and technologies. The companies in Silicon Valley in California provide large-scale, ongoing support for universities such as Stanford University and the California Institute of Technology to partner in a variety of product development and testing projects. The same situation is true for many institutions such as MIT, Purdue, Johns Hopkins, and Vanderbilt that take on extensive research projects in the sciences, medicine, engineering, and business. Traditionally these grant activities were mutually beneficial in nature (colleges get funds, foundations get research and development projects) and were well-understood as part of the culture of American higher education. However, there is a growing concern that the line separating higher education and commercial enterprise is blurring. Jennifer Washburn, in *University, Inc.* (2005), observed:

> The problem is not the university-industry relationships, which have existed for a long time; it is the elimination of any clear boundary line separating academia from commerce ... market forces are dictating what is happening in the world of higher education as never before.
>
> (p. xi)

Corporate financing via grants and contracts are driving a lot of the efforts of some segments of higher education, while colleges and universities are engaging in more direct relationships with commercial enterprises in developing and endorsing products. As Washburn (2005) goes on to state:

> On the vast majority of our nation's campuses today, the most valued professors are not the ones who devote their time and energy to teaching, they are the ones who bring in the most research money, and whose ideas can be turned into lucrative commercial products and licensed to industry.
>
> (p. xii)

Washburn's comment goes right to the heart of the question: Is higher education, in seeking and participating in commercial grants and contracts, compromising its basic mission to educate?

In recent years, there has been another type of higher education foundation grant that has received attention because of the extent of the sponsors' involvement with academic programs including curricular development and faculty hiring. These are not necessarily research-oriented but designed to promote a particular ideology. In May 2011, an article appeared in the *Washington Post* describing one such situation:

> John Allison, former chairman of the bank holding company BB&T, admired author Ayn Rand so much that he devised a strategy to spread her laissez-faire principles on U.S. campuses. Allison, working through the BB&T Charitable Foundation, gives schools grants of as much as $2 million if they agree to create a course on capitalism and make Rand's masterpiece, *Atlas Shrugged*, required reading.
>
> Allison's crusade to counter what he considers the anti-capitalist orthodoxy at universities has produced results—and controversy. About 60 schools, including at least four campuses of the University of North Carolina, began teaching Rand's book after getting the foundation money. Faculty at several schools that have accepted Allison's terms are

protesting, saying donors shouldn't have the power to set the curriculum to pursue their political agendas.

(Lubove & Staley, 2011)

Normally curriculum decisions, including courses to be offered and reading assignments are within the purview of the faculty. On the other hand, the enticement of $2 million is difficult for many presidents to refuse and so there have been conflicts at a number of colleges as the article mentions.

An even more significant question regarding the prerogatives of faculty occurred at Florida State University when the Charles Koch Foundation made a donation of $1.5 million to create two new programs in the Economics Department on "political economy and free enterprise" and "excellence in economic education." In addition to the establishment of the programs, the memorandum of agreement for the grant stipulated that the Foundation would have a say in hiring two faculty members to teach in the program (Hundley, May 10, 2011). Specifically, the Foundation would be represented on an Advisory Board that would participate in the selection of the new faculty hires. While the Advisory Board could be made up of faculty from the university and others, at least one member would be appointed by the Foundation. Furthermore, the faculty hires would have to be "unanimously" approved by the Advisory Board giving the Foundation, via its one member, veto power. In 2011, after the two new faculty were hired, a number of faculty and organizations both inside and outside Florida State University questioned this arrangement. A Faculty Senate Committee established by Florida State University President Eric Barron to examine the appointments concluded that the two individuals were well-qualified and that the hire process was in compliance with the procedures established by Florida State University. The Committee also found that the memorandum of agreement gave the Foundation-appointed members of the Advisory Board too much decision making power and could have opened up the possibility of undue outside influence within the hiring process. The Committee's Report also recommended that there be no future hiring of faculty under the existing memorandum of agreement unless modified in accordance with existing university hiring policies that give approval for faculty hiring and evaluation to the Department's Executive Committee (Florida State University, 2011).

Think Tanks

Think tanks are primarily concerned with funding research and policy reports designed to influence public thinking. There is a thin line between the work of foundations and think tanks. Conservative think tanks are often supported by conservative foundations. Think tanks operate from a "trickle-down" theory of ideas with think tank policymakers trying to influence media and politicians who are to pass on their ideas to the public. The end goal of think tanks is to influence the thinking of politicians, administrators, and the voting public. Since the 1970s conservative think tanks have promoted free market ideas including free markets or choice for education, and including choice of for-profit education. In his 1991 book *The Idea Brokers and the Rise of the New Policy Elite*, James Smith described this development: "In the early 1970s, executives in a handful of traditionally conservative foundations redefined their programs with the aim of shaping the public policy agenda and constructing a network of conservative institutions and scholars" (p. 181). One of the leaders and articulate spokespersons of this movement was William Simon, who left his job in 1976 as Secretary of the Treasury in the Nixon and Ford administrations to become head of the John Olin Foundation whose purpose, in Simon's words, "is to support those individuals and institutions who are working to strengthen the free enterprise system" (Simon, 1978, p. 233).

The new age of conservative attempts to influence American thinking about the economy and schools is outlined in Simon's 1978 book, *A Time for Truth*, which warned that public thinking was dominated by a liberal establishment. This argument was reflected in the book's foreword written respectively by free market advocates Milton Friedman and Friedrich Hayek. In the Preface, Friedman, who is maybe the first person to advocate school choice using vouchers, sounded the warning that intellectual life in the United States was under the control of "socialists and interventionists, who have wrongfully appropriated in this country the noble label 'liberal' and who have been the intellectual architects of our suicidal course" (Friedman, 1978). Applying concepts of the marketplace to intellectual life, Friedman argued that the payoff for these "liberals" was support by an entrenched government bureaucracy. In other words, the liberal elite and the government bureaucracy fed off each other. Using a phrase that would be repeated by conservatives throughout the rest of the 20th century, Friedman contended that "the view that government is the problem, not the cure," is hard for the public to understand (Friedman, 1978). According to Friedman's plea, saving the country required a group of intellectuals to promote a general understanding of the importance of the free market.

To undermine the supposed rule of a liberal intelligentsia, Simon urged the business community to support those intellectuals who advocate the importance of the free market. Simon called on businesspeople to stop supporting colleges and universities that produced "young collectivists by the thousands" and media "which serve as megaphones for anticapitalist opinion." In both cases, Simon insisted, businesspeople should focus their support on university programs and media that stress procapitalist ideas (Simon, 1978, pp. 232–233).

In his call for action, Simon calculated that the first step should involve businesspeople rushing "multimillions to the aid of liberty, in the many places where it is beleaguered." Upon receiving the largess of business, he insisted, "Foundations imbued with the philosophy of freedom … must take pains to funnel desperately needed funds to scholars, social scientists, writers, and journalists who understand the relationship between political and economic liberty" (Simon, 1978, p. 230).

This attempt to gain public support for free market ideas including free market ideas regarding education is described by David Ricci in *The Transformation of American Politics: The New Washington and the Rise of Think Tanks.* "Those who talked about developing conservative ideas," Ricci asserts, "were committed not just to producing them but to the commercial concept of a product, in the sense of something that, once created, must be placed before the public as effectively as possible" (1993, p. 166).

Today, think tanks continue efforts to mold public thinking and policies. Andrew Rich in his *Think Tanks, Public Policy, and the Politics of Expertise* (Rich, 2004) asserts think tanks are engaged in a "war of ideas." Rich classifies the 15 largest think tanks as either "Liberal, Centrist/No Identifiable Ideology" or "Conservative." He identifies the top three "conservative" think tanks as the Heritage Foundation, Hoover Institute, and American Enterprise Institute (Rich, 2004, Kindle Location 2572–2575). There are two important think tanks for educational policy that didn't make Rich's list of the top 10. These are the Progressive Policy Institute (liberal) and the Thomas B. Fordham Institute (conservative).

While there are ideological differences between conservative and liberal think tanks most advocate educational policies that benefit the educational-industrial complex. We will examine the ideas promoted by both conservative and liberal think tanks beginning with the Heritage Foundation which is listed by Andrew Rich as one of the 15 largest U.S. think tanks (Rich, 2004). Rich quotes the 1994 Speaker of the House Newt Gingrich regarding the Heritage Foundation, it "is without question the most far-reaching conservative organization in the country in the *war on ideas*, and one which has had a tremendous impact not just in Washington, *but literally across the planet* [emphasis added]" (Rich, 2004, pp. 64–67). In 2012, the Heritage Foundation explained its ideological position:

> Founded in 1973, The Heritage Foundation is a research and educational institution—a think tank—whose mission is to formulate and promote conservative public policies based on the principles of free enterprise, limited government, individual freedom, traditional American values, and a strong national defense.
>
> (Heritage Foundation, 2012)

The Heritage Foundation states that its mission is to influence public leaders: "Heritage's staff pursues this mission by performing timely, accurate research on key policy issues and effectively marketing these findings to our primary audiences: members of Congress, key congressional staff members, policymakers in the executive branch, the nation's news media, and the academic and policy communities" (The Heritage Foundation, 2012).

The Heritage Foundation's *Issues 2012: Candidate's Briefing Book* promotes policies that favor school choice and private schools (Heritage Foundation,2011; see also 2012). The purpose of the Briefing Book is to provide voters and political candidates with a conservative agenda for the 2012 elections. As part of war of ideas, the *Briefing Book* is intended to disseminate a particular ideology. The *Briefing Book* explains its purpose:

> As candidates begin their campaigns for office in 2012, they will need to define the key issues quickly and then present clear policy recommendations, supported by facts, for addressing those issues. Issues 2012: The Candidate's Briefing Book provides these issues, facts, and solutions in language every American will understand.
>
> (Heritage Foundation, 2011, p. iv)

Regarding education, the Briefing Book echoes the sentiment that public schools are failing and places part of the blame on the federal government. The Heritage Foundation advocates limiting the federal role in education and returning power to state governments and local school districts (Heritage Foundation, 2011, pp. 31–32).

Trying to influence the 2012 elections, the Heritage Foundation laid out a program designed, in their words, to "empower parents." This means school choice, including attending private schools at government expense and expanding the number of charter schools. The document states, "Expand private school choice by enacting or expanding such options as scholarships, vouchers, education tax credits for tuition or scholarship donations, or education savings accounts" (Heritage Foundation 2011, p. 33). This idea provides support for for-profit schools receiving government money. Expanding charter schools indirectly supports educational management organizations: "Lift caps on charter schools and pass strong charter-school laws to encourage a vibrant charter sector that also allows for fully online charter schools" (Heritage Foundation, 2011, p. 33).

Heritage Foundation's 2012 education recommendations favor changes that will aid the growth of the education-industrial complex by funneling public monies to for-profit schools. Specifically, the Heritage Foundation is trying to influence politicians to enact the following:

Expand private school choice by enacting or expanding such options as scholarships, vouchers, education tax credits for tuition or scholarship donations, or education savings accounts.

Lift caps on charter schools and pass strong charter-school laws to encourage a vibrant charter sector that also allows for fully online charter schools.

Expand public-school choice options such as school choice within and among school districts.

Create and expand education savings accounts such as those offered in
Arizona and for post-secondary education. (Heritage Foundation,
2011, pp. 33–34)

This agenda calls for expanding charter schools (which indirectly supports
educational management organizations), and supporting the use of public
money for private schools through vouchers, education tax credits and savings
accounts. When for-profit colleges were criticized in Congress in 2010, the
Heritage Foundation rushed to defend for-profit education:

> The roots of market-based education stretch as far back as classical Greece
> in the fifth century B.C., when proprietary schools and traveling teach-
> ers for hire … provided instruction to students willing to pay for their
> services. The Greek citizenry's growing demand for educational ser-
> vices combined with the freedom of educators to establish private for-
> profit schools led to the emergence of a nimble educational system.… In
> response to the needs of the students and their families, educators taught
> the subjects students wanted to learn.

(Burke, 2010)

The Heritage Foundation guide for voters and political candidates specifically mentions the for-profit online educational management organization
K12: "Expand online learning opportunities through statewide virtual schools,
fully online charter schools, and education savings accounts that can be used
for tuition at *private online K–12 schools* [emphasis added] in order to customize
programs to meet students' needs and allow students to work at their own pace"
(Heritage Foundation, 2011, pp. 33–34).

Conservative think tanks share common educational ideas like those in the
policy proposals of the Heritage Foundation and the Hoover Institute. Visiting the conservative Hoover Institute website on January 10, 2012, we were
greeted with the headline, "K-12 education task force members appear on Rick
Hess's top scholars list" (Hoover Institute, 2012c). A noteworthy feature of
this headline is that Frederick (Rick) Hess is director of education policy of
another important conservative think tank, the American Enterprise Institute.
The purpose of the article was to highlight the members of the Hoover Institute's Koret Task Force on K-12 Education who are on his list of top scholars.
The Chair of the Koret Task Force is Chester Finn who is president of both the
conservative Fordham Foundation and the Fordham Institute (Hoover Institute, 2012b).

The Koret Task Force's description highlights its dedication to pushing
for educational reforms that favor free enterprise solutions (e.g., for-profit
education).

The K-12 Education Task Force focuses on education policy as it relates to government provision and oversight versus private solutions (both within and outside the public school system) that stress choice, accountability, and transparency; that include systematic reform options such as vouchers, charter schools, and testing; and that weigh equity concerns against outcome objectives.

(Hoover Institute, 2012b)

Of particular interest for the education-industrial complex is the Koret Task Force's stress on charter schools, school choice, and testing which support educational management organizations, for-profit schools, and the testing and test preparation industries. School choice, of course, opens the door to for-profit schools and educational management organizations. This is highlighted in Chester Finn's contribution to the Koret Task Force's vision of education in the year 2030 (Hoover Institute, 2012b). As chair of the Task Force, Chester Finn focused on what school choice should look like by 2030. One of the things envisioned by Finn was the development of consumer choice in education with schools being operated by private firms.

Another high-profile organizational evolution was the spread of national "brand-name" schools, mostly run by sophisticated private firms, both for- and nonprofit. Part entrepreneurial venture and part virtual school system, they figured out how to replicate schools that adhere to specific models, supplying them with financial and human capital, providing essential business and curricular services, developing shared technologies and instructional materials, and affixing names that are gaining national recognition.

(Finn, 2010, p. 4)

In fact, Finn's consumerist branding model would result in marketing schools in the same way as automobiles and computers, including building brand loyalty. In the following, Finn specifically refers to "Our education industry."

Whereas Americans once thought of school systems as local and bureaucratic (e.g., the Dayton Public Schools), these new systems are far flung. A child whose family moves from Baltimore to Denver can transit painlessly from one "Gold Star" or "Green Dot" (or Edison, KIPP, High Tech High, etc.) school directly into another. Our education industry, like our hospitality, retailing, and communications industries, is developing recognizable brands that have spread across the nation and overseas, not unlike Holiday Inn, Macy's, and CNN. KIPP, for example, now has fifty-seven schools in India; High Tech High has thirty-two in metropolitan Shanghai alone.

(Finn, 2010, p. 4)

Therefore, Finn directly supports an expanded educational-industrial complex in the framework of consumerism and using brand names. He envisions the federal and state governments stimulating private investment in the education industry: "Federal and state tax regimes could provide incentives to encourage private venture capital investment in the entrepreneurial side of education, not unlike the inducements given to producers (and consumers) of renewable energy, fuel-efficient vehicles, and businesses that reduce their carbon footprints" (Finn, 2010, p. 6). Another member of the Hoover Institution's Koret Task Force, Williamson Evers, proposes changes that would benefit testing and test preparation companies, and software producers. Evers is a research fellow at the Hoover Institution and was the U.S. Assistant Secretary of Education for Policy from 2007 to 2009 and senior adviser to U.S. Secretary of Education Margaret Spellings during 2007 (Evers, 2010; Hoover Institute, 2012d). In his contribution to the Koret Task Force's vision for the year 2030, Evers sees increased use of adaptive testing that could be adjusted to the student's learning level. He specifically mentions testing companies as key components of future education developments: "Formative assessments on computers became pervasive, being offered by descendants of testing companies and textbook publishers. The new close relationship of curriculum and formative testing made old complaints about 'teaching to the test' irrelevant: the tests now test what is taught" (Evers, 2010, p. 4). In a vision that might please for-profit software companies along with publishers and testing companies, Evers predicts,

> Although many large publishers of tests remained in business, and some publishers who had not been in the testing business added that line of work, the new technologies facilitated large numbers of new entrants to the field of multimedia instructional materials. Most states with statewide adoption rules abandoned them because of the difficulty of managing the approval status of continuously updated, online textbooks.
>
> (Evers, 2010, p. 4)

Sharing these ideas is the previously mentioned Fredrick Hess, director of education policy at the American Enterprise Institute. The American Enterprise Institute declares its mission as promotion of ideas that protect free market competition: "The American Enterprise Institute is a community of scholars and supporters committed to expanding liberty, increasing individual opportunity and strengthening free enterprise" (American Enterprise Institute. 2012b). Among other affiliations, Hess is on the Boards of Directors of the National Association of Charter School Authorizers and 4.0 SCHOOLS (American Enterprise Institute, 2012a). The National Association of Charter School Authorizers is devoted to adding legitimacy to the charter school movement through the creation of standards: "The mission of the National Association of Charter School Authorizers is to achieve the establishment and operation of quality charter schools through responsible oversight in the public interest"

(National Association of Charter School Authorizers, 2012b). This organization is funded by the Gates, the Walton Family, Dell, and the Robertson foundations (National Association of Charter School Authorizers, 2012a). Exemplifying the interconnections between conservative foundations and think tanks, 4.0 SCHOOLS is funded by the Walton Family Foundation for the purpose of training school leaders (Walton Family Foundation, 2012).

Writing in the 2011 Annual Report of the American Enterprise Institute, Hess stresses the theme of competitive education markets, which would include for-profit schools and education companies, as the key to school improvement. He chides charter school advocates for not understanding markets: "We get a 'school choice' community that advocates charter schooling or school vouchers while showing remarkably little interest in what it takes for markets to work, or for 'choice' to yield good choices" (American Enterprise Institute, 2011, p. 30). Fulfilling the American Enterprise Institute's dedication to free markets and competition, Hess wrote in the same report about a book he wrote with Bruno Manno, senior advisor to the Walton Family Foundation, that the "volume that challenges us to push past the verities of school choice and school turnarounds and to embrace new opportunities to use technology, markets, and entrepreneurial solutions" (American Enterprise Institute, 2011, p. 31).

Another example of the interconnections is the previously mentioned Chester Finn, Jr. who is both chair of the Hoover Institute's Koret Task Force and president of the Fordham Institute. Similar to the previously discussed conservative think tanks, the Fordham Institute champions charter schools and advocates lifting all limits on their growth. In a special report, "Better Choices: Charter Incubation as a Strategy for Improving the Charter School Sector," the Fordham Institute (2012) suggests strengthening educational management organizations—their report uses the term *charter management organization*) (Cities for Education Enterprenuership Trust and the Thomas B. Fordham Institute, 2011). The report suggests "incubation" of new forms of charter schools in educational management organizations. This incubation period would include "strategic recruitment, selection, and training of promising leaders and the support of those leaders as they launch or expand new charter schools in cities or specific geographic regions" (Cities for Education Enterprenuership Trust and the Thomas B. Fordham Institute, 2011, p. 5). The reader will recall from chapters 4 and 5 that many educational management organizations operate for a profit managing large numbers of charter schools around the country.

By placing these management organizations at the center of the school choice and charter school discussion, the Fordham Institute is supporting this part of the educational-industrial complex. The report hopes that, "The initial efforts of a small number of charter incubators signal the potential for the creation of more high-quality educational options for needy students in cities throughout the country" (Cities for Education Enterprenuership Trust and the Thomas B. Fordham Institute, 2011, p. 5).

Do liberal think tanks contribute to the growth of the educational-industrial complex? Consider the Progressive Policy Institute which was created in 1989 by the Democratic Leadership Council. The Council formed the Progressive Policy Institute to support scholars formulating a new vision for the Democratic Party. The Institute defines its ideological position as:

> PPI's mission, modernizing progressive politics, hasn't changed. What has is the political context in which we operate. At our founding in 1989, progressives were in the political wilderness. Now we're in power. In fact, we may even be present at the creation of a new progressive majority in America—but only if we govern effectively.
>
> (Progressive Policy Institute, 2012b)

In "PPI [Progressive Policy Institute] Statement on Empowering Parents Through Quality Charter Schools Act," the Institute joined conservative think tanks in supporting the expansion of charter schools and choice: "PPI has long asserted that we need to spur faster growth of the best charter networks to lift overall quality in choice and open more slots to the neediest students" (Progressive Policy Institute, 2011). In fact, the Progressive Policy Institute believes that charter schools will help children from low-income families: "PPI has long championed public charter schools, which have expanded choice and educational opportunities for hundreds of thousands of poor families" (Progressive Policy Institute, 2012a).

A unique proposal from the Progressive Policy Institute could potentially expand the software, computer hardware, and gaming industries. The proposal is to create a "Digital Teaching Corps" that would focus on closing the literacy gap between children from low-income and high-income families. The Digital Teaching Corps would be voluntary and nonprofit and emphasize the use of technology in literacy instruction. Also, it is claimed in the policy proposal, "The Corps would also address a related 'digital participation gap' that is emerging from the explosion of new media tools that are now available to middle class kids."

While the support for charter schools aids educational management organizations, the use technology to teach literacy helps to expand digital learning industries. The proposal concludes, "American technological ingenuity gave birth to the Digital Age. Yet our public institutions—especially the vitally important institution of public education—have been slow to adopt online instruction, computer games, social networking and digital tools of all kinds." The policy statement describes the result of this failure as "a growing gap between how people acquire and process information, how they communicate with others, and how we educate our children" (Levine, 2011).

The Progressive Policy Institute also supports the extensive testing requirements of NCLB. When the reauthorization of NCLB in 2011 resulted in some members of Congress proposing to reduce the significance of standardized testing in determining failing schools and reporting annual yearly performance, the Progressive Policy Institute reacted with an article by Erik Adamiec, "Senate Guts School Accountability" (Adamiec, 2011). In defending testing, and indirectly the profits of test makers and test preparation companies, the article declared that NCLB's "signal achievement was to require local school authorities to measure the academic achievements of all students, including racial and ethnic subgroups. This provision meant that schools could no longer hide their failure to educate all students behind averages" (Adamiec, 2011).

It would be difficult to separate the influence of conservative think tanks from other possible factors in gaining public acceptance of free markets for education, including ideas of choice, vouchers, for-profit and charter schools, and the outsourcing of school services. Certainly, since the 1970s these organizations have attempted to shift public thinking in the direction of applying free market ideas to public schools. This free market thinking has been crucial in the expansion of the education-industrial complex. Even liberal think tanks like the Progressive Policy Institute support ideas regarding charter schools and technology that support for-profit education industries. Chester Finn's vision for 2030 of nationally and globally franchised schools captures free market thinking applied to education. Similar to other consumer products, Finn imagines a world of competition between schools that have been "branded" like any other consumer fast food franchise. While the public influence of visions like Finn's would be difficult to measure, one can say that these ideas do support an expansion of the educational-industrial complex.

Case Study—The Bill and Melinda Gates Foundation

The Gates Foundation deserves special attention in this chapter because of the assets at its disposal but also because it has operated in ways that epitomize the educational-industrial complex. It has become the face of large-scale foundation involvement in public education. There are many facets of the Gates Foundation operation that deserve our attention but we will examine three of them.

First, the Gates Foundation has sought to influence federal education policy to conform to its own view and ideology by promoting the appointment of its former employees and other collaborators to key positions in the U.S. Department of Education. A clear illustration of this was the appointment by Secretary Arne Duncan of James Shelton as Assistant Deputy Secretary for Education Innovation and Improvement. Before his appointment, he was a program officer at the Gates Foundation for almost 8 years, a partner in the New Schools Venture Fund, and president of the LearnNow Division of Edison Schools. He provides a direct pipeline from Gates to Arne Duncan and the rest of the administration at the U.S. Department of Education. Joining Shelton was Margot Rogers who served as Arne Duncan's Chief of Staff. Prior to joining the administration, she worked for foundations and nonprofit organizations on issues of education policy and practice for 15 years. Immediately prior to joining the U.S. Department of Education, she served as the special assistant to the director of education at the Gates Foundation. In this position she managed and co-led the development of the Foundation's education strategy and staff realignment, and served on the education division's investment committee and strategic leadership team. Rogers left the U.S. Department of Education in 2011, and was replaced by Joanne Weiss, who was a partner at the New Schools Venture Fund, which received tens of millions of dollars from the Gates Foundation. Prior to assuming the position as Duncan's Chief of Staff, Weiss was the Director of the Race to the Top Program, a $4.35 billion federal program that pitted state against state to develop strategies to turn around failing schools (Visconti & Thiam, 2009). An article in *Governing States and Localities* summarized the Gates Foundation relationship with the U.S. Department of Education as follows:

> Many of the ideas Duncan pushed states to adopt through Race to the Top, the $4 billion grant fund created by the 2009 federal stimulus law, come straight out of playbooks developed by Gates and other foundations. Top officials are now shuttling back and forth between the department and the Gates Foundation. Some critics say it's not too great a stretch to say that the Gates Foundation is, in effect, running the Department of Education.
>
> (Greenblatt, 2011)

Second, one of the Gates Foundation's major thrusts in school reform is to infuse technology in all aspects of school operations both instructional and administrative. Joanne Weiss, in an article titled, "The Innovation Mismatch: 'Smart Capital' and Education Innovation" provides a manifesto on how venture capital is the answer to spurring technological innovation in K-12 schools. Her conclusion was that venture capital "would finally bring millions of America's students the much-touted yet much-delayed benefits of the technology revolution in education" (Weiss, 2011). Weiss's article is a call for large-scale integration of technology into K-12 education. At a national meeting of the governors in 2005, Bill Gates stated that the nation's high schools are obsolete and need to be reinvented. Among the fixes he saw for the high schools and for public education in general was the development and expansion of technology for supporting instruction, for monitoring and collecting standardizing data on student assessments, and for developing large scale integrated longitudinal databases on student and teacher performance. In 2011, the National Governors Association announced support for the Shared Learning Collaborative that would establish the beginnings of a national clearing house of data on students and teachers. Initial funds for this project ($44 million) have been provided by the Gates Foundation in collaboration with the Carnegie Foundation. A contract has been issued to Wireless Generation, a company owned by Rupert

Murdoch's News Corporation, to develop the data framework for this system (Otterman, 2011). Four states have agreed to assist in the design and testing of the framework. The actual system, if developed fully and across the entire nation, will likely cost hundreds of millions of dollars.

The Gates Foundation has also been involved in funding the development of online course materials. In 2011, the Gates Foundation and the Pearson Foundation announced a project to create online reading and math courses aligned with the new K–12 academic standards adopted by 40 states. Twenty-four new courses will be developed that use video, interactive software, games, social media, and other digital materials to present math lessons for kindergarten through 10th grade and English lessons for kindergarten through 12th grade (Dillon, 2011a). As reported in the *New York Times*, Vicki Phillips, a director at the Gates Foundation, said:

> the partnership with Pearson was part of a suite of investments totaling more than $20 million that the foundation was undertaking, all of which involve new technology-based instructional approaches. The new digital materials, Ms. Phillips said, "have the potential to fundamentally change the way students and teachers interact in the classroom.... The partnership with the Gates Foundation could give Pearson a considerable advantage as textbook and learning technology companies position themselves in an education marketplace upended by the creation of the common standards.
>
> (Dillon, 2011a)

As alluded to in the article, Pearson has a lot to gain from this project in the years to come, but so does Gates. If every one of the 50 million students enrolled in these online courses, just think what this would mean for Microsoft, the company that sells and provides much of the software infrastructure (operating systems, browsers, search engines, etc.) for this technology.

A third important area of activity for the Gates Foundation has been education policy advocacy. The Gates Foundation uses its resources to advocate for policies compatible with its own goals and objectives. Furthermore, it does not always do this directly but through other organizations both public and private. In an insightful article in the New York Times, Sam Dillon relates the following story that occurred in Indiana:

> A handful of outspoken teachers helped persuade state lawmakers this spring to eliminate seniority-based layoff policies. They testified before the legislature, wrote briefing papers and published an op-ed article in The Indianapolis Star.... They described themselves simply as local teachers who favored school reform—one sympathetic state representative, Mary Ann Sullivan, said, 'They seemed like genuine, real people versus the teachers' union lobbyists.' They were, but they were also recruits in a

national organization, Teach Plus, financed significantly by the Bill and Melinda Gates Foundation.

(Dillon, 2011b)

This scenario, in which the Gates Foundation is funding a supposed grassroots activity in order to push its own education policy agenda, is playing itself out over and over again throughout the country. In the policy area, the Gates Foundation funds academic researchers, district data specialists, think tanks, and media organizations that tend to present Gates supported education policies in a most favorable light. In most cases, the receivers of the policy positions (legislators, school board members, parents) do not realize that Gates is funding the activity. Dillon in his piece goes on to mention that Allan C. Golston, the President of the Gates Foundation Advocacy Program in the United States, expects the Foundation to spend upwards of $3.5 billion on education, 15% or approximately $500 million of which will be used for advocacy (Dillon, 2011a). Among the organizations that Dillon identified as receiving substantial funding that result in advocacy-type activities included:

National Governors Association
Council of Chief School Officers
Fordham Institute
Harvard University's Strategic Data Fellows Program
A social action campaign to promote the film *Waiting for Superman* that sang the praises of a charter schools while demonizing teachers unions especially the president of the American Federation of Teachers, Randi Weingarten.
Foundation for Educational Excellence (headed by former Florida Governor Jeb Bush)
The New Teacher Project
Education Week
American Enterprise Institute

Dillon observes that by funding so many organizations, the Gates Foundation is assured of support for its policy positions. He also quotes Fred Hess who describes well the fine line that many educators walk when dealing with a major foundation willing to make substantive grants in return for direct or tacit support for its programs and policies.

> "It's Orwellian in the sense that through this vast funding they start to control even how we tacitly think about the problems facing public education" said Bruce Fuller, an education professor at the University of California, Berkeley, who said he received no financing from the foundation.
> [Fred] Hess, whose institute [American Enterprise Institute] received $500,000 from the Gates foundation in 2009 to influence the national education debates, acknowledged that he and others sometimes felt con-

strained. "As researchers, we have a reasonable self-preservation instinct," he said. "There can be an exquisite carefulness about how we're going to say anything that could reflect badly on a foundation.

(Dillon, 2011b)

References

Adamiec, E. (2011, October 20). *Senate guts school accountabiltity*. Retrieved from http://progressivepolicy.org/senate-guts-school-accountability

American Enterprise Institute. (2011). *American Enterprise Institute: 2011 annual report*. Washington, DC: Author..

American Enterprise Institute (2012a). *Frederick Hess*. Retrieved from http://www.aei.org/scholar/frederick-m-hess/

American Enterprise Institute. (2012b). *AEI's organization and purposes*. Retrieved from http://www.aei.org/about/

Barkan, J. (Winter 2011). Got dough? How billionaires rule our schools. *Dissent*. Retrieved from http://www.dissentmagazine.org/article/?article=3781

Burke, L. (2010, August 10). The assault on for-profit universities. Retrieved from http://blog.heritage.org/2010/08/10/the-assault-on-for-profit-universities/?query=The+Assault+on+For-Profit+Universities

Carnegie, A. (1889). The gospel of wealth. Retrieved from http://us.history.wisc.edu/hist102/pdocs/carnegie_wealth.pdf

Cities for Education Enterprenuership Trust and the Thomas B. Fordham Institute. (2011). *Better choices: Charter incubation as a strategy for improving the charter school sector*. Washington, DC: Thomas B. Fordham Institute.

Dillon, S. (2011a, April 27). Foundations join to offer online courses for schools. *New York Times*. Retrieved from http://www.nytimes.com/2011/04/28/education/28gates.html?nl=todaysheadlines&emc=tha26

Dillon, S. (2011b, May 21). Behind grass-roots school advocacy, Bill Gates. *New York Times*. Retrieved from http://www.nytimes.com/2011/05/22/education/22gates.html?_r=2&adxnnl=1&pagewanted=print&adxnnlx=1322465423-YRvgm8zUXA0JGY0doaKfGA

Evers, W. (2010). *American education in 2030: Standards and competitive rigor*. Palo Alto, CA: Stanford University.

Finn, C. (2010). *American education 2030: School choice*. Palo Alto, CA: Stanford University.

Florida State University. (2011, July). Koch Foundation memorandum of understanding. In *Faculty Senate ad hoc Committee review report*. Retrieved from http://president.fsu.edu/downloads/Full_Report.pdf

Fordham Institute. (2012). *The Fordham mission*. Retrieved from http://www.edexcellence.net/about-us/fordham-mission.html

Friedman, M. (1978). Preface. In W. Simon, *A Time for Truth* (p. xii). New York: Readers Digest Press.

Greenblatt, A. (2011, April 27). Billionaires in the classroom. *Governing the States and Localities*. Retrieved from http://www.governing.com/topics/education/billionaires-in-the-classroom.html#

Greene, J., & Symonds, W. C. (2006. June 26). Bill Gates gets schooled. *Business Week*. Retrieved from http://www.businessweek.com/magazine/content/06_26/b3990001.htm

Hammond, B., & Lednicer, L.G. (2008, June 23). Small-school experiment doesn't live up to hopes. *Seattle Times*. Retrieved from http://seattletimes.nwsource.com/html/education/2008012076_smallschools23.html

Heritage Foundation. (2011). *Issues 2010: Candidates briefing book*. Washington, DC: Author.

Heritage Foundation. (2012). *About us*. Retrieved from http://www.heritage.org/about

Hoover Institute. (2012a). *Task force and working groups: American education 2030.* Retrieved from http://www.hoover.org/taskforces/education/AE2030

Hoover Institute. (2012b). *Koret task force.* Retrieved from http://www.hoover.org/taskforces/education

Hoover Institute. (2012c). *K-12 Education task for members appear on Rick Hess's top scholars list.* Retrieved from http://www.hoover.org/news/103886

Hoover Institute. (2012d). Williamson Evers. Retrieved from http://www.hoover.org/fellows/10136

Hundley, K. (May 10, 2011). Billionaire's role in hiring decisions at Florida State University raises questions. *Tampa Bay Times.* Retrieved from http://www.tampabay.com/news/business/billionaires-role-in-hiring-decisions-at-florida-state-university-raises/1168680

Jenning, J. L., & Pallis, A. M. (2010). *Do New York City's new small schools enroll students with different characteristics from other NYC Schools?* Providence, RI: The Annenberg Institute for School Reform, Brown University.

Leibell, D. T. (2009, December 30). Gates embraces philanthro-capitalism: The world's largest private foundation bets big on venture philanthropy. Retrieved from http://trustsandestates.com/wealth_watch/gates-foundation-venture-philanthropy1230/

Letts, C. W., Ryan, W., & Grossman, A. (1997, March–April,). Virtuous capital: What foundations can learn from venture capitalists. *Harvard EducationBusiness Review,* 36–44. Retrieved from http://www.halftime.org/wp-content/uploads/2011/07/Virtuous_Capital_HB.pdf

Levine, M. (2011, September). *The digital teaching corps.* Retrieved from http://progressivepolicy.org/?s=21st+century+schools

Lewis, S. (1922). *The goose step.* Pasadena, CA: Author.

Lewis, S. (1924). *The goslings.* Pasadena,CA: Author.

Lubove, S., & Staley, O. (2011, May 14). College gifts now coming with strings attached. *The Washington Post.* Retrieved from http://www.washingtonpost.com/business/college-gifts-now-coming-with-strings-attached/2011/05/08/AF9TEf3G_story.html

National Association of Charter School Authorizers. (2012). *Funders.* Retrieved from http://www.qualitycharters.org/about/sponsors

National Association of Charter School Authorizers. (2012). *Mission.* Retrieved from http://www.qualitycharters.org/about/mission-2

Otterman, S. (2011, August 29). Subsidiary of News Corp. loses deal with state. *New York Times.* http://www.nytimes.com/2011/08/30/education/30wireless.html

Porter, M. E., & Kramer, M. R. (1999, November). Philanthropy's new agenda: Creating value. *Harvard Education Review.* Retrieved from http://hbr.org/1999/11/philanthropys-new-agenda-creating-value/ar/1

Progressive Policy Institute. (2011, September 14). *PPI statement on empowering parents through Quality Charter School Act.* Retrieved from http://progressivepolicy.org/ppi-statement-on-empowering-parents-through-quality-charter-schools-act

Progressive Policy Institute. (2012a). *New schools for the twentieth century.* Retrieved from http://progressivepolicy.org/education-reform

Progressive Policy Institute. (2012b). *Who we are.* Retrieved from http://progressivepolicy.org/about-us/who-we-are

Ravitch, D. (2010). *The death and life of the great American school system.* New York: Perseus.

Ricci, D. (1993). *The transformation of American politics: The new Washington and the rise of think tanks.* New Haven, CT: Yale University Press.

Rich, A. (2004). *Think tanks, public policy, and the politics of expertise* [Kindle version]. Cambridge, England: Cambridge University Press.

Simon, W. (1978). *A time for truth.* New York: Readers Digest Press.

Smith, J. (1991). *The idea brokers and the rise of the new policy elite.* New York: Free Press.

Visconti, V., & Thiam, S. (2009, December 3). Race to the top podcast: Diane Ravitch questions the new role. Retrieved from http://learningmatters.tv/blog/podcasts/race-to-the-top-podcast-play-money/3428/

Walton Family Foundation. (2012). *4.0 SCHOOLS*. Retrieved from http://www.waltonfamily-foundation.org/grantees/4.0-schools

Washburn, J. (2005). *University, Inc.* New York: Basic Books.

Weiss, J. (March 31, 2011). The innovation mismatch: "Smart capital" and education innovation. *Harvard Business Review*. Retrieved from http://blogs.hbr.org/innovations-in-education/2011/03/the-innovation-mismatch-smart.html

7

MEDIA

News Media, Edutainment, and the Education-Industrial Complex

Media disseminate information about education to the public and sell their products to schools. Media, as the term is used in this chapter, include movies, television, radio, newspapers, the Internet, and software. Media extend the education-industrial complex into the home. Concerned about school success parents buy education products or have their children view educational television programs that contain advertisements. Television and the Internet advertising accompanying educational television turn children into consumers. With education media the home is "curricularized" and turned into an extension of the school.

The marketing of media to schools follows a pattern we have described in previous chapters. When a new product is developed, sales to schools are considered a source of revenue that prompts companies to pressure government to fund the purchase of their new products. This pattern is particularly true for the movie and software industries.

A key concept in discussing media is edutainment or the combining of education with entertainment. Making learning fun is often claimed in media advertising. For instance in the 1920s and 1930s, *Parents* magazine promoted the purchase of toys such as wooden blocks and peg boards as early childhood learning tools (Ito, 2009, pp. 31–36). The promotion and marketing of education toys turns play into preparation for school. When edutainment media, radio and television, enter the home they are often accompanied by advertising directed at children. Radio and television advertising helped create a mass consumer culture among children. Today *Sesame Street*, which started as a noncommercial form of edutainment, licenses the sale of a range of products associated with the program (Sesame Street Store, 2012).

We will begin this chapter with a discussion of the key federal laws that aided the sale of media to schools and opened the door to advertising accompanying edutainment on noncommercial television. Then we will discuss the development of radio and television as forms of edutainment and the sale of classroom movies to schools. Eventually, classroom movies were replaced by the sale of edutainment software to schools and families. And finally, we will discuss news media's role in the education business and its influence on public thinking about education issues.

Government and Edutainment

The intention of this section is to provide a quick introduction to major federal actions that have linked government financing to media sales and advertising to schools and families. The consequences of this federal activity will be elaborated on in later sections of the chapter.

1. 1958 National Defense Education Act Title VII funded the development of education films and the purchase of audiovisual equipment and for educational television and radio programming.
2. 1965 Elementary and Secondary Education Act Titles II and III provided $100 million for libraries and $100 million for school resources including audiovisual and programmed materials. According to historian Geoff Alexander this legislation rapidly increased profits for producers of classroom films (Alexander, 2010, p. 41).
3. The Public Broadcasting Act of 1967 funded the Public Broadcasting Service (PBS) and National Public Radio (NPR), which provided noncommercial television and radio including children's programming in the form edutainment (Spring, 1992, pp. 231–250). Among the edutainment programs appearing on PBS were *Sesame Street*, *Mister Rogers Neighborhood,* and *Reading Rainbow* (Linn, 2004, p. 44).
4. The 1995 Congressional reduction of funding for PBS resulted in PBS seeking corporate sponsorship and other sources of funding. The result was to commercialize PBS's edutainment programs through corporate sponsorship and the licensing and sale of products associated with PBS edutainment programs (Linn, 2004, pp. 44–60).
5. The 2010 U.S. Department of Education's National Education Technology plan promoted the sale of information and communication technology to schools including learning software, hardware, and learning games (U.S. Department of Education, 2010).

As we will discuss, these federal actions helped education media companies to expand into homes and schools.

The Sale of Movies as Edutainment

Movies were the first modern media to be embraced as edutainment. The expansion of this industry into classrooms followed the pattern of first marketing to the general public and then seeking more profits through marketing to schools which resulted in lobbying government for school funds to buy movie projectors and films. The early movie industry considered schools an ideal place to sell their products. Movies, like later digital media products such as the iPad, sparked a belief that media could revolutionize the classroom. Thomas Edison, the inventor of the movie camera, claimed that "books will soon be obsolete in the schools ... our school system will be completely changed in ten years" (Alexander, 2010, p. 15).

Educators were slow to accept movies as a form of classroom learning and some worried that films would replace schools as the major influence on national culture (Spring, 1992, pp. 11–31). It was at the 1914 annual meeting of the National Education Association (NEA) that the film industry made its initial attempt to sell their products to schools. Alfred Saunders, the manager of Colonial Picture Corporation's Education Department, introduced the idea of edutainment in a presentation titled, "Motion Pictures as an Aid to Education." After discussing the types of films and movie projectors suitable for schools, he claimed that "every school that is equipped with a projecting machine may cover the cost of it by allowing the parents to attend exhibitions in the evening" (Saunders, 1914).

While worrying about the effect of movies on the public, NEA delegates embraced movies as edutainment. "In less than twenty years, the motion picture business has secured a hold on the minds of people," declared Peter Olesen, school superintendent from Cloquet, Minnesota. Olesen claimed the influence of movies was "almost equal to that of the school and the daily press" (Olesen, 1914). David Snedden, Commissioner of Education for Massachusetts claimed movies could bring real life images into the classroom and he stressed that educators should pressure the movie industry to ensure that films contained instructional values (Snedden, 1914). Echoing Snedden, Nathaniel Graham, school superintendent from South Omaha, Nebraska, asserted, "We all believe that encouragement by this body of educators will result in motion pictures being made available for every department of school work. Who can tell in how short a time motion pictures will be as great an accessory to education as is the printed text" (Graham, 1914)?

The NEA created a special committee to work with the industry's trade organization the Motion Picture Producers and Distributors of America (MPPDA). The MPPDA financed a meeting of this NEA committee in New York bringing together school and movie people. Indicative of the industry's interest in making money selling movies to schools, the MPPDA provided $5,000 for the committee to investigate the use of films for classroom instruction (Judd, 1923).

The NEA committee's 1923 report accepted the idea of schools being a new market for films. As a result, the NEA created a Department of Visual Instruction to study the classroom use of movies. The MPPDA asked educators to review old movies for use in classroom instruction in the hope that the commercial life of films could be extended. The MPPDA sponsored committees of teachers to select portions of old films that could be used in classrooms.

Also, the movie industry advanced the argument that many movies shown in theaters were a form of edutainment. Colonel Jason S. Joy, MPPDA's Director of Public Relations, told the delegates to the 1927 NEA annual meeting that education movies included historical and literary films like *Beau Geste, Ben Hur,* and *The Scarlet Letter* (Joy, 1927). Joy outlined what the movie industry was doing to make movies more attractive to educators and families, such as making films of "literary classics." Joy told NEA delegates, "This growing intimacy between the motion picture and the book has met with general although not universal approval. There have been those who feared that many people would 'take their reading out in looking'" (Joy, 1927, p. 967). Introducing the concept of education as entertainment, Joy claimed, "Books on the shelves of libraries make it possible for men to attain a certain amount of knowledge and information by hard work and application. But the moving picture, presented as an amusement, will in a few years make it impossible for any average man or woman to remain ignorant" (Joy, 1927, p. 967).

The evolution of education films illustrates how a new technology can result in profitmaking networks linking industrial leaders, school officials and government. Money was to be made selling hardware (movie projectors) and classroom films. Illustrating this evolving network Western Electric's Electrical Products, Inc. was established in 1928 to make education films; it was renamed Encyclopedia Britannica Films in 1943. In 1932, Electrical Products developed a cooperative relationship with the University of Chicago resulting in the production of 36 science films. A key source of profits for the company was the sale of projectors to 1,000 schools. In 1941, William Benton, the vice president of the University of Chicago, entered negotiations with the chairman of the board of Sears, Roebuck to purchase Encyclopedia Britannica. Benton, who previously headed the advertising agency Benton and Bowles, saw this as a win-win situation with the encyclopedia gaining prestige by its association with the University of Chicago and the University gaining revenue through the sale of the encyclopedia. In 1943, Benton arranged the purchase of Electrical Products and renamed the company Encyclopedia Britannica Films. Benton then invested $1.5 million in the company and acquired 300 education titles from Eastman Kodak. In 1944, the University took full control of Encyclopedia Britannica Films, buying out Benton's stake, and that year received royalty income of $300,000. In 1946, Benton became Assistant Secretary of State for Public Affairs during Truman's administration (Alexander, 2010, pp. 20–23).

Coronet Films, another major classroom film producer was founded in 1934 by the head of the *Esquire* magazine empire, David Smart. He established the largest privately owned movie studio east of Hollywood. During World War II Coronet filled its coffers making training films for the U.S. Navy. Similar to current efforts to produce online instruction aligned with the Common Core Standards, Cornet produced classroom films aligned with the textbook curriculum of schools. McGraw-Hill publishers entered the classroom film industry in 1946 (Alexander, 2010, pp. 29–31, 109).

In 1958 federal money expanded the education film industry. Similar to other parts of what would become the education-industrial complex, the education film industry had formed a trade association in 1943—Education Film Library Association. In 1958, the education film industry lobbied Congress to ensure funding for education films and money for schools to purchase audiovisual equipment. In the forefront of the lobbying effort was former Presidential candidate Adlai Stevenson who was on the board of Encyclopedia Britannica Films and would become its chairman in 1959. The lobbying was successful and the 1958 National Defense Education Act created under its Title VII a New Education Media program and provided funds for the purchase of equipment. This federal legislation was followed by the 1965 Elementary and Secondary Education Act which also provided funds for audiovisual equipment (Alexander, 2010, pp. 38–47).

The result of federal funding was a growth in the number of classroom film producers and an increase in their profits. During the first year of funding by the Elementary and Secondary Education Act, Encyclopedia Britannica Films' revenues increased from $10 million to $30 million. It was estimated that after the 1958 and 1965 federal legislation the total domestic market for education films included 3,000 public and private schools and libraries. Geoff Alexander writes, "Weston Woods Films' Morton Schindel recalls paying more money in taxes after the first year of ESEA funding than the company had made during the previous ten years" (2010, p. 41).

By the 1980s, classroom films began to be replaced by digital media and classroom television. The classroom film industry reflected what was becoming a tradition where for-profit industries would lobby government for financial support for the development and sale of their products. As digital classroom materials replaced classroom films their producers also recognized that lobbying government could result in financial support for development and the purchase by schools of hardware and software. Also, classroom films accustomed educators to the idea of edutainment.

Bringing Edutainment Advertising into the Home

Radio and television edutainment exposed children to advertising linking the curricularization of the home to a large number of noneducation products including toys, clothing items, and food. Early commercial radio and television was opposed by many educators. In the 1930s there was a debate between owners of radio companies and educators over the control of the airwaves. Would edutainment be accompanied by advertising directed at children?

Educators argued for radio being controlled by education institutions at government expense. In 1933, it was reported that over 40,000 schools actually held student debates about the value of the British system involving government funding of radio and American radio based on advertising (*Variety*, 1933). The radio industry claimed that commercial programming funded by advertising fostered a democratic culture by allowing listeners to vote for the type of culture they wanted by turning the radio knob to their favorite programs. Operated as a business, industry leaders argued, commercial radio responded to the choices made by listeners.

In 1930 the National Committee on Education by Radio was organized with representatives from 11 major national education organizations, including the National Education Association, the National Catholic Education Association, the American Council on Education, the National Association of State Universities, and the National Council of State Superintendents of Education. Joy Elmer Morgan, chair of the Committee, declared, "You will discover that the advertising agency is taking the place of the mother, the father, the teacher, the pastor, the priest, in determining the attitudes of children" (Morgan, 1934, p. 29). Morgan worried about the effect on the United States of a generation raised on commercial media. "No one knows what will happen," she warned, "when this country comes into the hands of those who have been exposed to the propaganda of the money changers and to the debasing material which they have broadcast into the lives of the people" (Morgan, 1934, p. 30).

In response, broadcasting companies claimed edutainment could be better served by commercial radio. At the 1934 NEA Annual meeting, Merlin H. Aylesworth, president of the National Broadcasting Corporation (NBC), spoke on "Radio as a Means of Public Enlightenment" (Aylesworth, 1934). Aylesworth contended that radio had joined the church, home, and school as a source of public enlightenment. Using questionable numbers, Aylesworth claimed that 50% of network radio was education. William Paley, president of Columbia Broadcasting System (CBS), claimed that CBS devoted 2,207 hours to education programming or edutainment during the first 9 months of 1934. Paley named CBS's "American School of the Air" and "Church of the Air" as education radio programs (Paley, 1934, p. 14). Paley defended edutainment by commercial broadcasters by claiming it could turn leisure time into education time. Paley stated, "We conceive of education by radio not in the narrow classical sense, but in the broadest humanitarian meaning. Nor, in our democratic society, is culture merely a matter of learning the difference between Bach and Beethoven ... but it is equally a knowledge of how to rear a family in health and happiness—or to spend leisure wisely and well" (Paley, 1934, p. 18).

Educators on the National Committee on Education by Radio believed that intellectual leaders should determine what was "good" or "best" for the education of the general public. On the other hand, leaders in the radio industry justified their control by claiming that if education by radio were to be effective it had to be packaged as entertainment that appealed to the masses. In other words, commercial broadcasters argued for the value of advertised sponsored edutainment.

Edutainment with advertising became the broadcasting norm for radio and later television. However, complaints about the effect of advertising on children occurred along with praise for edutainment programming. In the 1930s, Harold Milligan, chair of the Women's National Radio Committee of the National Council of Women, charged advertisers with exploiting children as consumers. Urging parents to counter the work of advertisers, she reported, "Some parents have met the box-top' problem by suggesting that if the child wants the prize offered for sending in a certain number of box tops, he pay for the package out of his own allowance" (Milligan, 1938, pp. 258–259). At the same time advertising was criticized, Women's National Radio Committee gave an award for CBS radio's edutainment historical program *Wilderness Road*. Some independent groups actually sponsored edutainment programming such as the American Legion Auxiliary support of a radio dramatization of James Adams's *The Epic of America* and offered prizes for the best children's essay on "What the 'Epic of America' Has Taught Me About the Future of America" (Milligan, 1938, p. 261).

Edutainment and advertising were already closely linked when television made its appearance in American homes after World War II. By this time, high school had become a mass institution resulting in the creation of a new consumer market for radio and television ads. Marketers coined the term *teenager* for high school students and *Seventeen* magazine advertised to the potential teenage market with slogans, such as "When Is a Girl Worth $11,690,499" (Schrum, 1998, p. 143).

In the 1950s children and teenagers were bombarded with television commercials on programs criticized for their lack of educational value. The result was a major change in children's education television after President John F. Kennedy's appointee to the Federal Communications Commission (FCC) Newton Minow in 1961 declared television "a vast wasteland." He described this wasteland as populated by "a procession of games shows, violence, participation shows, formula comedies.... And most of all, boredom." In part, Minow was reacting to an image of housewives ruining the minds of American children as TV became a baby sitter. Television was considered by Minow and others as a source of intellectual pap for the masses. Child care advocate Dr. Benjamin Spock wrote President Kennedy that instead of television instilling virtue in the citizen, "there is the constant search for the commonest level of taste in passive entertainment ... used, in turn, to sell goods, in a manner which breeds insincerity and cynicism, and which appeals always to more gratification" (Baugham, 1985, p. 33). Writing in the *Saturday Review,* critic Robert Lewis Shayon expressed disgust at a 1958 episode of *Leave It to Beaver* where the main character was upset at a school IQ test that accidentally classified him as a genius. "Beaver" was portrayed as shunning the title of genius. For Shayon, this was another example of television appealing to the masses by deprecating the intellect (Baugham, 1985, p. 33).

A result of this criticism was the creation of the noncommercial Corporation for Public Broadcasting and its model children's edutainment program *Sesame Street.* Prior to Minow's speech support had been growing for federal financing of education television. During the 1950s in another illustration of the linkages between foundations and federal policies, the Ford Foundation promoted education television and was, in part, responsible for the section of the National Education Defense Education Act which provided funds for "Research and Experimentation in More Effective Utilization of Television, Radio, Motion Pictures, and related Media for Education Purposes" (Spring, 1992, pp. 231–242).

In 1965, the Carnegie Corporation established the Carnegie Commission on Education Television whose work led to the Public Broadcasting Act of 1967 which funded the Public Broadcasting Service (PBS) and National Public Radio (NPR). Referring to the education potential of TV, the Commission's 1967 report asserted: "Important as this can be for adults, the informal education potential of Public Television is greatest of all for children" (Carnegie Commission on Education Television, 1967, p. 95). The Commission suggested that television focus on preparing preschool children for formal education. "Public Television programs," the report urged, "should give great attention to the informal education needs of preschool children, particularly to interest and help children whose intellectual and cultural preparation might otherwise be less than adequate" (Carnegie Commission on Education Television, 1967, p. 95). As a result of funding from the Carnegie Corporation, *Sesame Street* premiered on PBS in 1969 followed by *Mister Rogers' Neighborhood* and *Reading Rainbow.* PBS promised a new era of noncommercial edutainment on television. In 1993, PBS combined its edutainment under the brand name PBS Kids.

After the 1995 Congressional cuts in funding PBS was forced to reinvent itself. In 1998, PBS began adding promotional spots for commercial sponsors. PBS executives referred to the "new PBS" with the theme of "Doing good while doing well" (Linn, 2004). Seeking commercial sponsors for PBS Kids' programming a deal was reached with the Mills Corporation, a developer of shopping malls. The company's malls were trademarked as "Shoppertainment." Shoppertainment met edutainment when PBS began putting PBS Kids Pavilions in the Mills Corporation's malls. For the Mills Corporation the PBS Kids Pavilions served the function of attracting retail stores and customers to its malls. PBS earned royalties from the Mills Corporation's use of its logo and creative designs. PBS Kids claimed "we're not selling anything but [a] learn-ing message" (Linn, 2004, p. 47). Psychiatrist Susan Linn criticized PBS Kids' continuing assertion that it is noncommercial when its programming con-tains commercial messages. She writes, "For parents fielding pleas for Chicken Dance Elm and trips to Chuck E. Cheese (thanks to the PBS program "Clifford the Red Dog"), there's not much difference" (Linn, 2004, p. 47).

Children under 2 were exposed to the commercializing influence of tele-vision when in 1997 the BBC began showing *Teletubbies* which, according to British researchers into the effect of advertising on children, "opened up new opportunities for selling toys and associated material to ever younger age groups" (Gunter, Oates, & Blades, 2005, p. 2). After PBS aired the *Teletubbies* it began working with Microsoft to develop software and video products. Linn claims, "Teletubbies helped usher in the transformation of babies into a viable market for videos and computer software" (Linn, 2004, p. 53).

A 2012 visit to the Amazon website reveals the range of products sold through licensing agreements between PBS and other companies to use the brand names associated with *Teletubbies*, PBS Kids, and *Sesame Street*. Amazon offered 92 products after a search for "Teletubbies dolls" (Amazon, 2012a). These products are not cheap. For $159.99 parents can purchase for their infants a "TellyTummy Teletubbies—lala Doll Toy" (Amazon, 2012d) and for $149.99 a "Tomy Teletubbies Dance with Me Teletubby lala Doll Toy" (Amazon, 2012e). The TellyTummy Doll is described as: "Soft plush Teletubbies characters with a moving 'TV screen' in their tummies. Touch the hand and the aerial magically lights up while the TV screen shows all their favorite things! Also features fun character sounds and giggles" (Amazon, 2012d). The Tomy Teletubbies Dance Doll is described as "Teletubbies are brought to life through music, dancing with their distinctive Teletubby dance style just like on TV!" (Amazon, 2012e). A search for *Sesame Street* on Amazon produced 2,735 results with the most expensive being "Kermit the Frog Photo Puppet Replica" by *Master Replicas* for $1,500 (Amazon, 2012b). For $249.99 parents can buy their children a "Sesame Street Elmo Room in Box 5 Pc. Set Includes; Bed, Toy Organizer, Table and 2 Chairs" (Amazon, 2012c).

The PBS Kids website has a link to PBS Parents which has a link to PBS Kids Shop. Blocks, an original edutainment product for the home, are sold through the PBS Kids Shop as "A Foundation for Imagination the Creative Way with PBS Kids Exploration Blocks" with prices ranging from $29.99 to $39.99 (PBS Kids Shop, 2012a). Each children's edutainment program on PBS offers its own exclusive line of toys, games, videos, and even clothing. For instance in the shop for *Sid the Science Kid* parents can buy apparel with the show's logo including pajamas, sweat shirts, T-shirts, and tote bags. A "Sid the Science Kid 3-Piece Pajama Set" costs $14.97 (PBS Kids Shop—Sid the Science Kid, 2012b). You can even shop for clothing by age cohort: toddler, youth, and adult.

The PBS Teachers website offers DVDs for classroom use of programs originally shown on PBS. The DVD sales exemplify edutainment links between the home and the school. Listed as their best sellers are DVDs, such as *Nova: The Unknown World* ($17.99), *God in America: How Religious Liberty Shaped America* ($24.99), and *Richard Lavoie: It's So Much Work to Be Your Friend: Helping the Learning Disabled Child Find Social Success* ($49.95) (Shop PBS Educational Media, 2012a). The PBS Teacher website allows the user to shop by grade level, subject, or interest. Under "interest" the user is given many choices including "Educator's Top Picks" which includes *Naturally Obsessed: The Making of a Scientist*—DVD ($44.95); *The Motivation Breakthrough*—softcover book ($16.00); and *Odd Girl Out: The Hidden Culture of Aggression in Girls*—book ($14.00) (PBS Educational Media Educator's Top Picks, Shop 2012).

PBS Kids is also linked to government education policies highlighting the interconnections between media, government education policies, and for-profit companies; those companies licensed to use logos and characters from PBS edutainment shows. PBS is participating in developing digital games aligned with the federal government's stress on science, technology, engineering, mathematics subjects (STEM) in schools and funded by a grant from the U.S. Department of Education. In 2012, PBS Kids announced:

> PBS KIDS, in partnership with the Corporation for Public Broadcasting (CPB) is participating in the 2012 National STEM Video Game Challenge, an annual competition to motivate interest in STEM (science, technology, engineering and math) learning among America's youth by tapping into students' natural passion for playing and making video games. The contest is open to four different categories: Middle School students (5th grade–8th grade), High School Students, College Students and Teachers/Educators. Participants who wish to produce games as part of the PBS KIDS stream are encouraged to develop games for children ages 4–8 that focus on early math skills. This site is designed to provide information and resources to help guide game production. This project is part of the Ready To Learn Initiative, and funded by a grant from the U.S Department of Education.
>
> (PBS KIDS Stream, 2012c)

Among the contest's sponsors are Microsoft's XBOX 360, AMD Foundation, and the Entertainment Software Association. All three of these sponsors have an economic stake in developing edutainment games to be sold to schools. Microsoft's XBOX 360 would economically benefit from any edutainment game that could be played on its gaming platform which could be sold to schools. The AMD Foundation is one of those foundations similar to the Pearson Foundation that are created by companies to influence the sales of the parent company's products. The AMD Foundation gives its mission as:

- Provide opportunities for future generations to learn critical science, technology, engineering, and mathematics (STEM) skills and life skills
- Enrich AMD communities worldwide through employee engagement, matching gifts. and disaster relief programs (AMD Foundation, 2012b).

The parent company AMD designs "vivid digital experiences" with the claim that "AMD's graphics and computing technologies power a variety of solutions including PCs, game consoles and the servers that drive the Internet and businesses" (AMD, 2012a). And the Entertainment Software Association represents the economic interests of the digital game industry.

In summary, the one hope of separating edutainment from advertising on television was the Corporation for Public Broadcasting. When edutainment on PBS became commercial in the 1990s it duplicated the patterns we have described in other parts of the education–industrial complex. For-profit industries became involved through licensing of program logos and characters and sales through toy stores and PBS Kids which turned the home into a learning site for school and a site for selling edutainment products and associated DVDs, clothing, toys, books, and software. The Corporation for Public Broadcasting also receives federal government money to promote government education policies associated with STEM and with for-profit companies hoping to sell hardware and digital games to schools. In addition, through its promotion of gaming for STEM, the Corporation for Public Broadcasting is linked to the trade group Entertainment Software Association represents the economic interests of those wanting to sell edutainment games to public schools and the home.

Edutainment Media: Learning Software and Education Games

Developed in the 1970s, learning software was marketed to parents as education and to children as entertainment. However, similar to movies, producers of learning software saw schools as a source of revenue and state and federal governments as a source of financial support. Besides the actual software families and schools needed hardware, such as computers and gaming consoles. Today, many software products are adapted to gaming consoles sold by Sony, Microsoft, and Nintendo.

Learning software can be purchased at retail outlets, such as Wal-Mart, Costco, Best Buy, Toys "R" Us, Office Depot, and various computer stores. Learning software is marketed to parents as educational and to children as entertainment. Cultural historian Mizuko Ito argues, regarding learning software, "In marketing materials, parents are told that these products will ensure that their children will internalize the dispositions and cultural capital necessary for competitive academic success" (Ito, 2009, p. 43).

Government funding was behind the early development of learning software. In 1973 the State of Minnesota funded the Minnesota Education Computing

Corporation (MECC) which became a public corporation in 1985. MECC created and sold popular edutainment software including *MathBlaster* and the 1971 adventure learning game *Oregon Trail*, a new type of game that added the element of role-playing to learning games. Eventually The Learning Company acquired *Oregon Trail* and the very popular learning game *Carmen Sandiego* (Ito, 2009, pp. 36–43).

Pioneers of software learning games were often caught between a visionary goal of increasing children's opportunities to learn and the desire to earn money. One of the early and largest creators of software learning games was The Learning Company, founded in 1979 by Ann Piestrup (now McCormick). Her visionary goal was, "I want every child in the world to be able to get the basic skills they need to function thoughtfully…. We want lifelong learning for the entire world" (Ito, 2009, p.30). In 1998, The Learning Company was sold to Mattel for $3.8 billion highlighting the triumph of consumerism in learning software (Ito, 2009, p. 30).

Learning software became a big business with larger companies buying up software products from smaller companies. In 2001, the Learning Company was bought by Riverdeep, which was then bought by the publishing giant Houghton Mifflin Harcourt in 2006 (Houghton Mifflin Harcourt, 2011). Some of The Learning Company's products were adapted to other media such as movies and television. The Learning Company provides this history of its connections with other media:

- 1991–1996 *Where in the World is Carmen Sandiego?* Airs on PBS
- 1991—Series of Carmen Sandiego *Choose Your Own Adventure* books are written and published.
- 1993—PBS Series *Where in the World is Carmen Sandiego?* wins the George Foster Peabody Award for Excellence.
- 1994–1998—*Where on Earth is Carmen Sandiego?* animated series airs on Fox and other stations.
- 1996–1998—*Where in Time is Carmen Sandiego?* airs on PBS
- 1997–1994—*Carmen Sandiego Mystery* books are written and published
- 2004—*Carmen Sandiego: The Secret of the Stolen Drums*—Gamecube, Xbox & Playstation 2
- 2008—*Where in the World is Carmen Sandiego?* mobile adaptation is released by Gameloft
- Planetarium Movies: There were 2 Planetarium movies featuring Carmen produced. (Learning Company, 2011)

Knowledge Adventure is another example of the evolution of the learning software industry. The company began in the late 1980s with JumpStart which today is marketed as an online adventure-learning game. In the late 1990s, Knowledge Adventure merged with another education software firm Davidson & Associates which had bought *MathBlaster* and was developing education software for the toy giant Fisher-Price. The role of venture capitalism in developing learning games is contained in the financial history of Knowledge Adventure after 1996:

> Knowledge Adventure was purchased by Cendant in 1996 and acquired by Vivendi in 1998. In 2004, Knowledge Adventure spun out from Vivendi, led by Venture Investors. In September 2004, Knowledge Adventure completed a Series A financing led by venture capitalist firms Telesoft Partners and Azure Capital. In March of 2008, Knowledge Adventure completed a Series B financing, also led by venture capitalist firms Telesoft Partners and Azure Capital. These infusions of capital support Knowledge Adventure's continued innovation and expansion from education software to the new frontier of children's learning— adventure-based 3D virtual worlds.
>
> (Knowledge Adventure, 2011)

Cendant's 1996 purchase of Davidson & Associates made Knowledge Adventure part of a global conglomerate of companies that included the hotel chains Ramada, Howard Johnson's, Avis Rent-a-Car, and Day's Inn (Vivendi, 2011).

Also, software producers realized that profits could be made from selling learning apps for smart phones and iPads. For instance, an app for JumpStart is available through Apple's iTunes store with the description: "JumpStart Preschool Magic of Learning 1, an application designed for little hands and big imaginations! Your preschooler is invited to join Frankie the Dog on a magical learning adventure that will show just how fun learning can be" (JumpStart, 2011). In 2011, BlackBerry offered 347 education apps ranging from foreign language instruction to teaching math to toddlers (BlackBerry, 2011).

Today, many producers of learning software and games receive financial support and encouragement from the federal government. In President Barack Obama's administration, the U.S. Department of Education advocated the use of video games to promote national curriculum standards and STEM subjects (Spring, 2011, pp. 118–150). The 2010 U.S. Department of Education's National Education Technology Plan *Transforming American Education: Learning Powered by Technology* advocates the use of digital game design in schools (U.S. Office of Educational Technology, 2010). The Plan asserts, "Interactive technologies, especially games, provide immediate performance feedback so that players always know how they are doing. As a result, they are highly engaging to students and have the potential to motivate students to learn" (U.S. Office of Education Technology, 2010, p. xvii). The Plan's "Model of Learning, Powered by Technology" recommends "engaging environments and tools for understanding ... [in which] game-based courses use features familiar to game players to teach core subject content, such as history" (U.S. Office of Education Technology, 2010, p. 11). The plan also suggests the use of "education computer games" to teach literacy to preschoolers (U.S. Office of Education Technology,

2010, p. 21). Even research into using games for assessment of students is recommended in the Plan:

> Conduct research and development that explores how embedded assessment technologies, such as simulations, collaboration environments, *virtual worlds, games* [emphasis added], and cognitive tutors, can be used to engage and motivate learners while assessing complex skills.
>
> (U.S. Office of Education Technology, 2010, p. 37)

The National Education Technology Plan asserts that assessment can be done with edutainment games and virtual reality. The website for Virtual Performance Assessment provides this explanation of its goals:

> Science inquiry process skills are difficult to assess with multiple choice or constructed-response paper-and-pencil tests. This project will develop three single-user immersive three-dimensional (3-D) environments to assess middle school students' science inquiry skills. The investigators will *align these assessments to National Science Education Standards (NSES) and will develop the assessments to serve as a standardized component of an accountability program* [emphasis added].
>
> (Virtual Performance Assessment, 2011)

Foundations are backing the government's efforts to promote learning games. In 2010, the same year that the National Education Technology Plan was released, the Gates foundation sponsored a conference whose purpose, as described by the Foundation, was to discuss the development of games that would be aligned with the Common Core Standards for public schools. Attending were members of the commercial gaming industry. The Gates Foundation website states the conference was convened for the "purpose of creating a framework for developing game standards and a toolkit for developers to increase effectiveness of games in terms of alignment with the Common Core Standards, design principles, assessment, and other needed key elements (Gates Foundation, 2011).

The history of learning software parallels that of the movie industry with edutainment first being sold to the public and then to schools. In the next section, we explore this phenomenon with regard to Apple's iPad.

The iPad Goes to School

The 2010 introduction of Apple's iPad was a marketing triumph that eventually resulted in Apple marketing the product to schools. WebDesignCore claims that the iPad was the fastest ever selling consumer device. Within one month of its release 450,000 iPads had been sold with 3.5 million iPad Apps and 600,000 iBooks downloaded. Why did people buy the iPad? Fifty-six percent of purchasers said for entertainment while 42% gave the reason as the "cool factor" in owning one (WDCore Editorial, 2011).

Shortly after the iPad was introduced Apple held workshops with textbook publishers and teachers and school administrators on its educational use. Within one year of its introduction Apple offered 5,400 education applications with 1,000 being available for free. Houghton Mifflin Harcourt developed an iPad algebra program that includes a video on solving problems, individualized assessments, and practice problems (Hu, 2011).

Public schools using federal funds from the Race to the Top's competitive grant program began buying iPads. Educators acted like any other consumer gripped by the excitement of purchasing a new product. Millburn, New Jersey principal Scott Wolfe declared, "I think this could very well be the biggest thing to hit school technology since the overhead projector" (Hu, 2011). A Scottsdale, Arizona principal asserted, "Of all the devices out there, the iPad has the most star power for kids" (Hu, 2011).

Using federal money educators within the first year of production began buying iPads for their classrooms. These purchases were made despite the shortfall in funding that was causing many school districts to layoff teachers. A year after the release of the first iPad, the *New York Times* reported the following education purchases:

- New York's Roslyn High School hopes to provide iPads to all 1,100 of its students.
- New York City public schools have ordered more than 2,000 iPads.
- Two hundred Chicago public schools applied for 23 district-financed iPad grants totaling $450,000.
- Virginia Department of Education is overseeing a $150,000 iPad initiative to replace history and Advanced Placement biology textbooks at 11 schools.
- Six middle schools in four California cities (San Francisco, Long Beach, Fresno, and Riverside) are teaching the first iPad-only algebra course, developed by Houghton Mifflin Harcourt.
- Kindergartners are getting their hands on iPads in Scottsdale, Arizona in a lab containing 36 iPads. (Hu, 2011)

By 2012 there were 1.5 million iPads in use in education and 20,000 education apps in the iTunes store (Tomassini, 2012). Apple's website "Apple in Education" declares that the iPad is: "The device that changed everything is now changing the classroom" (Apple, 2011a). The sources of profit for Apple are not only the actual sale of iPads to schools but also the sale of apps from Apple's App Store and the sale of Multi-Touch textbooks. The sales pitch to school districts, particularly those with budget problems, is that iPad books will save money:

> Budget constraints force schools to use the same books year after year, long after the content is out of date. But with textbooks on iPad, students

can get a brand-new version each year—for a fraction of the price of a paper book. They can discover and download iBooks textbooks from the Textbook section of the iBookstore directly to iPad.

(Apple, 2011a)

A similar message appears in the textbook section of the iBookstore: "Paper textbooks are expensive to produce and expensive for schools to buy. Which is why schools are forced to use a book for several years to make the finances work" (Apple, 2011c).

Apples App Store offers iPad learning apps as edutainment. Its bestselling app, "How Rocket Learned to Read" is sold as edutainment: "Based on the best-selling picture book, this playful app is loaded with animation and interactive games to promote reading" (Apple, 2011b). It's "Math Bingo" app is also sold as edutainment: "Addition, subtraction, multiplication, and division have never been more fun. Get five Bingo Bugs in a row by correctly solving math problems" (Apple, 2011b). Also the science app "Britannica Kids: Volcanoes" is marketed as edutainment: "Learn about the world's major volcanoes while having fun with memory matching and puzzles" (Apple, 2011b). For second language learning Hangman Pro HD is sold as edutainment based on the classic Hangman game: "Think you have a good vocabulary? Find out with an app that captures the classic Hangman experience, right down to the chalk dust" (Apple, 2011b).

Some apps are sold as preparation for college entrance exams making Apple another company involved in making money from test preparation. An example of a test prep app is "AP US History 5 Steps to a 5": "This five-step study plan with strategies, flash cards, and tests will help you prepare for the AP U.S. History exam" (Apple, 2011b).

In 2012, Apple announced that it was forming a partnership with Pearson, McGraw-Hill, and Houghton Mifflin Harcourt to produce interactive textbooks that would be sold through Apple's iBook store at $14.99 or less. Apple would receive 30% of the revenue for each book sold. However, *Education Week* reports that textbook revenues would not decrease even with publishers giving a 30% cut to Apple. These electronic textbooks, of course, could be updated every year if school districts are willing to spend the money. What this alliance means is that Apple will gain revenue from both the textbooks sold through its iBook store and from sales of iPads to schools (Tomassini, 2012).

Paid for by local school districts, Apple's iPad and apps become another part of the education-industrial complex. However as school people rushed to buy iPads and apps for their classrooms, some educators questioned the value of Apple's product. *New York Times* reporter Winnie Hu wrote, "Elliot Soloway, an engineering professor at the University of Michigan, and Cathie Norris, a technology professor at the University of North Texas, question whether school officials have become so enamored with iPads that they have overlooked less costly options, like smartphones that offer similar benefits at a fraction of the iPad's base cost of about $500" (Hu, 2011).

Edutainment and Toddlers

As parents worry about their children's success in schools and the home is curricularized, toddlers become a market for edutainment through new technology. For instance, iPhones are now the toy of choice for toddlers. *New York Times* reporter Hilary Stout asserts, "But just as adults have a hard time putting down their iPhones, so the device is now the Toy of Choice — akin to a treasured stuffed animal—for many 1-, 2- and 3-year-olds" (Stout, 2010). According to Stout, Apple has built its reputation on creating products that are simple and intuitive. Consequently, it is easy for children as young as 2 to operate the phone.

Software producers quickly learned that apps could be created for children that would turn smart phones and iPads into edutainment. For instance, an app for JumpStart is available through Apple's iTunes store with the description: "JumpStart Preschool Magic of Learning 1, an application designed for little hands and big imaginations! Your preschooler is invited to join Frankie the Dog on a magical learning adventure that will show just how fun learning can be" (JumpStart Preschool, 2011a, 2011b). BlackBerry offers 347 education apps ranging from foreign language instruction to teaching math to toddlers. There are a whole host of apps for iPhones ranging from reference works for older students to teaching foreign languages to toddlers. With smart phone apps, children carry the school in their hands. The home is curricularized and with it a child's entire life. Education apps are marketed as edutainment; learning for adults and fun for kids. For instance a BlackBerry app is advertised as:

> TVO's Polka Dot Shorts is a sequence matching game for kids aged 2–5 that supports the early learning and kindergarten math curriculum and has been teacher and classroom tested. It will keep them entertained, help them to learn, and keep your BlackBerry device safely locked—your little one can't send emails or make phone calls.
>
> (BlackBerry, 2011)

Some apps are legitimized by the claim that they are teacher and classroom tested. The school is invoked to convince parents of the worth of buying the app. More importantly, the lines between school, home, and play disappear. As their favorite toy is carried in their pockets or held in their hands, the toddler lives in an integrated future of school, home, and work.

Major toy manufacturers sell online games as edutainment. Fisher-Price, owned by Mattel, one of the world's largest toy manufacturers, carries online games with the message that edutainment prepares children for school. Their online games are not only for toddlers but also for infants. Edutainment games for infants include "Laugh & Learn Animal Fun Game" and "Laugh & Learn Peek-a-Boo! Game." Toddler edutainment games include "Laugh & Learn Learning About Opposites Game" and "The ABC's Zoo Learning Game." Reflecting the curricularization of the home parents are urged by Fisher-Price:

> If you have some free time, you might find it's beneficial to get online and play a few of these learning games yourself before sitting down at the computer with your child. You know your child best; having a preview will help you determine which online learning activities are most appropriate for your infant, toddler, or preschooler's stage of development … and which games are so much fun your child will want to play them again and again!
>
> (Fisher-Price Online Games & Activities, 2012)

In and out of school edutainment becomes another product that is promoted as a panacea for education. Parents and educators rush to buy the latest technological products that promise success for students in school. The home becomes another source of revenue for the education-industrial complex. As the home is curricularized it uses the same education products, such as the iPad and apps, as the school.

The News Media and Education

News media play a dual role in education. Faced with declining revenues from newspaper and advertising sales, newspapers are seeking other revenue through expansion into the education business and the broadcasting of live video and video ads on the Web. In addition, news media disseminate education news to the public and, consequently, may play a role in shaping public opinion regarding education policies (Stelter, 2012).

In previous chapters we discussed some of the involvement of news media in the education business. In chapter 3 we discussed Rupert Murdoch's News Corporation's acquisition of Wireless Generation as the company's first step into the education business. At the time of purchase, Murdoch expressed his belief in the potential of the education market, "We see a $500 billion sector in the U.S. alone," he said, "that is waiting desperately to be transformed by big breakthroughs that extend the reach of great teaching" (Quillen, 2010). In chapter 4 we discussed the *Washington Post*'s acquisition of the test preparation company Kaplan and its expansion into higher education and online learning through K12.

The *New York Times* has also entered the education business through the creation of the "Knowledge Network" which it describes as offering "a wide range of distinctive adult and continuing education opportunities, including online courses, programs and Webcasts. Some of our programs are offered directly by *The Times*, while others are presented in collaboration with universities, colleges and other educational institutions" (2012a).

To offer online courses the *New York Times* uses the for-profit online platform service of Epsilen Global Learning Environment. Similar to other complex education–business relationships discussed in this book, the Epsilen Global Learning Environment links the *New York Times* to other education businesses including the testing and publishing giant Pearson. Besides the *New York Times*, the company is partnered with SunGard Higher Education, MERLOT, Blackboard Collaborate, Intern U, Oracle, Pearson, and The Center for Strategic and International Studies (CSIS) (Epsilen, 2012a).

Similar to Rupert Murdoch's entrance into the education business through the purchase of Wireless Generation, the New York Times purchased majority ownership of Epsilen (Epsilen, 2012b). In 2012, using Epsilen Global Learning Environment, the *New York Times* offered a wide range of courses ranging from those in an arts and culture program to a wine program (*New York Times*, Online Learning, 2012). Some of the courses are linked to degrees, credit, and noncredit courses offered by the City University of New York, Ball State University, and the University of Toronto. Specifically, the courses offered in conjunction with the City University of New York are in health information management and information systems; those offered at Ball State University are in media studies; and those offered with the University of Toronto are in creative writing (*New York Times* Knowledge Network, 2012a, p. 9).

The *New York Times* also offers a postbaccalaureate teacher education program for elementary, secondary, and special education in cooperation with the online Rio Salado College. Rio Salado is one of 10 community colleges in Phoenix, Arizona. The online college's postbaccalaureate teaching degree claims to lead to a teaching certificate in most states:

> The Post-Baccalaureate Teacher Preparation Programs, approved by the Arizona State Board of Education, are designed for working adults who wish to earn a teaching certificate and enter the teaching profession. If you already have a four year degree from a regionally accredited post-secondary institution, or are about to receive one, these programs enable you to obtain a teaching certificate in early childhood, elementary, secondary or special education that is accepted in the majority of states besides Arizona.
>
> (Rio Salado College, 2012)

As news corporations expanded into the education business, they came under criticism for their limited coverage of education policies. A 2009 Brookings Institute study concluded: "despite the importance of media coverage for public understanding of education, news reporting on schools is scant ... there is virtually no national coverage of education" (West, Whitehurst, & Dionne, 2009, p. 1). The study found that in 2009 "only 1.4 percent of national news coverage from television, newspapers, news Web sites, and radio dealt with education" (West et al., 2009, p. 1). This was actually more than 2007 and 2008 when only 1.0 and .7%, respectively, of national news covered education issues. Most of this reporting has little to do with education policy issues. The report asserts, "This makes it difficult for the public to follow the issues at stake in our education debates and to understand how to improve school performance" (West et al., 2009, p. 1).

The Brookings' report suggests financial causes to the general decline in reporting in all areas besides education. Television news and newspapers cannot afford the staff required to assign reporters to education issues and to cover schools. The report recommends that: "Newspapers and other media outlets that have cut back on education reporting should reconsider these decisions both on public interest grounds, and also because there is widespread interest in the issues surrounding education" (West et al., 2009, p. 3). Also it recommends that: "Foundations and non-profit organizations should focus on developing alternative forms of education coverage both nationally and locally" (West et al., 2009, p. 3).

There are also problems when media report on education. Cynthia Gerstl-Pepin studied the 2000 presidential election when Gallup polls indicating public interest in education caused politicians to focus on education issues. From her perspective how media functions is important for maintaining an informed electorate: "Because most voters increasingly use the media as their primary source of information, their role in electoral politics is key to the functioning of our democracy" (Gerstl-Pepin, 2002, p. 37).

How did media respond to the 2000 election focus on education? Gerstl-Pepin concluded that reporters focused on candidates' positions on education. Seldom, if ever, did the media offer any analysis of what politicians said were the education problems and solutions. She wrote,

> They turn to others to make those assessments as a result of the "veil of objectivity." Oftentimes, the candidates or their advisors or supporters are designated to represent their side of the debate.... Rather than informing the public, the media serve to represent the issues as framed by the candidates of the two main political parties.
>
> (Gerstl-Pepin, 2002, pp. 49–50)

One of her interesting examples of media's failure to inform the public about education issues was the controversy over test scores in Texas. Republican candidate George W. Bush claimed that he was the Texas "education governor." During the 2000 election, Gerstl-Pepin writes, national media just accepted Bush's claim of improving Texas schools as evidenced by higher student test scores. Gerstl-Pepin asserts, "There is no substantive proof that higher test scores will improve instruction, address racism and poverty, or lead to a stronger economy. All of these arguments overlook that social inequities are directly linked to school performance" (Gerstl-Pepin, 2002, p. 50). From her perspective real improvement in schools requires addressing, "Long-term, substantive changes such as addressing poverty, racism, and gender discrimination are rendered invisible in shortsighted campaign rhetoric" (Gerstl-Pepin, 2002, p. 50). The media's focus on superficial items like test scores, she claims, was uninformative. A critical media should have examined whether or not test scores were an indicator of school improvement or failure.

By merely mouthing the claims of politicians, Gerstl-Pepin argues, the media reduces public understanding of complex issues and prepares the public to accept simple remedies and test scores as an indication of quality. To exemplify the reductionist nature of media and political education discussion, Gerstl-Pepin quotes a letter written by a teacher to the *Los Angeles Times*:

> As I listened to the second debate on Wednesday night and heard George W. Bush's simplistic platitudes like "we won't leave any child behind" and Al Gore's "accountability for students and teachers," I was astounded at what a superficial understanding these "educated" men have of the work I do. There is no two-minute sound-bite answer to the myriad of education issues facing our communities—so don't give one!
>
> (Gerstl-Pepin, 2002, p. 50)

In summary, faced with declining revenues some newspaper companies, such as the *Washington Post*, News International, and the *New York Times*, have entered the education business through purchase of test prep companies, online schools, for-profit colleges, digital services to schools, and online courses. The result is to put these major news companies squarely into the education-industrial complex. Will these newspaper companies join other members of the education industry in pressing for more public money to be spent on for-profit education products and services? Under Rupert Murdoch's control News International sponsors the openly conservative Fox News. Will Fox News support government policies that enrich Murdoch's investments in the education industry? Or will the news media continue, as Gerstl-Pepin suggests, giving only superficial coverage of education issues and simply mouth the words of politicians. Of course, superficial coverage based on political rhetoric could result in persuading the public to support government funding of the education industry.

Conclusion: Profiting From Schools and Homes

Media companies followed the same path as many of the other education businesses discussed in this book. Sometimes with support from foundations, media companies sought increased revenues by selling edutainment to schools and the home. They have lobbied for and received government money. In search of new revenues newspaper companies, such as News International, *Washington*

Post, and the *New York Times*, have entered the education business while critics complain about the lack of in-depth reporting of education news.

As schools and homes embrace edutainment the home becomes curricularized. The marketing of edutainment follows a pattern first established by the movie industry where profits were sought by selling films to schools. This opened the door to public money being funneled from government funds to the movie industry. After World War II, lobbying by the classroom film industry contributed to government funding for the purchase of equipment and films with the passage of the 1958 National Defense Education Act and the 1965 Elementary and Secondary Education Act.

Foundations played a role in gaining government funding for education television. At first, edutainment on radio and television was accompanied by commercials. The Carnegie Commission on Education Television made possible noncommercial edutainment over PBS and NPR. After government budget cuts in the 1990s, PBS and PBS Kids succumbed to commercialization. The result was tying television edutainment to the sale of noneducational products such as clothing and food.

Today, the education-industrial complex is expanding with the sale of learning software and games along with the required hardware. Learning software started with a vision of improving education rather than making a profit. But this quickly changed as for-profit companies bought up makers of learning software. Like the movie industry, these companies saw sales to schools as an important source of revenue. Most recently this has been exemplified by Apple's efforts to sell its iPad and apps to schools. These efforts reproduce the pattern of for-profit companies seeking government funds for the development and sale of their products.

References

Alexander, G. (2010). *Academic films for the classroom: A history.* Jefferson, NC: McFarland.

Amazon. (2012a). *Teletubbies dolls.* Retrieved from http://www.amazon.com/gp/search/ref=sr_st_scat_phl_165793011?rh=n%3A165793011%2Ck%3Ateletubbies+dolls&sort=-price&keywords=teletubbies+dolls&ie=UTF8&qid=1328214602&scn=165793011&h=a389d34fe0ad4870b8186ba4a3c264beceda8a54

Amazon. (2012b). *Kermit the frog puppet replica.* Retrieved from http://www.amazon.com/Kermit-Frog-Photo-Puppet-Replica/dp/B000J680AM/ref=sr_1_1?s=toys-and-games&ie=UTF8&qid=1328279173&sr=1-1

Amazon. (2012c). *Sesame Street Elmo room in box 5 pc.* Retrieved from http://www.amazon.com/SESAME-STREET-ORGANIZER-ASSEMBLY-REQUIRED/dp/B001KZBMK6/ref=sr_1_3?s=toys-and-games&ie=UTF8&qid=1328279173&sr=1-3

Amazon. (2012d). *Tellytummy Teletubbies—La La doll toy.* Retrieved from http://www.amazon.com/Tellytummy-Teletubbies-Doll-Toy/dp/B003WUKQEK/ref=sr_1_1?s=toys-and-games&ie=UTF8&qid=1328214849&sr=1-1

Amazon. (2012e). *Tomy Teletubbies dance with me Teletubby lala doll toy.* Retrieved from http://www.amazon.com/Tomy-Teletubbies-Dance-Teletubby-Doll/dp/B002RJESPA/ref=sr_1_2?s=toys-and-games&ie=UTF8&qid=1328214849&sr=1-2

AMD. (2012a). *About AMD*. Retrieved from http://www.amd.com/us/aboutamd/Pages/AboutAMD.aspx

AMD. (2012b). *AMD foundation*. Retrieved from http://www.amd.com/us/aboutamd/corporate-information/corporate-responsibility/community/foundation/Pages/information.aspx

Apple. (2011a). *Apple in education*. Retrieved from http://www.apple.com/education/ipad/

Apple. (2011b). *Thousands of apps. Endless potential*. Retrieved from http://www.apple.com/education/apps/

Apple. (2011c). *iBooks textbooks for iPad*. Retrieved from http://www.apple.com/education/ibooks-textbooks/

Aylesworth, M. (1934). Radio as a means of public enlightenment. In National Education Association, *Proceedings* (pp. 99–102). Washington, DC: National Education Association.

Baugham, J. (1985). *Television's guardians: The FCC and the politics of programming, 1958–1967*. Knoxville: University of Tennessee Press.

BlackBerry. (2011). *Appworld: "TVOKids Polka Dot Shorts."* Retrieved from http://appworld.BlackBerry.com/webstore/content/26663?lang=en

Carnegie Commission on Education Television. (1967). *Public television: A program for action*. New York: Harper & Row.

Epsilen. (2012). *About*. Retrieved from Epsilen: http://corp.epsilen.com/about/

Fisher-Price. (2012). *Online games & activities*. Retrieved from http://www.fisher-price.com/fp.aspx?st=30&e=gameslanding&mcat=game_infant,game_toddler,game_preschool&site=us

Gates Foundation. (2011). *Grants*. Retrieved from http://www.gatesfoundation.org/Grants-2010/Pages/New-York-University-OPP1019503.aspx

Gerstl-Pepin, C. (2002). Cynthia I. GeMedia (mis)representations of education in the 2000 presidential election. *Education Policy, 16*, 37–55.

Graham, N. (1914). Discussion. In National Education Association, *Proceedings* (p. 746). Ann Arbor: National Education Association.

Gunter, B., Oates, C., & Blades, M. (2005). *Advertising to children on TV: Content, impact, and regulation*. Mahwah, NJ: Erlbaum.

Houghton Mifflin Harcourt. (2011). *Executive leadership*. Retrieved from http://www.hmhco.com/leadership.html

Hu, W. (2011, January 4). Math that moves: Schools embrace the iPad. Retrieved from http://www.nytimes.com/2011/01/05/education/05tablets.html?sq=iPad schools&st=nyt&scp=1&pagewanted=print

Ito, M. (2009). *Engineering play: A cultural history of children's software*. Cambridge, MA: MIT Press.

Joy, J. (1927). Motion pictures in their relation to the school child. In National Education Association, *Proceedings* (pp. 964–969). Washington, DC: National Education Association.

Judd, C. (1923). Report of Committee to Cooperate with National Education Association, *Proceedings* (pp. 243–244). Washington, DC: National Education Association.

JumpStart. (2011). Preschool magic of learning. Retrieved from http://ax.itunes.apple.com/us/app/jumpstart-preschool-magic/id395058540

Knowledge Adventure. (2011). Financing history. Retrieved from http://www.knowledgeadventure.com/CompanyInfo.htm

Learning Company, The (2011). *History of Carmen Sandiego brand*. Retrieved from http://carmensandiego.com/hmh/site/carmen/home/articles?article=2560

Linn, S. (2004). *Consuming kids: Protecting our children from the onslaught of marketing and advertising*. New York: Anchor Books.

Milligan, H. (1938). Mrs. Harold Milligan. In C. Marsh (Ed.), *Educational broadcasting 1937* (pp. 258–261). Chicago, IL: University of Chicago.

Morgan, J. (1934). A national culture: By-product or objective of national planning? In National Education Association, *Proceedings* (pp. 29–36). Washington, DC: National Education Association.

New York Times. (2012a). Knowledge network. Retrieved from http://www.nytimesknownow.com/

New York Times. (2012b). Take an online course with the *New York Times* and see where that course takes you. In *The New York Times Knowledge Network Winter and Summer 2012 Catalog.* New York: Author.

New York Times. (2012c). *About us.* Retrieved from http://www.nytimesknownow.com/index. php/about-us/

New York Times. (2012d). *All courses.* Retrieved from http://www.nytimesknownow.com/index. php/category/subject/all-courses/

Olesen, P. (1914). Discussion. In National Education Association, *Proceedings* (p. 747). Ann Arbor, MI: National Education Association.

Paley, W. (1934, October 17). Radio as a cultural force. *CBS Reference Library.* New York: CBS Reference Library.

PBS Educational Media, Shop. (2012). *PBS teacher shop.* Retrieved from http://teacher.shop.pbs. org/family/index.jsp?categoryId=3710164

PBS Educational Media, Shop. (2012). *Educator's top picks.* Retrieved from http://teacher.shop.pbs. org/family/index.jsp?categoryId=1411597&clickid=header&cp=1398013

PBS Kids Shop. (2012a). *Toy blocks.* Retrieved from http://pbskidstoys.shop.pbskids.org/toys-games/blocks.html?dir=desc&order=price

PBS Kids Shop. (2012b). *Shop—Sid the science kid.* Retrieved from http://sidscience.shop.pbskids. org/clothing.html

PBS KIDS (2012c). *2012 National STEM video game challenge.* Retrieved from http://pbskids.org/ stemchallenge/

Quillen, I. (2010, December 8). Rupert Murdoch moves into K-12 tech. market. *Education Week*, p. 16.

Rio Salado College. (2012). *Teacher education.* Retrieved from http://www.riosalado.edu/pro-grams/education/postbacc/Pages/default.aspx

Saunders, A. (1914). Motion pictures as an aid to education. In National Education Association, *Proceedings* (p. 744). Ann Arbor: National Education Association.

Schrum, K. (1998). Teena means business: Teenage girls' culture and "Seventeen Magazine," 1944–1950. In S. A. Inness (Ed.), *Delinquents and debutantes: Twentieth-century girls' cultures* (pp. 136–156). New York: New York University Press.

Sesame Street. (2012). *Sesame Street store.* Retrieved from http://store.sesamestreet.org/

Snedden, D. (1914). Discussion. In National Education Association, *Proceedings* (p. 746). Ann Arbor, MI: National Education Association.

Spring, J. (1992). *Images of American life: A history of ideological management in schools, movies, radio, and television.* Albany, NY: SUNY Press.

Spring, J. (2011). *The politics of American education.* New York: Routledge.

Stelter, B. (2012, February 6). Print news media go live with video programming. *New York Times*, pp. B1–2.

Stout, H. (2010, October). Toddlers' favorite toy: The iPhone. Retrieved from http://www. nytimes.com/2010/10/17/fashion/17TODDLERS.html?scp=1&sq=toddler+iphone&st= nyt

Tomassini, J. (2012, January 25). Apple unveils e-textbook strategy for K-12. *Education Week*, p. 8.

U.S. Department of Education. (2010). *National education technology plan 2010: Transforming Ameri-can education: Learning powered by technology.* Washington, DC: U.S. Department of Education.

Variety. (1933, August 29). British vs. American radio slant, debate theme in 40, 000 schools. *Variety*, p. 1.

Virtual Performance Assessment (2011). Using immersive technology to assess science inquiry learning. Retrieved from http://vpa.gse.harvard.edu/about/

Vivendi. (2011). *Group.* Retrieved from http://www.vivendi.com/vivendi/-Group

WDCore Editorial. (2011). *A brief history of the iPad-infographic.* Retrieved from http://www.web-designcore.com/2011/04/30/a-brief-history-of-the-ipad-%E2%80%93-infographic/

West, D., Whitehurst, G., & Dionne, E. (2009). *Invisible: 1.4 percent coverage for education is not enough.* Washington, DC: Brookings Institute.

8

CONCLUSION

"A Nation at Risk" Redux

In 2011, the Occupy Wall Street (OWS) movement was a major news story. On the surface, it seemed to be a protest directed against "big money" individuals and corporations. Its theme was "the 99% versus the 1%" since the protesters saw themselves as individuals who represented 99% of the income earners versus the top 1%. Its popularity grew considerably and what started as a local phenomenon in Zuccotti Park in downtown Manhattan mushroomed into a national and international movement. But contrary to popular opinion, OWS is not antirich people or corporate America per se. It was concerned about those well-to-do individuals and corporations who came to dominate much of our national, state, and local public policies. In the first two paragraphs of its declaration, OWS stated:

> As we gather together in solidarity to express a feeling of mass injustice, we must not lose sight of what brought us together. We write so that all people who feel wronged by the corporate forces of the world can know that we are your allies.
>
> As one people, united, we acknowledge the reality: that the future of the human race requires the cooperation of its members; that our system must protect our rights, and upon corruption of that system, it is up to the individuals to protect their own rights, and those of their neighbors; that a democratic government derives its just power from the people, but corporations do not seek consent to extract wealth from the people and the Earth; and that no true democracy is attainable when the process is determined by economic power. We come to you at a time when corporations, which place profit over people, self-interest over justice, and oppression

over equality, run our governments. We have peaceably assembled here, as is our right, to let these facts be known.

(Occupy Wall Street Declaration, 2011)

The key phrase in the declaration is "run our governments." The focus is on those corporations that manipulate the government for their own profits and ideas. In essence OWS questioned how "We the people..." came to be replaced by "We the vested interests...."

In this same spirit, the material in the preceding chapters of this book has not been an indictment of the rich and corporate America but a look at how some segments in the population have sought to "play" and control the political system for their own financial and ideological benefit. We are specifically concerned about the influence of vested interests on the education of our children. It is a concern when companies team with the Pentagon to promote the wants of the military-industrial complex, it is of far greater concern when vested interests play with our children's lives and futures. George Lakoff (2002) in his seminal work, *Moral Politics*, used the metaphor of a family to represent policy processes in this country. He referred to the disagreement between nurturing families (liberal view) and strict parents (conservative view) over the best way to raise children as similar to the way policy is developed in this country. This is not necessarily a perfect metaphor but for our purposes it resonates very well. When we consider our feelings for our own children, grave concerns arise when they are viewed not as young minds to be developed but as markets from which to derive profits and ideological fodder. In the preceding pages we presented a number of examples in which the confluence of education policy and profit raised alarms with respect to the motives of certain individuals and corporations. It would be important to summarize some of these in this conclusion and offer some recommendations to limit the exploitation of government funds meant for public schooling.

The Public Purse and the Education-Industrial Complex

At the heart of the education-industrial complex is the public purse held by federal, state, and local school district governments. Collected from tax revenues, the public purse tempts education entrepreneurs interested in profiting from taxpayers' money. One key to opening the public largess to for-profit companies are education policies that favor for-profit schools and colleges, educational management organizations, the purchase of school equipment, books, tests, and software, and the use of supplementary education services such as tutoring. In addition, certain government policies can result in parents curricularizing their homes by buying edutainment products to help their children succeed in school. Technology fuels most of these services, facilities, equipment, and products. Education policies that enable for-profit companies have substantial backing from the foundations that engage in venture philanthropy or are justified by ideas propagated by think tanks. One important idea spread by conservative foundations and think tanks is that competition and the invisible hand of the marketplace will lead to better and less expensive schools. This is highly debatable.

Flexians are an important part of the networks linking education businesses, trade associations, foundations and think tanks to the public purse (Figure 8.1 is an enhancement of the flexian network introduced in chapter 1). Flexians are not necessarily pursuing just their own economic interests as they move between positions in schools, foundations, think tanks, and education businesses. They may be dedicated to an intellectual interest or a selfless desire to improve schooling. As flexians move through the network of the education-industrial complex, they create personalized relationships with contacts in local, state, and government bureaucracies that make it easier to advance the agenda of a foundation or think tank or to promote government policies that favor their education-business employers. They are most effective at the federal and state levels of education policy making, as well as in the large urban school districts such as New York, Chicago, and Los Angeles where education expenditures are very high.

As noted in chapter 2, flexian movement through the network can lead to a convergence of interests between government policymakers, education businesses, foundations, and think tanks. This convergence of interests can

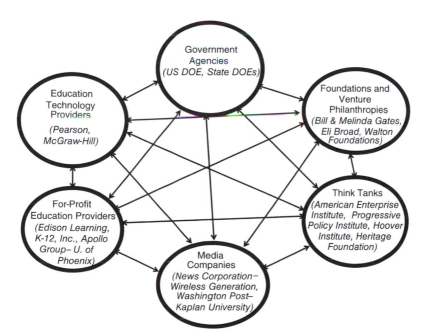

FIGURE 8.1 Networks and Alliances of the American Education-Industrial Complex.

encompass profitmaking, careerism, and ideology. For instance, two organizations woven through this book's chapters are the Gates Foundation and the publishing and textbook/testing giant Pearson. Both organizations have an interest in technology, online instruction, and the Common Core. Pearson created the Pearson Foundation to promote its products to government officials and to develop online courses in conjunction with the parent company, seeking increased profits as its ultimate goal. The Gates Foundation partially funded the Pearson Foundation as part of its championing of fully online course instruction. A legitimate interpretation of this activity might stress Bill Gates's financial holdings in Microsoft, a company that would benefit from more online instruction through the sale of hardware, game consoles, and software. Another illustration of this convergence of interests is the previously discussed U.S. Department of Education's Assistant Deputy Secretary for Innovation and Improvement James H. Shelton, a flexian who moved through a network linking education businesses and the Gates Foundation, where he was program director, and on to his present position of providing grants for learning technology. His coworker in the U.S. Department of Education, Karen Cator, Director of the Office of Educational Technology and previously of Apple, Inc., links this network to the trade organization Software & Information Industry Association where she served on the Board of Directors. This coincidence of interests involving the careerism, ideals, and intellectual interests of these two individuals, the Gates Foundation, and the profit motives of Pearson, Apple, and members of the Software & Information Industry Association, serves as a prime example of the power of this network.

A coincidence of interests is also illustrated in chapter 3 where the flexian network sought to use the public purse to benefit for-profit companies selling hardware, software, and computerized administrative services. The underlying ideas here are that schools should operate like businesses and that techniques such as data-driven decision making should determine student learning, teaching methods, school administrative decisions, and government education policies. Data-driven decision making is made possible only by significant investments in computer related technology and advances in analytic software. Furthermore, at the heart of data-driven school decision making are assessments of student performance that tie the business of schooling to the business of test makers like McGraw-Hill and Pearson. An example of the convergence of economic interests and the belief that schools should operate as businesses is the case study of Wireless Generation in chapter 3. This company was contracted by the New York City school system to participate in and eventually lead the Achievement Reporting and Innovation System (ARIS). After its sale to Rupert Murdoch's News Corporation, Murdoch hired the Chancellor of the New York schools to head the News Corporation education division, which included Wireless Generation. All of these players espoused through their actions and public statements the transformation of schools into data-driven businesses for the benefit of children.

Where is the evidence that these investments will lead to better instruction and learning? Why do the public and government policymakers blindly support unproven ideas that policies governing student learning should be entirely data-driven and nested in schools operated as businesses? Chapter 6 details the activities of venture foundations like the Broad Foundation and the Walton Family Foundation along with other foundations, like the ubiquitous Gates Foundation, in supporting data-driven solutions for learning. A number of conservative foundations and think tanks are disseminating the idea that business corporations always operate more efficiently than government bureaucracies. This image of corporate efficiency provides justification for turning government services over to for-profit enterprises and for hiring business people to run schools. Are all corporations operated efficiently? If so, how does one explain the bailouts by the federal government in 2008 to the tune of hundreds of billions of dollars to the banks, financial services companies, General Motors, and Chrysler? Perhaps government bureaucracies are intrinsically different from corporations and they operate differently because their goal is not profit but serving the public interest.

As discussed in chapter 5, ideologies supporting free market economics and claims of corporate efficiency were used to justify the growth of for-profit K-12 schools and for-profit higher education. While for-profit trade schools have a long history in the United States, large for-profit universities are relatively recent. It is hard to imagine anyone in the Western world in the 19th century advocating for-profit higher education when the traditional goals were the development of character through intellectual culture or religious in nature. A popular 19th century justification of higher education is exemplified by Cardinal John Newman's *The Idea of a University*. This volume of lectures considered theology the queen of university subjects and urged a general education (Newman, 1990). In the United States, the Yale report of 1828, which set the tone of collegiate education into the 20th century, provided the goals of developing character and an intellectual culture. In other words, 19th century colleges and universities were, in part, devoted to the development of religious and secular character (Rudolph, 1962).

By the late 19th and early 20th century, American higher education adopted social and economic goals, as corporations used public supported university research and hired graduates educated to meet their needs. This set the stage for the eventual evolution of for-profit higher education. The Morrill Act of 1862 added a vocational goal to the rhetoric of higher education. It provided that money derived from lands granted under the act would be used "to teach such branches of learning as are related to agriculture and the mechanic arts, in such manner as the legislatures of the States may respectively prescribe, in order to promote the liberal and practical education of the industrial classes in the several pursuits and professions in life (Spring, 2011a, p. 289). Writing in *Outlook* magazine in 1906, the editor Lyman Abbot explored the role of the American University. He concluded that while English universities emphasized culture and the education of aristocrats and German universities focused on scholarship and the education of scholars, American universities emphasized service to society and education for a life of social service (Rudolph, 1962, pp. 356–357). In 1963 the service and vocational functions of higher education were emphasized by Clark Kerr, President of the University of California, in a series of lectures published as *The Uses of the University* (Kerr, 2001). Kerr likened universities to service stations providing help to business, government, and other private organizations. Coining the term *multiversity*, Kerr asserted that Cardinal Newman's vision of the university had been replaced with a multiversity that provided research to businesses and government and promoted equality of opportunity through its vocational functions. In other words, Kerr reiterated a growing trend to see higher education as preparation for employment that would allow students to increase their incomes as compared to their parent's incomes. By the end of the 20th century the mantra heard by many students was "go to college to get a good job." The combination of vocationalism in higher education and free market ideologies spurred the growth of for-profit higher education as students needed to combine their education goals with their careers and work responsibilities. To advance their careers they found online learning programs especially at for-profit colleges such as the University of Phoenix that offered courses that could fit into their incredibly busy lives. Unfortunately, their trust in some of these for-profit colleges and universities was betrayed. Rather than developing the skills and credentials to advance their careers, these students, many of whom were adults with family responsibilities, found themselves burdened with significant debt and no college degrees.

For-profit colleges depend on the public purse. The fact that government money is a revenue source for for-profit higher education reflects free market ideologies and ideas supporting the privatization of government services. As noted in chapter 5, for-profit colleges received 66% of their revenues from federal student aid in 2008–2009. Government funding of for-profit schools results in their lobbying government through their trade organization the Association of Private Sector Colleges and Universities, for more funds and favorable policies.

The media, as discussed, in chapter 7, has not helped the public understand the implications of free market ideology applied to education or the growth of the education business sector. In fact, newspaper companies like the Washington Post, the News Corporation, and the New York Times have joined the rush to earn profits from education. In addition, edutainment media in the form of television programming, software, and hardware have entered homes with the promise of school success and, consequently, future employment success. In addition, as discussed in chapter 4, parents can contract for for-profit supplementary education services that promise school success through tutoring and test preparation. The combination of edutainment and supplementary education services curricularizes the home and makes the home an extension of the education-industrial complex.

In summary, networks link the public purse to education businesses, trade associations, government policies, and promoters of supporting ideologies from foundations and think tanks. Flexians move along the lines of this network as taxpayers fill the public purse and trade associations for education businesses lobby for government money to be spent on their members' products. Education businesses also directly lobby lawmakers. Foundations and think tanks provide the justification to channel money from the public purse to educational profiteers. The student is a captive in this economic and ideological network that we call the education-industrial complex.

What to Do?

How do we stop this hemorrhaging of public money flowing to the education-industrial complex? Schools have always bought textbooks, maps, globes, and other classroom materials. What's different now is that the public purse is more vulnerable to exploitation through the combination of technological advances, free market ideology, school privatization, stress on assessment, and a shadow elite moving between government, for-profit companies, trade associations, foundations, and think tanks. The central question is how to ensure greater public control over the spending of the education dollar. There is no silver bullet. To the contrary, resolution will have to be achieved along the many levels of education policy development in this country.

First, we maintain that the greater centralization of power over schools and the dispersal of influence along a network of flexians not only reduce public control over what is taught in schools but also over how school money is spent. We propose that the federal government's role in education be limited to things it does well and that it sever itself from things it has muddled. This is not a new concept. John Stuart Mill, in his famous essay "On Liberty" (1859/1956) warned:

> A general State education is a mere contrivance for moulding people to be exactly like one another: and as the mould in which it casts them is that which pleases the predominant power in the government, whether this be a monarch, a priesthood, an aristocracy, or the majority of the existing generation, in proportion as it is efficient and successful, it establishes a despotism over the mind, leading by natural tendency to one over the body.

> (Mill, 1859/1956, p. 129)

The federal government's greatest contributions have been and can continue to be in insuring civil rights of students and school personnel, establishing and funding financial aid programs, and protecting students from fraudulent practices. Its attempt in 2011 to rein in the exploitive operations of some for-profit colleges and universities is an example of what it has done well. It can do more in this area. On the other hand, it should leave to the states and localities issues related to curriculum, testing, assessment, and building student and school database systems. The No Child Left Behind policy that has dominated federal involvement in public education for much of the 21st century has both opened schools to for-profit companies and lessened public control of the school curriculum and classroom assessments.

Second, state education departments are in a critical position between the federal government and local school jurisdictions. They have the important responsibility to establish statewide policies and direction. They can and should establish policies related to a wide range of practices involving personnel, curriculum, assessments, and data collection; however, they need to share these powers with local jurisdictions be they school boards, town boards, or cities under mayoral control. Some state education boards, as demonstrated by their relationships with large testing companies, have been as culpable as the federal government in allowing education to become the playing field of less than scrupulous profiteers. On the other hand, state boards can be extremely helpful in facilitating federal funding and helping to coordinate the goals of local school districts.

Third, it would be too simple to expect that giving more control over education policies to local school districts would make it easier for the public to monitor the flow of monies to the education-industrial complex. There is, however, an element of truth in this recommendation. Since it is the localities that supply the majority (about 60%) of the funding for education, they should have a major say in how the funds are distributed. Local school budgets in most communities are subjected to an annual review and public vote. Their closeness to the community makes their decisions and operations far more transparent to their constituents and less prone to exploitation by large national and international companies. In addition, by returning curriculum, testing, and other decisions to the communities and sharing same with state boards, corporations are forced to work with many separate entities and cannot easily manipulate the system by having one or several flexians operate at the highest levels of government as they are doing now. Nevertheless, returning more control to local school boards is not a panacea. In the past, local school boards in districts with heterogeneous populations have been criticized for representing community elites to the detriment of low-income and minority families; this is not necessarily a problem in communities with homogenous populations (Spring, 2011b, pp. 51–84). If this is true then local school board elections need to be examined to make them more representative of the entire community and not just local elites.

The influence of local elites is not accidental but the result of changes made in school board election rules in the early 20th century. These early changes were justified as keeping control of schools out of the hands of the uneducated and unsuccessful and placing power in the hands of the "best" people who supposedly would be better educated and, consequently, would know what was best for the education of children. The result of this was for school board elections that were to be at-large, nonpartisan, and held at different times than general elections (Cronin, 1973). At-large elections require school board candidates to have the resources to campaign throughout the district. The authors would replace at-large elections with representive elections from smaller precincts within a district whose boundaries might be determined by the enrollment boundaries of district schools. With representation determined through small precincts, a school board candidate only needs to have the resources to campaign in a small area instead of running a campaign thoughout the school district. This change will make it easier for average citizens to campaign within a small geographical area. Eliminating the nonpartisan requirement for school board elections would recognize the reality that politics plays an important role in educational policy (Hawley, 1973). Scheduling school board elections at the same time as other general elections would increase voter participation and, consequently, ensure that elected board members represent a larger population.

We propose minimizing state and federal control of public schools, but retaining state and federal regulations that ensure protection of the civil rights of students and school personnel. In the past a major problem created by local control of schools was racial segregation, justified by politicians waving the banner of states rights. We do not advocate returning to an era when local control and states' rights meant a denial of civil rights. In addition to ensuring the protection of the civil rights of students and school personnel, the federal and state governments can play an important role in the equal funding of schools by providing local school districts with flat grants. Currently, federal monies carry requirements that state and local schools must implement. In the 1950s the U.S. Congress explicitly rejected the idea that local school districts could be granted money whose use would be decided by the district. Instead, Congress adopted the strategy of giving categorical grants with the proviso that districts that wanted the money would implement federal policies. This has been the pattern of federal funding beginning with the 1958 National Defense Education Act through President Barack Obama's Race to the Top. We would like to return the control of the public purse to the local school board. In other words, state and federal funding of local schools would be for the purpose of reducing disparities in funding between rich and poor school districts. Decisions about how the money would be spent would rest largely in the hands of locally elected school board representatives.

In the 21st century, there has also been a movement in large cities to eliminate locally elected school boards replacing them with mayoral control of education. This has been accomplished in places like New York and Chicago with mixed results. In New York City, the Panel for Education Policy (PEP) that was designed to represent community interests as part of the change to mayoral control has been the object of intense criticism and protests by parents, students, and teachers. PEP has even sparked an Occupy Department of Education movement over the Panel's rubber-stamping of any proposal backed by Mayor Michael Bloomberg without listening to community or parental concerns (Phillips, 2012). The concept of mayoral control is still being evaluated but its implementation in places like New York has left communities and parents feeling powerless and disenfranchised.

Unfortunately, we do not believe that there is any foolproof system for protecting against education policies that invite for-profit companies to raid the public purse. Local school board members could still be exploited by the marketing methods of education businesses. However, by placing education funds in the hands of locally elected representatives there is less chance of exploitation by the education-industrial complex and the existing maze of exploitive networks described in this book.

Fourth, teacher unions and professional organizations can provide valuable leadership and financial resources to counter the power of large corporate entities. Recently, however, these organizations, especially the teachers unions are being portrayed as the enemy of sound education practice interested only in protecting their prerogatives. To counter media-based outlets, they must take the offensive with their own public relations campaigns that highlight the dedication and service that so many teachers provide to our children. These organizations also need to be flexible in their respones to innovations; they cannot continue to appear to be immovable obstacles resisting any changes whether they be technological advances or policies. The power of the teachers and their organizations should not be underestimated. Steven Brill, an award-winning author, documented the education reform movement in a highly acclaimed book, *Class Warfare: Inside the Fight to Fix America's Schools* (2011), which examined many of the actions and connections of policy makers, teachers, and administrators most involved with changes in American education. His conclusion was most interesting in that all of the reforms enacted in the past 20 or so years, including charter schools, alternative teacher preparation programs, and infusions of technology cannot change the immense system of American education without the help and cooperation of teachers, their unions, and their organizations. He even went so far as to recommend that the person best qualified to lead a large urban school system such as New York City would be Randy Weingarten, the current president of the American Federation of Teachers, and before that, president of the United Federation of Teachers. His point was that she would have the most clout to influence the tens of thousands of teachers working in the New York City public school system. Charter schools, which received a good deal of focus in Brill's book, cannot change the education system. Some charter schools are incredibly innovative but some are worse than the public schools they are suppose to replace, and in the end they cannot scale up enough to resolve all the issues facing American education. Teachers, principals, and other education professionals who work in schools every day are at the fulcrum of education and they need to be a part of and partners in the solutions.

Final Word

In closing, it has been the intention of this book to raise issues and examine practices that have been at best quesitonable and may in fact be hurting our children, their education, and their futures. In 1983, *A Nation at Risk: The Imperative for Educational Reform* was published by The National Commission on Excellence in Education. It described a floundering education system that threatened America's social and economic systems even its way of life. Its panicky language was extreme:

> Our Nation is at risk. Our once unchallenged preeminence in commerce, industry, science, and technological innovation is being overtaken by competitors throughout the world. This report is concerned with only one of the many causes and dimensions of the problem, but it is the one that undergirds American prosperity, security, and civility. We report to the American people that while we can take justifiable pride in what our schools and colleges have historically accomplished and contributed to the United States and the well-being of its people, the educational foundations of our society are presently being eroded by a rising tide of mediocrity that threatens our very future as a Nation and a people.

Nonetheless *A Nation at Risk* generated movements filled with unbridled criticism of American public education that continue to this day. It is interesting to note that much of the data for *A Nation at Risk* compared the public school systems in the 1960s and 1970s. In the 1990s, the United States enjoyed one of the greatest periods of economic prosperity ever experienced by any nation in the history of humankind, which, in turn, generated significant improvements in the lifestyles of tens of millions of Americans. It is our position that a case can be made that the quality of the public school systems in the 1960s and 1970s played a part in germinating this prosperity and were not an all-encompassing "rising tide of mediocrity" as depicted in *A Nation at Risk*. Today, the American people are again hearing the cries for education reform to stem global competition that threatens our economy and our society. It is our position that the threat to the American way of life is seeing our schools and our children as markets from which to derive profits. In the words of Rupert Murdoch of the News Corporation, the American education sector is a "$500 billion market that's largely been untapped" (Mencimer, 2011). Or this quote from the *Our Times Press*, "Education is the new growth industry," said one City Hall source. "All the business giants, including Bill Gates, want to find the one product that will revolutionize education" (Witt, 2011). We are again facing *A Nation at Risk* created by individuals, companies, and organizations that travel carefully along the boundaries of legality, unethical behavior, and in some cases, unscrupulous practices and who are trying to turn our public school systems into vehicles for profiteering. Our children, who should be enjoying wonder, experiencing excitement, and gaining an appreciation of lifelong learning, are instead being subjected to the manipulation of the players in the American education–industrial complex.

References

Brill, S. (2011). *Class warfare: Inside the fight to fix America's schools.* New York: Simon & Schuster.
Cronin, J. (1973). *The control of urban schools.* New York: Free Press.
Hawley, W. (1973). *Nonpartisan elections and the case for party politics.* New York: Wiley.
Kerr, C. (2001). *The uses of the university* (5th ed.). Cambridge, MA: Harvard University Press.
Lackoff, G. (2002). *Moral politics: How liberals and conservatives think* (2nd ed.). Chicago, IL: University of Chicago Press.
Mencimer, S. (October 14, 2011). Rupert Murdoch compares US education system to Third World country's. *Mother Jones.* Retrieved from http://motherjones.com/mojo/2011/10/rupert-murdoch-compares-us-education-system-third-world-countrys
Mill, J. S. (1956). On liberty. Indianapolis, IN: The Liberal Arts Press (Original work published 1859)
National Commission on Excellence in Education. (1983). *A nation at risk: The imperative for educational reform.* Washington, DC: Author. Retrieved from http://www2.ed.gov/pubs/NatAtRisk/index.html
Newman, J. (1990). *The idea of a university.* South Bend, IN: University of Notre Dame Press.
Occupy Wall Street. (2011, September 30). *Declaration of the occupation of New York City.* Forum Post: First official release from Occupy Wall Street. Retrieved from http://occupywallst.org/forum/first-official-release-from-occupy-wall-street/
Phillips, A. M. (2012, February 10). Amid protesters disruptions, City board votes to close 18 schools and truncate 5 others. *New York Times.* Retrieved from http://www.nytimes.com/schoolbook/2012/02/10/amid-protesters-disruptions-city-board-votes-to-close-18-schools-and-truncate-5/
Rudolph, F. (1962). *The American college and university.* New York: Knopf.
Spring, J. (2011a). *The American school: A global context from the Puritans to the Obama era.* New York: McGraw-Hill.
Spring, J. (2011b). *The politics of American education.* New York: Routledge.
Witt, S. (July 21-27, 2011). On the Bloomberg-Murdoch trail: Influence peddling reportedly swirling around the DOE's $22 billion cash cow. *Our Time Press.* Retrieved from http://www.ourtimepress.com/upload/July212011sm

About the Authors

Anthony G. Picciano is a professor and executive officer of the PhD Program in Urban Education at the Graduate Center of the City University of New York. He is also a member of the faculty in the graduate program in Education Leadership at Hunter College, the doctoral certificate program in Interactive Pedagogy and Technology at the City University of New York Graduate Center, and CUNY Online BA Program in Communication and Culture. He has extensive experience in education administration and teaching, and has been involved in a number of major grants from the U.S. Department of Education, the National Science Foundation, IBM, and the Alfred P. Sloan Foundation. In 1998, Dr. Picciano cofounded CUNY Online, a multimillion dollar initiative funded by the Alfred P. Sloan Foundation that provides support services to faculty using the Internet for course development. He was a founding member and continues to serve on the Board of Directors of the Sloan Consortium.

Dr. Picciano's major research interests are school leadership, education policy, Internet-based teaching and learning, and multimedia instructional models. Dr. Picciano has conducted three major national studies with Jeff Seaman on the extent and nature of online and blended learning in American K-12 school districts. He has authored numerous articles and 10 books including *Educational Leadership and Planning for Technology* (5th ed., 2010, Pearson), *Data-Driven Decision Making for Effective School Leadership* (2006, Pearson), *Distance Learning: Making Connections across Virtual Space and Time* (2001, Pearson), and *Educational Research Primer* (2004, Continuum). In 2007, he coedited a book on blended learning with Chuck Dziuban titled, *Blended Learning: Research Perspectives* (The Sloan Consortium). He is currently coediting a follow-up to this book with Chuck Dziuban and Charles Graham. In 2010, Dr. Picciano received the Sloan Consortium's National Award for Outstanding Achievement in Online Education by an Individual.

Joel Spring is a professor at Queens College and the Graduate Center, City University of New York, whose scholarship focuses on educational policy, the politics of education, and educational globalization. Joel Spring is an enrolled member of the Choctaw Nation. His great-great-grandfather was the first Principal Chief of the Choctaw Nation in Indian Territory and his grandfather, Joel S. Spring, was a district chief at the time Indian Territory became Oklahoma. He is a citizen of the Choctaw Nation I.D. #1274408293.

Joel Spring has published over 20 books on American and global school policies, including *Political Agendas for Education: From Change We Can Believed in to Putting America First* (2010), *Globalization of Education: An Introduction* (2009), *A New Paradigm for Global School Systems: Education for a Long and Happy Life* (2007), *Wheels in the Head: Educational Philosophies of Authority, Freedom, and Culture from Confucianism to Human Rights* (3rd. ed., 2008), *Deculturalization and the Struggle for Equality: A Brief History of the Education of Dominated Cultures in the United States* (6th ed., 2010) and *American Education* (14th ed., 2010). His most recent book is *Education Networks: Power, Wealth, Cyberspace and the Digital Mind* (2012). He lived for many summers on an island off the coast of Sitka, Alaska. His novel, *Alaskan Visions*, reflects these Alaskan experiences.

Joel Spring has been given numerous educational awards including the Society of Professors of Education Mary Anne Raywid Award for Distinguished Scholarship in the Field of Education; the University of Wisconsin Alumni Achievement Award, Gerald H. Read Distinguished Lecturer, Center for Intercultural and Intercultural Education, and the Presidential Lectureship, University of Vermont; He frequently gives invited lectures which in 2010 included the Mitstifer Lectureship at the annual meeting of the University Council for Education Administration, the keynote for the 30th Bilingual/ESL Conference, and an invited lecture tour of China including the University of Hong Kong, Szechuan Normal University, Tsinghua University, Beijing Normal University, and the Central University of Nationalities.

INDEX

184 Index

Florida State University, 127
Florida Virtual School, 6, 29, 55, 97–98
Foglesong, Robert "Doc", 59
for-profit colleges, 7, 110–11, 112, 116. *See also* higher education privatization
Ford Foundation, 120, 124, *124*, 150
Fordham Foundation, 131
Fordham Institute, 129, 131, 134
Foundation for Excellence in Education, 22–27
foundations and think tanks: overview, 12–13, 119–20; foundations and higher education, 125–27; major foundations, 123–25, *124*; think tanks, 127–36; and venture philanthropy, 120–23. *See also* the Gates Foundation
Fox News, 163
free enterprise and American Way campaign, 82–83
free market ideology: and privatization of education services, 64, 65–66; and think tanks, 127–29
Friedman, Milton, 66, 128
Full Sail University, 111–12
Fuller, Bruce, 139
funding: corporate funding of nonprofits, 30; and current state of American education, 11; Hudson Institute, 57; public funding and the education-industrial complex, 168–73; public funding control, 173–76. *See also* foundations and think tanks

games: learning software and education games, 153–56; and online instruction, 30; television and edutainment, 152–53; toddlers and edutainment, 159–60; and virtual schools, 97–98
Gates, Bill, 21, 137
the Gates Foundation: and Broad Foundation, 24; and education funding, 123–24, *124*; and education policy advocacy, 138–40; and educational games, 156; and expansion of online education, 23; and flexians, 15, 16; and Foundation for Excellence in Education and Pearson Foundation, 22, 25–27; and school reform, 7; and shadow government, 21–22, 29–31; technology and school reform, 137–38; and U.S. Department of Education, 136–37; and venture philanthropy, 121–23
Gates, Robert, 1–2

Gephardt, Richard, 112
Gerstl-Pepin, Cynthia, 162–63
GI Bill and higher education, 105
Gingrich, Newt, 129
Global Education Advisors, 86–87
Global Education Initiative (GEI), 34–35
global governance. *See* shadow elite
Global Information Technology Report 2010– 2011, 35
Golston, Allan C., 139
Google, 30
The Goose Step (Sinclair), 120
The Goslings (Sinclair), 120
"The Gospel of Wealth" essay, 119–20
Gotbaum, Betsy, 59–60
governance. *See* shadow elite
government and edutainment, 144
graduation rates and credit-recovery tutoring, 96
Graham, Nathaniel, 145

Hagström, Mikael, 35–36
Hayek, Friedrich, 66, 128
Heavener, Bill, 112
Heritage Foundation, 7, 129–31
Hess, Rick, 131, 133, 139–40
Hewlett Foundation, 124, *124*
higher education privatization: and American universities, 171–72; and deregulation of online colleges, 113–16, *115*; and the education-industrial complex, 111–13; higher education and foundations, 125–27; history of for-profit higher education, 103, 105–6, *106*; and rising enrollment, 102–3, *103*, *104*; student demographics, 106, *107*, 108, *109*, 110–11
Hoover Institute, 129, 131–33
Houghton Mifflin Harcourt, 25, 154, 157
Hudson Institute, 57
"Human Network", 15

IBM, 59
The Idea Brokers and the Rise of the New Policy Elite (Smith), 128
The Idea of a University (Newman), 171
ideology: and education-industrial complex, 2, 3–5, *3*; and for-profit privatization of education services, 65–66; higher education and foundations, 126–27; and technology in American education, 53–54; and think tanks, 127–36
information and communications

Meyer Memorial Trust, 122
Microsoft, 151, 152
Middle East and North Africa (MENA), 34
military-industrial complex, 1–2, 58–59
Mill Corporation, 150–51
Mill, John Stuart, 173
Milligan, Harold, 149
Minnesota Education Computing Corporation (MECC), 153–54
Minow, Newton, 149, 150
Mister Rogers' Neighborhood, 144, 150
Molnar, Alex, 63, 80
Molnar, Andrew, 45
Moral Politics (Lakoff), 168
Moreno, Glen, 77
Morgan, Joy Elmer, 148
Morrill Act, 171
Mosaica Education, 73
Motion Picture Producers and Distributors of America (MPPDA), 145–46
motivation: and the education-industrial complex, 52; learning and effectiveness of technology, 49–50
movies and edutainment, 145–47
Mubarak, Hosni, 10
multiversity, 172
Murdoch, Rupert, 160, 163, 177

A Nation at Risk report, 13, 53, 177–78
National Association for the Advancement of Colored People (NAACP), 9
National Association of Charter School Authorizers, 133–34
National Association of Manufacturers (NAM) and American Way campaign, 82–83
National Broadcasting Corporation (NBC), 148
National Committee on Education by Radio, 148–49
National Council of Women, 149
National Defense Education Act, 4, 144, 147, 150
National Education Association (NEA): movies and edutainment, 145–46; and politics, 5; radio and edutainment advertising in the home, 148–49; technology and education policy, 54
National Education Technology Plan (NETP): and flexians, 15, 17; and Pearson publishing, 26; and personalized bureaucracy, 20–21; promotion of learning software and

games, 144, 155–56; and transformation of education, 48–52
National Heritage Academies, 53
National Public Radio (NPR), 144, 150
networks: and education-industrial complex, 9–10, 169–70, *169*; flexians, 15–16, 169–70, *169*; World Economic Forum meetings, 33–34. *See also* shadow elite
The New Arab Journalist (Pintak), 10
New Schools Venture Fund, 136–37
New Teacher Project, 21
New York Times Company, 7
New York Times Knowledge Network, 160–61
Newark school district, 86–87
Newman, John, 171, 172
News Corporation, 59
News International, 7
news media. *See* media
No Child Left Behind: and charter schools and EMOs, 69–74; and data-driven decision making, 47–48; and Edison Schools, 67–69, 85–87; and for-profit privatization of education services, 65–66; and privatization of government services, 18; and the Progressive Policy Institute, 135–36; and school choice, 4; and technology funding, 55; testing and assessment software and services, 99–102; and tutoring services, 95–96
"Not School", 39

Obama, Barack, 64, 72, 100, 155
Occupy Wall Street (OWS) movement, 167–68
Olchefske, Joseph, 73
Olesen, Peter, 145
online education: in college and universities, 50–51; and the Gates Foundation, 138; growth in, 46–47, *47*; and IQity, 25; Pearson Foundation, 25–27
Oracle, 30
Oregon Trail game, 154
Organization for Economic Cooperation and Development (OECD), 39
outcomes and productivity, 53–54

Paley, William, 148
Panel for Education Policy (PEP), 175–76
Papert, Seymour, 45
Parent-Teacher Association (PTA), 8
parochial school systems, 92